THE

BOOK CLUB
COMPANION

THE
BOOK CLUB
COMPANION

A Comprehensive Guide to the
Reading Group Experience

Diana Loevy

BERKLEY BOOKS, NEW YORK

THE BERKLEY PUBLISHING GROUP
Published by the Penguin Group
Penguin Group (USA) Inc.
375 Hudson Street, New York, New York 10014, USA
Penguin Group (Canada), 90 Eglinton Avenue East, Suite 700, Toronto, Ontario M4P 2Y3, Canada
(a division of Pearson Penguin Canada Inc.)
Penguin Books Ltd., 80 Strand, London WC2R 0RL, England
Penguin Group Ireland, 25 St. Stephen's Green, Dublin 2, Ireland (a division of Penguin Books Ltd.)
Penguin Group (Australia), 250 Camberwell Road, Camberwell, Victoria 3124, Australia
(a division of Pearson Australia Group Pty. Ltd.)
Penguin Books India Pvt. Ltd., 11 Community Centre, Panchsheel Park, New Delhi—110 017, India
Penguin Group (NZ), Cnr. Airborne and Rosedale Roads, Albany, Auckland 1310, New Zealand
(a division of Pearson New Zealand Ltd.)
Penguin Books (South Africa) (Pty.) Ltd., 24 Sturdee Avenue, Rosebank, Johannesburg 2196,
South Africa

Penguin Books Ltd., Registered Offices: 80 Strand, London WC2R 0RL, England

This book is an original publication of The Berkley Publishing Group.

The publisher does not have any control over and does not assume any responsibility for author or third-party websites or their content.

PRINTING HISTORY
Berkley trade paperback edition/August 2006

Berkley trade paperback ISBN: 0-425-21009-X

An application to register this book for cataloging has been submitted to the Library of Congress.

PRINTED IN THE UNITED STATES OF AMERICA

10 9 8 7 6 5 4 3 2 1

PUBLISHER'S NOTE: The recipes contained in this book are to be followed exactly as written. The publisher is not responsible for your specific health or allergy needs that may require medical supervision. The publisher is not responsible for any adverse reactions to the recipes contained in this book.

To Philip

Contents

Introduction   1

CHAPTER ONE
THE BELOVEDS   5

The Ten Indispensable Titles   7

No Leader, No Problem: Discussion Basics   19

Club Rules: May We Knit?   22

When Pets Misbehave: Flying Minnies and Slobbering Horaces   25

Club Rules: When Pets Meet the Club Checklist   28

The Unexpected Meeting Place: The Botanical Garden   29

Hosting Basics: How to Be Popular   31

Angry, Often Desperate Housewives: The Novels   33

The Beloved Cocktail   35

An Anne Tyler Celebration   37

Time Travel: If You Were in a 1920s Book Club   45

CHAPTER TWO
THE BOOK CLUB CLASSIC   47

The Twenty Indispensable Titles   49

Four Questions for Isabel Allende   72

No Leader, No Problem: Your Next Book   74

Club Rules: E-mail Stylings   76

When Pets Misbehave: Baddest Kitty   77

Book Club Style: Flowers from
The Hours and *Mrs. Dalloway's* Hothouse 78

The Costume Drama 80

The Bell Jar by Sylvia Plath: An Appreciation 82

The Tween Book Club 101 84

A Bel Canto Evening 86

Time Travel: If You Were in a 1930s Book Club 93

CHAPTER THREE

CLASSIC FICTION

95

The Twenty-one Indispensable Titles 97

What Is a Classic? 122

Club Rules: How True! Mark Up Your Book without Mercy 124

When Pets Go Missing 126

The Tween Book Club:
The Lion, the Witch and the Wardrobe by C. S. Lewis 128

The Many Favorites of Ernest Hemingway 130

Classic Fiction Anniversary Party 131

CHAPTER FOUR

BRIT LIT 101

145

The Ten Indispensable Titles 147

Touring Thematically: Channeling Jane Austen 159

Meeting Thematically: Form a Spin-Off Literary Society 161

When Pets Preen 163

The Tween Book Club: *The Witches* by Roald Dahl 165

P. G. Wodehouse 101 171

Luncheon at the Club 174

Time Travel: If You Were in a 1940s Book Club 178

CHAPTER FIVE
RED, WHITE AND NOIR   181

The Ten Indispensable Titles   183

No Leader, No Problem: Customizing Discussion Questions   194

When Pets Misbehave: The Fearful Guest   196

Touring Thematically: Authors at the Lectern   198

The Indispensable Short Story Collection   200

Peyton Place by Grace Metalious: An Appreciation   203

The Indispensable Platter: Vegetables All Year Long   206

Time Travel: If You Were in a 1950s Book Club   209

CHAPTER SIX
LITERARY RESPITES   213

The Ten Indispensable Titles   215

Six Questions for Alexander McCall Smith   227

The Best Generic Questions for Discussing Series   229

New Year's Resolutions for Book Clubs   230

Book Club Craft Essentials   232

The Tween Book Club: *A Christmas Memory* by Truman Capote   234

Book Club Style: *Gift from the Sea*   236

Holiday Celebration   238

Snacking at the Club   240

Time Travel: If You Were in a 1960s Book Club   243

CHAPTER SEVEN
BLACK LIT 247

The Ten Indispensable Titles 249

Five Questions for Bebe Moore Campbell 262

No Leader, No Problem: The Flip Side 264

Book Club Style: A Color Purple Flower Celebration 265

The Indispensable Reading List: Memoir and Nonfiction 266

The Tween Book Club:
Roll of Thunder, Hear My Cry by Mildred D. Taylor 268

Casting Call 270

Book Club Supper 271

Time Travel: If You Were in a 1970s Book Club 276

CHAPTER EIGHT
NONFICTION THAT READS LIKE FICTION 279

The Ten Indispensable Titles 281

No Leader, No Problem: Meeting Style 292

The Indispensable Reading List: Biographies 293

Savannah Style 294

The Indispensable Reading List: The Arcane Thriller 295

A Restaurant Meeting 296

Best Generic Discussion Questions for Nonfiction 298

Supper at the Club 299

Time Travel: If You Were in a 1980s Book Club 303

CHAPTER NINE
THE MEMOIR   305

The Ten Indispensable Titles   307

Five Questions for Ann Patchett   319

The Cultural Revolution, Before and After   322

Enchanted Summer Book Club   324

Seasonal Fruit Platters   326

Supper at the Club   327

Time Travel: If You Were in a 1990s Book Club   332

Bibliography   335

Acknowledgments   337

INTRODUCTION

Here's the plan: The book club will take place at Brideshead, the old Marchmain place in Evelyn Waugh's *Brideshead Revisited*. Julia will pick all of us up in Sebastian's Morris-Cowley and someone will hold his teddy bear. She will make several round trips so the entire club can arrive before dinner. We will light her cigarettes at her request. Wilcox will open the cellars for us while we wait for Charles Ryder to come and give us the *real* story. And if we are very, very lucky, we might be able to catch a glimpse of Miss de Bourgh's little phaeton and ponies trotting by.

Our clubs may not always be the stuff of dreams, but the characters we meet seem to become the ones we cherish the most. Maybe it's because we are all in this together and it's a busy, portentous road we're all on. Being in a club makes the experience of reading deeper, more magical and—when you really stop to think about it—positively inspirational. And though there is no such thing as a perfect book club, each club is in a continual process of becoming the club it always wanted to be.

We want our clubs to be homey but with an edge of suspense. We tweak the formula while maintaining the expected routine. And is there a better environment in which to show off? A newly developed themed dish, a recently adopted four-legged, impeccably groomed member, a betrothal sapphire slipped on a finger with nails painted in homage to Terry McMillan's

Robin Stokes or Barbara Kingsolver's Rachel Price—it's never hard to get the club's complete attention.

But no one can compete with the main event: the book. Your ideas for the most enticing book club books, like mine, come from every source: superb librarians, acquaintances met on the street, encyclopedias of forgotten lore, or booksellers who leap at the chance to tell you about the latest "great read" as well as their most favorite. But the very best ideas for books come from other book clubs, near and far.

We have a special language, an instantaneous oral tradition that creates the latest "it" books. How does everyone know? They just do—and the "it" books rarely fail. You might not adore every one of them—you *are* defending your point of view to the bitter end, aren't you?—but a mirthful time is had by all.

While the current "it" books become part of our collective memory, what about the other eleven selections? The Internet lights up with one possibility after another; it's very much okay to choose the "it" book of the 1983, 1952 or 1920—or 1860. Many people haven't read these other kinds of classics (*The Far Pavillions, Sophie's Choice* or *The French Lieutenant's Woman*, anyone?), so it may be time to designate a yearly slot in the schedule to do so.

Celebrations R Us as we ring in the holidays, a big club anniversary, a twentieth member. Or we may just be feeling "gala." Whether it's a special occasion or pure merry making, you will commemorate it with a page or two in your newly established club scrapbook or a sleek, modern, easy-to-use portfolio. Your ever-growing book lists, handcrafted invitations from the member whose life's work it is to do these things for you, priceless quotes on cocktail napkins or vellum all count as tangible club memories.

The book club of your dreams will feature a bevy of hosts who care deeply about the group. Not that anyone has time to perfect a dish that Flaubert describes with exquisite precision, but the host of the first rank demonstrates awareness that the club is actually coming over. That might mean making copies of maps for everyone, preparing a last-minute, any-time pasta or cookies, or wrapping herb bouquets and flowers of the color purple to hand over to each member as he or she leaves. It might also mean taking charge of the restaurant meeting, the picnic or the enchanted garden trip.

And if you take the extra time to think of just one key discussion point, or print out the publisher's discussion questions from barnesandnoble.com, or find an acerbic but brilliant quote about the author or the work, you might just mesmerize the entire club.

Friendship, surprise, club shorthand and chemistry. These are the ingredients that we are fortunate enough to possess. We have help, of course, with the usual vintage or a classic cocktail made in swell-looking batches of vermilion or liquid emeralds. If our favorite authors can set the scene, dress their protagonists with great specificity and send them off to favorite watering holes, we can certainly pay tribute in the best way we know how. (Attention club: Just because we read books, we're not excluded from the designated driver rule. But you knew that.)

Members come and members go, but we have an excellent plan for new recruits or maintenance of the core group. While some book clubs are open to new members and are downright civic-minded, other clubs are closed societies. "We don't want nobody that nobody didn't send" is the motto. If your club is picky about new members, you are in good company. One of the first book clubs, the Literary Club, was started in London in 1764. Joshua Reynolds and Samuel Johnson held forth once a week at a tavern called the Turk's Head in Soho. When the tavern became a house, the club moved around town for the rest of the century. The other members? Edmund Burke, Thomas Percy, James Boswell, Edward Gibbon, Oliver Goldsmith and Adam Smith.

One of the most famous clubs of all time was P. G. Wodehouse's the Drones, the fictional club where Bertie Wooster repairs with Catsmeat Potter-Pirbright, Gussie Fink-Nottle and the rest of the gang. We might lack their fleet of leather chairs for the after-luncheon sleep, but we are as familiar with the comfy sofa as the next club person. Perched in our usual spot, we look forward to the knowing commentary from a certain friend and are surprised by another who might be seized with a luminous thought. If it is one of our favorite books and we fear giving up the characters, we get one more chance to spend some time with them. And if we just didn't care for the book, it will soon be over.

Best of all, your club has read and discussed a group of books that you can refer to for the life of the club—and often that is a lifetime. You remember what happened that night and you reminisce while you move on to the next book, the next club trip and more merriment, more memories. One evening, a friend might be amiable and cogent. The next time, he seems as if he were apprenticed to a Dark Arts wizard at Hogwarts. And sometimes even you are the sorcerer's apprentice.

No problem! Your book club will embrace you and embolden you, and it will enable you to create lifelong friendships. Pick a new book, create a new setting, discover a new character or rediscover and share a cherished one, and start again. You know it will be the best time you have ever had with the best group you will ever know.

I

THE BELOVEDS

"And yet I remembered. Two Indian-head pennies, chewing gum,
soap dolls, a rusty medal, a broken watch and chain."
—*To Kill a Mockingbird*

First, we are captivated. And in the end, we can't forget. These are the books many of us love most of all. Our ardor may be the result of sticking with the protagonists through the good times and the bad times—we've been through all of it together. They are so endearing we have created our own family album filled with the life stories of our favorites: Scout Finch, Chiyo, Lily Owens, Leah Price, Cassandra Mortmain, Amir and Hassan are among the fierce semi-orphans we care so much about. The corners of their images might as well be dog-eared with all the loving care with which they have been handled.

The characters in Beloved Book Club Lit are often cruelly betrayed, though sometimes they do the betraying. Their childhoods become the dimmest memory as they are faced with one loss after another. Though often touched by suffering, the characters' lives in Beloved Lit are filled with meaning and adventure. Resilience is often their only recourse and that's why they have won us over.

Scout, Leah and Cassandra must think, struggle, strategize, sometimes journalize and attempt to survive. For they are characters filled with humanity and flaws. They remember and regret, or simply hit the road to remember and regret. Race matters deeply as schoolteacher and unlikely hero himself, Grant Wiggins, continually reminds us. In *A Lesson Before Dying* he poses what may be our ultimate discussion question: What is a hero?

Your own pantheon of beloveds may be up for review. In the meantime, throw on your togas or any old priceless kimono, consult with the Daughters of Mary, Delia Grinstead, Adah Price, Leah Price, Sayuri, Hatsumomo and your other muses—and begin the parley.

The Ten Indispensable Titles

▪▪▪

Gilead

(2004) by Marilynne Robinson

Open any page of *Gilead* and you will find crystalline prose, whole passages to contemplate and wisdom to share. Marilynne Robinson's novel takes the form of a letter written by a dying seventy-seven-year-old Congregational minister, Reverend John Ames, to his seven-year-old son. Ames will never see him grow up and this is his last communication. The story Ames tells stretches back to the 1830s, when his grandfather, another John Ames, left Maine for Bleeding Kansas and preached with a pistol in his belt. But Ames is writing to his son in placid, contemplative 1950s Iowa during the age of Eisenhower.

This Ames had married a much younger woman, and she and his young son are the joys of his life. He savors every day left to him. "You are drawing those terrible little pictures that you will bring me to admire and which I will admire because I have not the heart to say one word that you might remember against me," Ames observes.

Is this a book about life or death? Falling squarely in the "life" category is the appearance in town of Jack Boughton, John Ames's namesake and son of his dear friend, a Presbyterian minister. Jack has been a kind of hellion, and now middle-aged, poses some thorny theological and life questions for Ames. His appearance sparks real drama and a surprise you will surely want to analyze. What does Ames mean when he says "remembering and forgiving can be contrary things"? Take a walk through a good woman's owl garden and consider all that Marilynne Robinson has created in this deep, short work.

Discussion questions, Picador: Excellent, helpful and thought provoking. One question discusses the Biblical references to Gilead, a region near the

Jordan River that has healing properties, but as a word means "rocky area." Another asks what the Reverend would think of today's religious controversies.

Furthermore: *Gilead* is Robinson's first novel in decades. Her last was the critically acclaimed *Housekeeping* (1981), recently republished and rediscovered by clubs. It is the story of two sisters growing up near a glacial lake in the West where their mother drove to her death.

I Capture the Castle
(1948) by Dodie Smith

Charming teen diarist Cassandra Mortmain narrates the story of her family's cheerful destitution in an increasingly derelict but romantic castle complete with moat for moonlight swims. Enter two wealthy, adorable Americans who inherit the land and nearby hall to become the family's landlords, and a whimsical, Austen-tinged romantic comedy ensues. Husband-stalking sister Rose wants to live in a Jane Austen novel, and we want to live in this novel. (Cassandra would prefer to be in a Charlotte Bronte.) Book clubs will delight in the many literary references. "Ah, but you're the insidious type," the Vicar tells Cassandra. "Jane Eyre with a touch of Becky Sharp. A thoroughly dangerous girl. I like your string of coral."

Clubs will also adore the pluckiness of our narrator who writes in her journal by candlelight—in the 1930s! Discussions may begin with Cassandra's coming of age story and could end with an appreciation of the English eccentric. There are many here to appreciate or denigrate, including Cassandra's father, one-book author James Mortmain. Cassandra "captures" it all: the dating career of Rose, village life and the changing seasons, and a few controversial decisions, especially regarding Cassandra and the too-wonderful Stephen Colly who saves the family from utter destitution. A more mature Cassandra emerges, or maybe that is what she wants us to believe. Enchanting black-and-white illustrations by Ruth Steed, based on sketches by the author, complete the scene.

Discussion questions, St. Martin's Press: Good. Most worthwhile is the question about the new Americans in the neighborhood, their mannerisms and the mutual curiosity between both parties.

Drinking thematically: Cassandra has her first cherry brandy when out with the gang at "The Keys" inn while Rose has a crème de menthe. Cassandra downs another cherry brandy when visiting the rooms of sublime librarian and schoolmistress Miss Marcy, conveniently located above the inn.

Note to dog people: Cassandra's snowy white bull terrier, Heloise, is a true companion and foil. (Her cat is named Abelard, "a beautiful pale ginger.") "All right, Heloise darling, you shall have your blanket. She gazes at me with love, reproach, confidence and humour—how can she express so much just with two rather small slanting eyes?" Dodie Smith was also the author of *101 Dalmations* (1956). And wouldn't *that* be a great discussion book?

■ ■ ■

The Kite Runner
(2003) by Khaled Hosseini

Book clubs have made *The Kite Runner* the "it" book of several seasons and it's easy to see why. The vanished world of Afghanistan in the 1960s and early 1970s is the setting for this story of a childhood friendship beset by small and large events. The sultans of Kabul are two motherless boys: Amir enjoys a privileged life while Hassan is his friend—and personal servant. Amir's first word was "Baba" meaning "father." Hassan's first word was "Amir." This unequal relationship, where Amir can read and write, and Hassan, who is a lower-cast Hazara, cannot, is one of the most poignant in all of books.

The two boys share a love of kites, and the annual kite tournament throughout Kabul is the highlight of their young lives. It's not a sport for the weak, and Hosseini uses the kite-running and kite-fighting metaphor to ultimate advantage. The year Amir wins the tournament—in an attempt to win his father's love—is also the time he witnesses an event that will change his relationship with Hassan and his life.

Clubs love to discuss the story of Amir and Hassan, and the portrait of this friendship makes this novel beloved. Is Amir just being a kid or do his actions indicate less-excusable motivations? How does the event play out throughout the book and into the California sections where the small family emigrates? Is this a modern version of a folktale? Many club members simply want to put their arms around the characters and hug them.

Penguin Reading Group Guide: Very good, though there is a spoiler in the first question. The rest touch on almost every aspect of the book, from the kite running scenes and the Afghan rituals to the role of each family member in this poignant story.

Entertaining thematically: Amir's favorite: hot black tea with three sugar cubes and toasted *naan* topped with sour-cherry marmalade.

Furthermore: Look for Khaled Hosseini's next book, *Dreaming in Titanic City*, about the long friendship of two Afghan women.

Selling *The Kite Runner* to the club: A tale of humanity set against some brutal scenes, it's a contemporary fable made for discussion.

■■■

Ladder of Years
(1995) by Anne Tyler

The sage of Baltimore gives us one of her wisest, funniest, most profound books. Anne Tyler gets it right about so many things—marriage, teenagers, family relations, time travel—it's as if the author has visited every house everywhere and asked, "Who's for more chicken?"

One fine, sunny beach day, Delia Grinstead, a forty-year-old wife and mother who has never lived outside of her father's house, walks away from her physician husband and almost-grown children and keeps going. It's the adventure of a lifetime, though she has no idea what awaits her. Delia ends up in historic Bay Borough, only a few hours from her home in Baltimore. At first it's a Twilight Zone town, and the dreamy, alienating quality Tyler is so adept at conveying is in full bloom.

When Delia's Bay Borough life begins to take shape, the questions begin. What kind of life is it? Will she ever return to the old one, and isn't it delicious to contemplate this new, glamorous world of simplicity, spinsterhood and self-invention? Compare and contrast early Delia with "Miss Grinstead." Are they the same person? There are several Tyler-style fairy tales in *Ladder of Years*; can you identify them all?

Discussion questions, Random House: All over the place. There are so many questions, you are bound to find at least a few useful. Spoiler alert: Questions about the ending are lodged in the middle of the list.

Note to cat people: Has an author ever described cat behavior more lovingly? And did you know cats love the word "beautiful"? In *Ladder of Years*, Vernon and George each have a role to play. Tyler describes exaggerated purring, cuddling, following Delia around, avoiding her, investigating the furniture, weaving around her ankles, marching and vanishing. And then there is the ultimate reward: a warm snuggle by a sleeping ball of fluff.

■ ■ ■

A Lesson Before Dying
(1993) by Ernest J. Gaines

A black man in 1940s Louisiana takes the wrong ride to the wrong place at the wrong time. A murder is committed and he is promptly arrested and sentenced to die. But *A Lesson Before Dying* is not a courtroom drama or a police procedural. It is a book about ideas: Can Grant Wiggins, a teacher in the local black school, help the doomed prisoner Jefferson die as a man after his own attorney compares him to a hog in supplication to the all-white jury? Prodding Grant to his reluctant task are Jefferson's dignified mother Miss Emma and his own Tante Lou.

One of Ernest Gaines's supremely elegant achievements is to make Grant a cynical, questioning hero in the hard-boiled detective mode. The author sets up the tension inherent in all of Grant's relationship, readying him for the hard task ahead. Questions abound: What are the lessons learned and who learns them? Who is the real teacher in this book? Grant's "What is a hero?" conversation is one of the best in all book club discussions. Jefferson's simple, eloquent diary entries where he tells the story of his all-too-brief life and present circumstances ("day breakin . . . sun comin up . . . the bird in the tre soun like a blu bird . . .") provide the magnificent, heartbreaking response.

Discussion questions, Vintage Books: These questions are so good, they are a required, parallel reading experience. Lessons of faith and the grim choices the characters must make in this Jim Crow setting are posed beautifully.

Cocktails: Grant and Vivian meet at the incomparable Rainbow Club, a dark bar and café described in such loving detail you can actually hear the cars driving up on the crushed seashells. Grant's drink of choice is brandy with a side of ice water, and "Miss Lady" orders the same.

Entertaining thematically: Meanwhile, back at the Rainbow Club, Thelma serves Grant shrimp stew, "a green salad of lettuce, tomato and cucumber, a piece of corn bread and glass of water on the counter." Are you paying attention? Thelma has given you the menu for the perfect, complementary supper at the club.

Furthermore: Gaines won the National Book Critics Circle Award for this book and is well known for his equally lauded *The Autobiography of Miss Jane Pittman* (1971) and *A Gathering of Old Men* (1983). *A Lesson Before Dying* starring Don Cheadle, Mekhi Phifer and Cicely Tyson is available on DVD.

In a recently published collection of essays, *Mozart and Leadbelly: Stories and Essays,* Gaines writes about his wide-ranging cultural influences. In that spirit, take time to revisit the story that greatly influenced Grant, "Ivy Day in the Committee Room," by James Joyce. Included in *Dubliners*, the short story portrays a group of squabbling politicians on the birthday of Charles Stewart Parnell. What is its significance to *A Lesson Before Dying*?

Memoirs of a Geisha
(1997) by Arthur Golden

An orphaned girl with unusual gray eyes is taken at nine years old from her tipsy house and is plunged headlong into a tough, catty apprenticeship in Kyoto's geisha district. The poor girl emerges as the beautiful, intelligent geisha Sayuri. From each layered kimono to the strict structure of geisha society, *Memoirs of a Geisha* depicts a sensual, glamorous world that book clubs have loved to explore.

Arthur Golden's writing is filled with apt metaphors and symbols, often embodied in the artful robes now ensconced in museums around the world. A juicy, bitter conflict between rivals Sayuri and the evil, gorgeous Hatsumomo is the delicious core of the novel. "I know perfectly well how Hatsumomo treats you: about like a serpent treats its next meal, I should think," Mameha, the most glamorous geisha of them all, tells her protégé, Sayuri. And the protégé is up to the challenge. "Every night I lay on my futon scheming," Sayuri confides in us, as she always does, especially about her love for the elusive Chairman. Geisha careers rise and fall, making the story an energetic and suspenseful portrayal of a society that has all but disappeared. And you will also understand once and for all that geishas are not prostitutes. But in geisha training of maximum subtlety, the seductive arts can be just as dangerous.

Discussion questions, Vintage Books: Excellent and thorough, with several provocative questions concerning the language and symbols of the geisha system, and the differences between the young Chiyo and the Sayuri she becomes. How do the secondary characters such as Mother, Auntie, Nobu and Pumpkin enhance the story?

Entertaining thematically: It's too easy to order the usual sushi—what kind of *okiya* are you running anyway? Concentrate on the unique dishes described in the novel such the snack *umeboshi ochazuke* (rice and pickled sour plums soaked in tea). Consult your local saki specialist about *amakuchi*, Hatsumomo's favorite.

Selling *Memoirs of a Geisha* to the club: Required reading for all viewing parties.

■■■

My Antonia
(1918) by Willa Cather

Drawing on semi-autobiographical incidents of the Nebraska frontier, Willa Cather tells an elegiac, graceful tale of a vanished time in her youth. Jim Burden, who has just lost his mother and father, is sent to live with his grandparents on a farm near Black Hawk. In the late nineteenth century, Nebraska is a region of sometimes terrible magnificence, a changeable "tawny landscape" where men eat like Vikings. Jim develops a friendship with a lovely and spirited Bohemian immigrant, Antonia, and her strange and difficult family. While the prairie frontier is a lonely place, it can also be one of the most convivial, as Cather amply demonstrates when Jim and his family move to town.

The definition of the pioneer spirit is bound up in the character of Antonia and her friend Lena. Whose Antonia is portrayed in *My Antonia*? Discussions of faith will revolve around Jim's wise grandfather, especially in his relationship with the doomed Mr. Shimerda. Spellbinding descriptions of the light, the seasons and even the passing of the day, and the hour "of triumphant ending," have made *My Antonia* a favorite to read aloud and to savor. Just follow the sunflower trail.

Penguin Reading Group Guide: Excellent, a parallel reading experience. Questions are arranged chronologically, beginning with the introduction of the unnamed narrator and range through the reasons for Mr. Shimerda's suicide, the possible romantic infatuation between Jim and Antonia, and a reflection of all the mirror images in the book.

Editions that make a difference: Look for any edition that features the timeless illustrations of W. T. Benda, striking in their depiction of loneliness and friendship amid the fierce beauty of vast prairie.

Furthermore: Clubs love to return to Cather, sometimes after a very long absence. Consider Cather's other classics about the West: *O Pioneers!*, *The Song of the Lark* and *Death Comes for the Archbishop*. For a lovely companion book or successive selection, consider Sarah Orne Jewett's *The Country of the Pointed Firs*. This story collection about a Maine seaport town in the late nineteenth century was beloved by Cather.

■ ■ ■

The Poisonwood Bible
(1998) by Barbara Kingsolver

The natural and political world of Africa meets the Bible and the Price family in Barbara Kingsolver's tour de force, *The Poisonwood Bible*. It's 1959 and Baptist preacher Reverend Nathan Price, his long suffering wife Orleanna and their four daughters (Rachel, twins Leah and Adah, and youngest, Ruth May) leave Bethlehem, Georgia, bearing Betty Crocker cake mixes for a mission in the Congo. Reverend Price, about whom you will not stop talking, is obsessed with baptizing the Kilanga—in a country on the brink of revolution. *The Poisonwood Bible* is famously told from the point of view of the four Price sisters and their mother.

"Man Oh Man, are we in for it now," Rachel remembers with her customary princess-logic. Rachel's beauty-queen personae, counterbalanced by the fierce warrior Leah and the braniac Adah, is but one of the reasons *The Poisonwood Bible* is beloved. The novel is a dazzling example of how a complicated international situation is brought to life by each character telling her own truth. Leah, perhaps the conscience of the book, relates the story in realpolitik point of view as she grows from her father's favorite to an African warrior, wife and mother ("the Bride of Africa," in Rachel parlance). The brilliant Adah begins her portion in word games reminiscent of her literary hero, Emily Dickinson ("Sunrise tantalize"). Ruth May's impressions are heartbreakingly simple and clear-eyed. Orleanna strikes a defensive posture and tries to explain why in the name of God she did not leave her husband when she had the chance.

What happens to the Price family is a tragedy but pales next to the fate of the Congo itself. Kingsolver makes this point repeatedly and clubs have been arguing about it ever since.

Discussion questions, Harper Perennial: Very good. Questions range from Kingsolver's use of symbolism to the different voices of the sisters and how they drive the narrative.

Cocktails: Double Singapore Slings at the Equatorial, charge to Rachel and show her your nails: Immoral Coral.

Furthermore: As a young girl, Kingsolver lived for several years in the Congo, and lucky for us, she kept a journal. Her parents were public health officials, and the author has repeatedly stated they are not at all like the parents in *The Poisonwood Bible*.

***The Poisonwood Bible* suggested reading list**: *Things Fall Apart* by Chinua Achebe, *Heart of Darkness* by Joseph Conrad, *The Complete Poems of Emily Dickinson* by Emily Dickinson, *Children of Wax: African Folk Tales* by Alexander McCall Smith.

■ ■ ■

The Secret Life of Bees
(2002) by Sue Monk Kidd

Sue Monk Kidd has made apprentice beekeepers of us all. Her method? Create an unexpected, mystical bee queendom in Tiburon, South Carolina, populate it with a creative family of black sisters (May, June and queen bee August Boatwright), set it all during the civil rights struggle in 1964—and add a feisty, strategy-minded runaway, fourteen-year-old Lily Owens. Then, teach us all about beekeeping, honey production, real families and love.

Clubs adore every corner of this book, from the bee colonies and their human counterparts to the now-classic characters. Monk hits her theme from the very beginning, when Lily hears bees in the wall. Lily is a surprisingly wise and good-natured adolescent, considering that she has to live with her mean dad T. Ray, an ingenious punisher, and that, as a four-year-old, she may have accidentally killed her mother, for whom she still yearns. When she hears a voice say, "Lily Melissa Owens, your jar is open," she knows she must leave home to rescue Rosaleen, her black caregiver who is in the clutches of the town rascists. A girls' adventure ensues leading the pair to the convent/spa/bee farm of the Boatwrights.

One of Kidd's greatest characters is May Boatwright, the emotionally fragile sister who feeds a homemade wailing wall with slips of paper ("Birmingham, Sept 15, four little angels dead") while she absorbs all the bad news of the world. Don't miss the Daughters of Mary, bearing food and comfort. Beware of their potentially lethal pocketbooks.

Penguin Reading Group Guide: Very good. It leads with a terrific interview with the author in which she informs on all matters from growing up in the South during the civil rights era to the story surrounding the Black Madonna and all other queenly symbols. The questions are thorough and provocative: What will happen to Lily when the novel ends?

Book design that makes a difference: Fans of book design appreciate the enigmatic cover painting of the honey jar with the Black Madonna label, the bee graphics and the decorative chapter breaks mingled with the scientific epigrams about bee behavior, especially that of the queen. Discuss the whole package.

Entertaining thematically: Start the club with August's official welcome: Jelly glasses filled with orangeade, served on a tray of course. Next, May's specialty, sweet-potato biscuits, followed by the Daughters' funeral lunch: fried chicken, deviled eggs with paprika, sliced ham, green beans, turnips, macaroni and cheese, and caramel cake.

Dressing thematically: Daughter of Mary signature hats, including Lunelle's "purple felt the size of a sombrero with fake fruit on the back."

To Kill a Mockingbird

(1960) by Harper Lee

Perhaps the most beloved of all the beloveds, Harper Lee's Pulitzer Prize–winning novel may define the coming-of-age story. It's the depths of the Great Depression in Maycomb, Alabama. Outspoken tomboy Scout and her older brother Jem, "a born hero," are being raised by their father, small-town lawyer Atticus Finch, and the family's black housekeeper Calpurnia. In the course of this world-famous tale filled with symbolism, descriptions of racial strife in the Deep South and the violence that accompanies it, Scout learns many things, often the hard way, but always the literary way.

From the courtroom drama where Atticus must fight a losing battle for the life of Tom Robinson, accused of raping a white woman, to one of the last scenes with Scout dressed up as a ham after a Halloween pageant, *To Kill a Mockingbird* seems to be a part of our own family history. This time around, consider whether Atticus is the hero you remembered him. How does Lee develop character through dialogue and how does she use the exuberant secondary characters such as Aunt Alexandra, Miss Maudie Atkinson and Mrs. Dubose to further her portrait of life in Maycomb? Don't miss the glorious friendship of Scout, Jem and movie-picture obsessed Dill (modeled on Lee's childhood friend Truman Capote), especially when the trio tries to lure the wondrous, mysterious shut-in Boo Radley out of his house.

Discussion questions, Harper Perennial: Good. A question about the title and its symbolism throughout the book is well phrased. There is a fascinating look at the challenges and criticisms of *To Kill a Mockingbird* over the years and a succinct biography of Harper Lee.

Fun fact: A Brooklyn theater company performs an adaptation of *To Kill a Mockingbird* on six porches and sidewalks in the borough.

Selling *To Kill a Mockingbird* to the club: It may be your favorite book of all time, but have you shared it with your present club? It will kick off your beloved-books discussion series—and you may cry in different places this time around.

No Leader, No Problem:
Discussion Basics

Minimal requirements: At the beginning of the club, you will offer a brief summary of the book, which you will make intriguing and concise. You may include a short roundup of the critical response and a fascinating, highlights-only author biography that puts him or her in a specific time, place, literary school, or on the best-seller list.

Preparation: The more you put into the discussion before you get to the club, the more you and the group will get out of it. Discussion questions prepared by the publisher but tailored by you, quotes from the book including sparkling dialogue, notes from the introductions, critical responses—it will all be appreciated more than you will ever know. You may not get to all of it, but ideas never expire.

Maps for everyone: Don't scurry around at the last minute looking for an atlas. Have one right in front of you or make sure everyone has access to copies of the Region in Question. Even a map you might consider obvious, such as the position of West Egg and East Egg in many editions of *The Great Gatsby*, should be copied and distributed. A visual prompt is never wrong.

The spirit of exploration: You don't have all the answers, nor should you. Your discussion should be viewed as a voyage of discovery. Attention know-it-alls, popinjays, quidnuncs and pontificators: You may not know who you are, but the rest of the group does. Put on that pith helmet and join the group. After all, you will have to face the same people next month.

If you chose the book, show up: Nothing annoys members more than the person who nominates the book and then goes AWOL. Open the discussion with why you chose the book and what you think of it now that you have read it.

When antlers lock: Some clubs live for the moment when there is a truly divided room. Only when the discussion gets personal and everyone is having those annoying side conversations does it digress into an unworkable morass. If you are hosting, step up and stop the side conversations and get everyone back on track.

Maintain your defense while going it alone: Book clubs are social groups that naturally want to arrive at a consensus. You can see the members switching sides mid-club. You don't have to change your mind just because everyone but you loved/hated the book. Keep fighting the good fight with even better reasons. You are not crazy.

Best mid-defense-of-book plea: "Leap with me."

Best in-summary line for the entire room: What is your abiding memory of this book?

Shrinking violets: If the club's violets are being trampled by the more aggressive plant species, institute a roundtable discussion format where each member has a chance to speak in turn. This is especially effective in the beginning of the meeting.

Reading aloud: In order to dissect, it is best to hear the author's words as he or she intended them, often in spoken dialogue. There are usually one or two wonderful readers in a group. Call on them if they are not volunteering, though they usually do.

Appalling expressions and epithets in classic fiction: Wishing them away never works. Adapt the sangfroid of NPR's Diane Rehm and incorporate the vile things into your discussion. And consider this: What might be considered offensive to book clubs in the year 2525 or in a galaxy far away?

Personal responses: It's very much okay to relate a book to your personal experience—books and their meaning to you is what the club is all about. Every discussion is unique to every club. But watch digressions into unrelated subjects or boasts ("I *invented* Women's Studies . . .") that stop the discussion dead.

Club killer: Many book clubs disband because the meetings have moved so far away from discussing the book. Remember why you chose to form a book club in the first place.

Continue the conversation online: If you have further thoughts on last night's discussion, send an e-mail to the group or the individuals you know have an interest in literary topics. Avoid gossiping at all costs, especially on e-mail.

Leave your club with these thoughts: It was an exhilarating meeting and I am leaving wanting more even though it is so late . . . Everyone made such good points and participated . . . I have a feeling of friendship sustained . . . I can't wait to read next month's book . . . Each book is a winner . . . The controversy was impassioned but somehow inspiring . . . There were different points of view but it was enjoyable to hear each club member present her arguments . . . What shall I serve next?

Club Rules: May We Knit?

Professor Azar Nafisi is visiting your club. Will you be taking up that half-finished sweater or the birthday scarf you are knitting on deadline? We all remember Professor Nafisi ran a classroom where self-expression flourished amid Iraqi bombs and worse, which she described in *Reading Lolita in Tehran*. Knitting was not only permissible, it may have been a necessity. So the good professor would completely understand if you took up your knitting.

What about a visitation from Professor Vladimir Nabokov? Well, he was quite clear on the subject when he addressed his Cornell students: "All satisfied with their seats? O.K. No talking, no smoking, *no knitting*, no newspaper reading, no sleeping, and for God's sake take notes." (italics added)

In *Vanity Fair*, Becky Sharp reaches for her sewing only to make a point. "Whenever Mrs. Rawdon wished to be particularly humble and virtuous, this little shirt used to come out of her workbox. It had got to be too small for Rawdon long before it was finished, though." And Charles Dickens created the most evil knitter of them all: Madame Defarge, a vengeful revolutionary known as a "tricoteuse." Madame stitches an enemy list within the day's knitting while not missing any of the festivities at the guillotine.

Want even more ominous? When Marlow receives his contract from the Company office in *Heart of Darkness*, he notices and is haunted by two women feverishly knitting black wool. One of the knitting women, described as the somnambulist, leads our narrator into the waiting room—while still knitting with downcast eyes! Marlow concludes these knitters are guarding the door of Darkness.

Meanwhile, back at the book club, our knitters may not be such fateful harbingers, but they are equally intent on combining their two favorite obsessions. Other knitters wouldn't dream of being distracted from fellow members' every utterance, feeling that the lack of eye contact would somehow detract. Some of the most experienced and best knitters (the ones with the websites) say they need a break once and a while. Still others, nonknitters included, defend everyone's right to multitask.

To knit or not to knit at your book club? If you knit during a book club that is not also a knitting club, consider the following observations from the field.

Not to knit:

- You think it's rude not to make consistent eye contact with the club.

- You feel marginalized by the club if you knit.

- You feel easily distracted if you are not fully concentrated on either your knitting or the club.

- You think your comments are more easily dismissed than those of the nonknitter sitting next to you.

- To the question "Would you knit if Barbara Kingsolver or Oprah herself were in the room?" you answer, "Certainly not."

- You knit everywhere you go anyway; you need a break.

On the other side of the needles:

- Why ever not knit? If the piece you are working on is not complicated, your club consists of old friends, and there is no counting involved, knitting enhances the experience. You get into the rhythm of the talking and knitting.

- You are now an expert knitter and can count stitches in your sleep, discuss books and plan every menu for the next month, all at the same time.

- You find it relaxing to knit and to watch other people knit and talk about books.

■ You feel talking and knitting looks very Brontë sisters, although if you had time on your hands in the first half of the nineteenth century, you would be doing your fine needlework. Even Elizabeth Bennet wryly took up some needlework during her visit to Netherfield, bemusedly observing Mr. Darcy.

When Pets Misbehave:
Flying Minnies and
Slobbering Horaces

Item: Flying Minnie jumps out of nowhere and lands on your arm. Bad kitty! But unbeknownst to you, you are sitting in her chair. The host, Minnie's owner (but really, who is owning whom?), tries to encourage a dialogue. Soon, Minnie is back to her favorite chair and giving you one of those "I so won" looks.

Item: It's your holiday party and everyone is dressed to impress. Horace, too, is excited as each guest comes in. He's so excited in fact that he blows his nose on your silk skirt. And it's the most glamorous night of the year for your book club.

Item: Perdida, a skilled and lithe leaper from way back, lands on the perfectly themed, *covered* dishes on the counter at least several times, and guests are starting to notice.

Item: Topper wants only love and attention. All attempts to put him out of the room when the book discussion starts results in literary baying that ratchets up to operatic. Pig's ears and biscuits are proffered, eaten and considered a delicious *amuse bouche* for the evening of snacks ahead.

Nothing makes Minnie, Horace, Perdida or Topper more excited than the irresistible combination of arriving club members and food—they simply forget every single thing they ever learned in charm school. They leap, slobber, and throw their bodies around. They refuse to leave gracefully or make very bad choices once they do. Shrieking? Check. Circling tails?

Check. Body language involving claws? Righto. Baying that you cannot believe comes out of your beloved one? That's our boy!

On a good day—maybe even most days—you think you have picture-perfect pets that are true ladies and gentlemen. But when the club arrives, even you must curb their enthusiasm.

"All pet owners who want to expose their animals to other people in social settings should have their pet under leash or voice control at all times," instructs Dr. Merry Crimi, past president of the American Animal Hospital Association and the owner of a veterinary clinic in Portland, Oregon. "If the dog isn't trained well enough to stay off of guests, the owner needs enough physical control over the dog to prevent jumping, salivating and other behaviors that are tiresome even for the best dog lover.

"We have to remember that people join book clubs because they love to read and network with others who love to read. They probably don't have a primary objective of interacting with your pet, as cute and intelligent as you think it may be. Many people enjoy dressing up, which is a ruined experience when you come home with snagged hose, pet hair everywhere and saliva stains on previously clean clothes."

The consensus of the experts? Many club members crate their dogs as a matter of course. Because so many clubs serve food, the club rules should allow only well-behaved dogs or cats that are well groomed and that may come and go as they please but will not bother the guests.

If you are hosting, perhaps for the first time, and you have a pet, inform members of the group via e-mail. Describe what kind of pet it is, what your plans are for its participation in the club (he will be in the room, he will visit part time, she will roam in and out) and ask up front whether any members have any allergies, asthma or fears. These members can reply off-line or call so that arrangements can be made.

All club members should have input as to what the club rules should be on pet attendance, just as you might for small children who need supervision. Be kind, courteous and understanding—enjoy what you're really there for, and if need be, give the dog the night off.

Behavior management begins at home, and hosts and other guests should not be subjected to "training" events held at club night that go badly due to insufficient time invested up front at home and in dog-training classes.

Regarding seating assignments, don't even think of getting up for kitty or pooch, no matter how they look at you. "Humans need to assert their rightful alpha position and seating is no different," says Dr. Crimi. "Our pets behave much better when we reinforce the fact that we are 'top dog.' Many animal behavior problems occur when we fail to do that. It's the humans that read the books and are interested in book club—they should probably have preferential seating! As I tell my dog occasionally, 'sometimes you just have to be the dog.'"

TREATS FOR EVERYONE

Pig's ears and other treats may do more harm than good, and offering them reflects a quick fix and not proper training unless it is part of a bigger training strategy. And that plate of food, combined with the excitement of the guests, might be all too irresistible for your pet. William Berloni, an animal behavior specialist and celebrity pet trainer whose pupils can be seen in Broadway shows such as *Annie* and *Chitty Chitty Bang Bang*, suggests treats for everyone—at the same time. "When the food comes out, the dog can be treated to a bone with peanut butter inside—served in the kitchen or another room."

As a test before the club comes, place the hors d'oeuvres on a coffee table a day or two before to test the animal's willingness to sit and stay. If he or she passes the test, she may be club ready.

Club Rules: When Pets Meet the Club Checklist

■ Communicate with the club as early as you can. Only you know the level of training of your pet. Be honest with yourself and ask, what is best for the club.

■ For best behavior, vigorously exercise your pet before the club comes.

■ Consider using a leash when the guests enter.

■ Crate the animals as much as you wish—it is not a punishment, it is their room. Keep crates close to the club activities so the pet does not feel isolated.

■ Keep all food and platters wrapped and away from pets, safe and sanitary. Creative placement of platters may be necessary if your pet has a "history" of going for food.

■ Have chew toys of various types available in the pets' areas. Avoid toys that leave stains on the carpets.

■ Use common sense as you would with your children, and respect the fact that people who share your time and common interests may not enjoy having to interact with your pets.

The Unexpected Meeting Place: The Botanical Garden

Springtime in Kyoto meant all the top geishas headed to Maruyama Park to view the incomparable blossoming cherry trees. Have you considered your own viewing party a la *Memoirs of a Geisha* or any other book that features flowers as prominent plot points or dramatic symbols? When you think of it, almost every book has a floral theme, some more ominous than others.

So well before the cherry blossoms, oleanders or English gardens are at their peak, start making plans for a meeting at the heart of the action. After all, how could your club resist the forty-five varieties of blossoms at the Brooklyn Botanic Garden's Cherry Blossom Festival?

For a poetic and aesthetic experience, consider having a seasonal book club meeting in a natural environment, beautifully landscaped and close to home.

BOTANICAL GARDEN CHECKLIST

- Review the botanical garden's website carefully. Check for hours of operation and special outdoor rooms on the site where your club could meet. The Denver Botanic Gardens, for example, has gazebos in the Romantic Gardens where enterprising clubs might gather. Then it's off to the Monet Deck, where food is served in the spring and summer months.

- Gardens are not parks, so picnics are usually discouraged and alcohol invariably is as well. Check to see if and when meals and drinks are served and where in the garden you are permitted to meet. In most gardens it is the café, so plan your club around its hours. And at certain institutions, such as the Getty Center in Los Angeles, a special picnic lunch can be ordered in advance.

- If the best spot to be in the garden is, for example, the Evening Island at the Chicago Botanic Garden, you can bring your books but no picnics. Plan a meal before or after somewhere offsite, and ask the garden for suggestions ahead of time.

- Beware of wedding receptions, usually held on the weekends. Make your club plans for a weekday.

- If you are planning to see a seasonal bloom attraction based on a book, call the garden in advance—the institution might offer a docent who can further explain the flower and plant, especially the one you are there to see.

- Consider becoming a member of the garden. Some gardens have special members rooms where you might be able to hold a club, special meeting or social event such as a summer or holiday party.

Hosting Basics:
How to Be Popular

Though everyone claims to be casual when the club comes over, the truth is that guests want to be guided—and even coddled a bit. Even at the book club. And though many of your fellow book club members can also be your bestest friends, you still need to take charge.

Before you volunteer to host the club, make absolutely sure you can do it. Nothing is more aggravating than having the club scramble at the last minute for a replacement host. Emergencies are one thing; normal everyday scheduling is another. If you don't have an official roster of hosting assignments, make sure your word is as good as your crudités.

At the very minimum, you as the host should

- Finish your food preparation and room arrangements before everyone comes so that you may be available for the "Where is the . . . ?" questions. This is especially crucial if a meal is involved and members are bringing dishes.

- Never neglect your drinks duties—from bartending to water pouring. A basic beverage bar includes water and soft drinks; it's your decision whether to serve tea or coffee—you know your group.

- Ensure that everything from recipes to gadgets have been tested and work. It's tragic to have to fantasize about a hammer or spend the evening picking cork out of wine bottles with butter knives because the new wine opener doesn't work or the old one can't be found.

- Provide one coherent seating arrangement for the discussion so that members will know exactly where to sit at a glance. This is especially important when clubs rotate houses. Hint: The book under discussion should be prominently displayed—along with pens and paper—on the coffee table or larger table.

■ Arrange enough seating to accommodate the number of people you expect. It's true that everyone pitches in and drags chairs over at discussion time, but they should spend the precious minutes catching up with one another or attending to the soufflé they brought instead.

■ Provide a place near almost every person on which to set down a cup and saucer or cold drink.

■ Set out napkins, big and small.

Angry, Often Desperate Housewives: The Novels

The Amateur Marriage★
  by Anne Tyler
Angry Housewives Eating Bon-Bons★
  by Lorna Landvik
The Breakdown Lane★
  by Jacqueline Mitchard
Brick Lane★
  by Monica Ali
Diary of a Mad Housewife
  by Sue Kaufman
Distant Shores
  by Kristin Hannah
Divine Secrets of the Ya-Ya Sisterhood★
  by Rebecca Wells
The Doctor's Wife
  by Elizabeth Brundage
Everything She Thought She Wanted★
  by Elizabeth Buchan
The First Wives Club
  by Olivia Goldsmith
The Future Homemakers of America★
  by Laurie Graham
The Good Wife Strikes Back★
  by Elizabeth Buchan

How to Cook a Tart
  by Nina Kilham
An Italian Affair★
  by Laura Fraser
Keeping Faith★
  by Jodi Picoult
Lady Oracle★
  by Margaret Atwood
The Last Girls★
  by Lee Smith
Le Divorce★
  by Diane Johnson
The Life and Loves of a She-Devil
  by Fay Weldon
Lost in the Forest★
  by Sue Miller
Madame Bovary
  by Gustave Flaubert★
The Mermaid Chair ★
  by Sue Monk Kidd
Mrs. Bridge
  by Evan S. Connell
Mrs. Dalloway★
  by Virginia Woolf

★Publisher discussion questions available.

*Open House**
  by Elizabeth Berg
*Our Kind**
  by Kate Walbert
*Persian Pickle Club**
  by Sandra Dallas
Pull of the Moon
  by Elizabeth Berg
*Revenge of the Middle Age Woman**
  by Elizabeth Buchan

*The Saving Graces**
  by Patricia Gaffney
The Stepford Wives
  by Ira Levin
Tara Road
  by Maeve Binchy
Thursdays at Eight
  by Debbie Macomber
A Wedding in December
  by Anita Shreve

Beloved Cocktail:
The Cosmopolitan

Though Carrie Bradshaw lay down her swizzle stick long ago, many book clubs simply cannot resist mixing up a batch of these pinkest ladies beloved by the *Sex and the City* gang, and apparently by you.

These cosmopolitans call for cranberry juice, "not cranberry cocktail, for God's sake," according to mixologist Peter Armstrong on whose recipes these are based. Cranberry juice can be found at health food and gourmet groceries.

THE COSMOPOLITAN

MAKES 8 DRINKS

1½ cups vodka
1 cup Cointreau
½ cup cranberry juice
⅓ cup fresh squeezed lime juice

Mix ingredients in large pitcher and refrigerate. When ready to serve, pour into cocktail shaker. Shake with ice and strain into chilled martini glasses.

COSMO PUNCH

SERVES 14

4 cups premium vodka
2½ cups Cointreau
½ cup fresh squeezed orange juice
1 cup fresh squeezed lime juice
1 cup cranberry juice

Mix all ingredients in a punch bowl. You can make the punch up to an hour in advance and refrigerate. When ready to serve, pour into punch cups and add ice.

An Anne Tyler Celebration

When Delia walked out of the café, she felt she was surrounded by a lighter kind of air than usual—thinner, more transparent—and she crossed the street with a floating gait.   *—Ladder of Years*

Everyone has a favorite Anne Tyler book—even Colin Firth. He selected *Saint Maybe* as one of his favorite books in the January 2005 edition of *O* magazine. The actor who played Mr. Darcy in the BBC version of *Pride and Prejudice* and Mark Darcy in the *Bridget Jones* movies even poses an excellent discussion question: "How do you evaluate a deed that has brought catastrophe?" Firth would be a welcome addition to any book club, yes?

Debate the merits of your favorite Anne Tyler, from the recent novels (*The Amateur Marriage, Back When We Were Grownups*) to the early masterpieces (*Dinner at the Homesick Restaurant, The Accidental Tourist*). Some club members will fight for their right to call *A Patchwork Planet* her masterpiece, and you should come prepared with the book—and specific passages—to which you are most devoted.

Optional but worth it: Look for the Fotofolio postcard featuring Anne Tyler in her Baltimore home, holding her cat. If you locate the card in a bookstore or online, buy in quantity and send to the club, informing them of the Tyler festivities and what each member should bring.

Choose a date for your club's Anne Tyler Founder's Day Celebration, get out the scalloped paper placemats in honor of Rick-Rack's Café, serve crab cakes and coleslaw, and send everyone home with Cats' Tongue cookies in festive paper bags.

Take-Home Cookie

EDNA LEWIS AND SCOTT PEACOCK'S
CATS' TONGUES

MAKES ABOUT 2½ DOZEN COOKIES

⅔ cup all-purpose flour
1⅔ cups confectioners' sugar
1 teaspoon ground ginger
⅛ teaspoon salt
2 egg whites
½ cup heavy cream

Preheat the oven to 400 degrees.

Sift together in a bowl the flour, confectioners' sugar, ginger and salt. Whip the egg whites in one bowl and the heavy cream in another, just until both are frothy. Pour the beaten egg whites over the sifted ingredients, and stir until well blended. Pour in the heavy cream, and stir just until blended.

Drop 1 level teaspoon of the batter onto a well-buttered cookie sheet. Draw the dull blade side of a butter knife downward through each teaspoon of batter until you form a cookie that is approximately 2½ inches long and tapered to a fine point on one end. Repeat with the remaining batter, allowing about 1½ inches between cookies.

Bake in the preheated oven for 5–8 minutes, until the edges of the cookies begin to brown. Remove from the oven, and allow to cool for 1–2 minutes, then lift the cookies from the cookie sheet with a thin spatula and place them on a wire rack to cool. (If the cookies cool too much and become difficult to remove, place the baking sheet back in the oven for about 1 minute to soften.)

Store the cooled cookies in an airtight container for up to 4 days.

TAKE-HOME COOKIE PREPARATION

These are delicate cookies, so the take-home treats work best if you use a bag-within-a-bag method.

1. Place from 3–5 cookies in a clear mini bag, about 4 × 6 inches. Close the bag with a small disc sticker.

2. Place the mini bag in a small paper sack, 4¾ × 2¾ × 9⅜ inches. Color of the bag is host's choice. Seasonal or holiday colors work well, and if there is a color theme to the book you are discussing, leap at the chance to gift thematically.

3. Make a ½-inch fold at the top of the paper sack, fold/over and place a thematic sticker to close. Best in theme are the "stuffed crab" stickers from Mrs. Grossman's (mrsgrossmans.com), but sticker people can go wild with the infinite variety. If the bag is too heavy for the sticker, apply a dot of glue to sticker and bag.

4. Line the colorful bags next to the door in a basket and give them away as you say good-bye.

Ina Garten's Chicken Stew with Biscuits

SERVES 8

Note: In paragraph 2, the recipe calls for a sheet pan lined with parchment or wax paper. Wax paper might smoke in a hot oven, so parchment paper would work best.

For the Stew:

3 whole (6 split) chicken breasts, bone in, skin on

3 tablespoons olive oil

Kosher salt and freshly ground black pepper

5 cups chicken stock, preferably homemade (recipe follows)

2 chicken bouillon cubes

12 tablespoons (1½ sticks) unsalted butter

2 cups chopped yellow onions (2 onions)

¾ cup all-purpose flour

¼ cup heavy cream

2 cups medium-diced carrots (4 carrots), blanched for 2 minutes

1 10-ounce package frozen peas (2 cups)

1½ cups frozen small whole onions

½ cup minced fresh parsley

For the Biscuits:

2 cups all-purpose flour

1 tablespoon baking powder

1 teaspoon kosher salt

1 teaspoon sugar

¼ pound (1 stick) cold unsalted butter, diced

¾ cup half-and-half

½ cup chopped fresh parsley

1 egg mixed with 1 tablespoon water, for egg wash

Preheat the oven to 375 degrees.

Place the chicken breasts on a sheet pan and rub them with olive oil. Sprinkle generously with salt and pepper. Roast for 35 to 40 minutes, or until cooked through. Set aside until cool enough to handle, then remove the meat from the bones and discard the skin. Cut the chicken into large dice. You will have 4 to 6 cups of cubed chicken.

In a small saucepan, heat the chicken stock and dissolve the bouillon cubes in the stock. In a large pot or Dutch oven, melt the butter and sauté the onions over medium-low heat for 10 to 15 minutes, until translucent. Add the flour and cook over low heat, stirring constantly, for 2 minutes. Add the hot chicken stock to the sauce. Simmer over low heat for 1 more minute, stirring, until thick. Add 2 teaspoons salt, ½ teaspoon pepper and the heavy cream. Add the cubed chicken, carrots, peas, onions and parsley. Mix well. Place the stew in a 10 × 13 × 2-inch oval or rectangular baking dish. Place the baking dish on a sheet pan lined with parchment or wax paper. Bake for 15 minutes.

Meanwhile, make the biscuits. Combine the flour, baking powder, salt and sugar in the bowl of an electric mixer fitted with the paddle attachment. Add the butter and mix on low speed until the butter is the size of peas. Add the half-and-half and combine on low speed. Mix in the parsley.

Dump the dough out on a well-floured board and, with a rolling pin, roll out to ⅜ inch thick. Cut out 12 circles with a 2½-inch round cutter.

Remove the stew from the oven and arrange the biscuits on top of the filling. Brush them with egg wash, and return the dish to the oven. Bake for another 20 to 30 minutes, until the biscuits are brown and the stew is bubbly.

To make in advance, refrigerate the chicken stew and biscuits separately. Bake the stew for 25 minutes, then place the biscuits on top, and bake for another 30 minutes, until done.

CHICKEN STOCK

MAKES 6 QUARTS

3 5-pound roasting chickens

3 large yellow onions, unpeeled, quartered

6 carrots, unpeeled, halved

4 celery stalks with leaves, cut in thirds

4 parsnips, unpeeled, cut in half (optional)

20 sprigs fresh parsley

15 sprigs fresh thyme

20 sprigs fresh dill

1 head garlic, unpeeled, cut in half crosswise

2 tablespoons kosher salt

2 teaspoons whole black peppercorns

Place the chickens, onions, carrots, celery, parsnips, parsley, thyme, dill, garlic and seasonings in a 16- to 20-quart stockpot. Add 7 quarts of water and bring to a boil. Simmer uncovered for 4 hours. Strain the entire contents of the pot through a colander and discard the solids. Chill the stock overnight. The next day, remove the surface fat. Use immediately or pack in containers and freeze for up to 3 months.

Gramma's Crab Cakes

MAKES 12 MEDIUM CRAB CAKES

If crab cakes could be described as light, these would definitely qualify. This recipe was adapted from a neighbor, Charlaine Fontelieu, who received it from her Baltimore-bred daughter-in-law.

3 tablespoons unsalted butter

1 small red onion, finely diced

4 stalks of celery, small diced

¼ cup parsley

1½ teaspoons Old Bay Seasoning

½ teaspoon Tabasco sauce

½ teaspoon Worcestershire sauce

½ pound lump crabmeat, shells removed

½ medium lemon

½ cup smashed saltines (about 10 crackers)

1 teaspoon paprika

1 teaspoon dry mustard

1 egg

½ cup mayonnaise

salt and pepper to taste

¼ cup oil for frying

Melt the butter over medium heat in a large pan. Add the onion, celery and parsley and saute with Old Bay Seasoning, Tabasco sauce, and Worcestershire sauce until the onions have a slight brown edge. Set aside to cool.

In a separate bowl, break up crabmeat, pick out any remaining shells and transfer to a paper towel to drain. Squeeze a small amount of lemon over the crabmeat, then combine with saltines, paprika, dry mustard, egg and mayonnaise. Salt and pepper to taste. Form the mixture into 1½-inch di-ameter cakes, the size of very small hamburgers.

Heat the oil over medium heat. Saute the crab cakes for 3–4 minutes per side, or until they are golden brown. Drain on a paper towel.

Serve with tartar sauce or cocktail sauce, sliced lemon and your favorite coleslaw.

If You Were in a
1920s Book Club

1920

The Age of Innocence
   by Edith Wharton
Bull-Dog Drummond
   by Cyril McNeile
Flappers and Philosophers
   by F. Scott Fitzgerald
Main Street by Sinclair Lewis
Poems by Wilfred Owen
This Side of Paradise
   by F. Scott Fitzgerald
Women in Love by D. H. Lawrence

1921

Alice Adams by Booth Tarkington
The Beautiful and the Damned
   by F. Scott Fitzgerald
Collected Poems
   by Edwin Arlington Robinson
Crome Yellow by Aldous Huxley

1922

Babbitt by Sinclair Lewis
The Ballad of the Harp-Weavers
   by Edna St. Vincent Millay
The Garden Party by Katherine
   Mansfield
One of Ours by Willa Cather
Queen Victoria by Lytton Strachey
Tales of the Jazz Age
   by F. Scott Fitzgerald
The Wasteland by T. S. Eliot

1923

Cane by Jean Toomer
The Flower Beneath the Foot
   by Ronald Firbank
Horses and Men
   by Sherwood Anderson
*New Hampshire: A Poem with Notes
   and Grace Notes* by Robert Frost
Stella Dallas by Olive Higgins Prouty
Three Stories and Ten Poems
   by Ernest Hemingway
Tulips & Chimneys by e. e. cummings
Whose Body? by Dorothy L. Sayers

1924

A Passage to India by E. M. Forster
So Big by Edna Ferber
The Tattooed Countess
   by Carl Van Vechten

1925

An American Tragedy
   by Theodore Dreiser
Arrowsmith by Sinclair Lewis
Barren Ground by Ellen Glasgow
The Great Gatsby
   by F. Scott Fitzgerald
The Informer by Liam O'Flaherty
Mrs. Dalloway by Virginia Woolf
The Professor's House by Willa Cather
When We Were Very Young
   by A. A. Milne

1926

Beau Geste by P. C. Wren

Enough Rope by Dorothy Parker

Gentlemen Prefer Blondes
 by Anita Loos

The Murder of Roger Ackroyd
 by Agatha Christie

Show Boat by Edna Ferber

The Sun Also Rises
 by Ernest Hemingway

1927

The Bridge of San Luis Rey
 by Thornton Wilder

Death Comes for the Archbishop
 by Willa Cather

Elmer Gantry by Sinclair Lewis

Men without Women
 by Ernest Hemingway

The Plutocrat by Booth Tarkington

To the Lighthouse by Virginia Woolf

We by Charles Lindbergh

1928

Ashenden, or: the British Agent
 by W. Somerset Maugham

Decline and Fall by Evelyn Waugh

John Brown's Body
 by Stephen Vincent Benet

Home to Harlem by Claude McKay

Orlando by Virginia Woolf

Parade's End by Ford Maddox Ford

Point Counter Point by Aldous Huxley

Scarlet Sister Mary by Julia Peterkin

1929

All Quiet on the Western Front
 by Erich Maria Remarque

The Bishop Murder Case
 by S. S. Van Dine

Dodsworth by Sinclair Lewis

Elizabeth and Essex
 by Lytton Strachey

A Farewell to Arms
 by Ernest Hemingway

Goodbye to All That by Robert Graves

A High Wind in Jamaica
 by Richard Hughes

Is Sex Necessary?
 by James Thurber and E. B. White

The Last September
 by Elizabeth Bowen

Little Caesar by W. R. Burnett

Look Homeward Angel
 by Thomas Wolfe

Passing by Nella Larsen

The Sound and the Fury
 by William Faulkner

THE BOOK CLUB CLASSIC

"I time travel. Involuntarily."
—Henry DeTamble, *The Time Traveler's Wife*

The fiercest wars rage, the plots are of biblical propor-tions, the largest passions are in play, emotions are operatic and women often get the choicest roles. The big concepts of the Book Club Classic are tinted in mean reds, blues and grays. Bold colors are splashed across endless, open seas. The arias are as wondrous—and poisonous—as an exotic songbird or voices from a distant galaxy. A classic book club is so intensely focused on its theme, it can often be reduced to a sensational headline: "Murdered Teen Tells All from Heaven," "Hostage! Roxane Coss Held in Terrorist Plot," "Smyrna Burns, Michigan Girl Switches Sex," "Boleyn Girl Loses Throne, Head."

And the apocalyptic battle scenes are not just on the field of war. In the Book Club Classic, even the novellas are writ large. Can there be a bigger icon than chic, mysterious Holly Golightly? Compared to her, Mrs. Dalloway or La Stupenda Roxane Coss are icons in training.

In many of the Book Club Classics, we return to one of our fa-vorite discussion questions: What is a hero? Characters are in varying degrees of crisis and there are often two protagonists. Consider the seductive and strange mirror images of both Boleyn girls, Calliope and Cal Stephanides, and Kavalier and Clay. Their futures are perilous, buffeted by natural and political disasters and the effects of time and space. If our protagonists prevail, character is destiny. And if not, well, you'll just have to discuss among yourselves.

Last season's "it" book gains a permanent perch in our library of book club classics, an evolving canon. We are establishing a permanent collection, an ever-lengthening reading list for new clubs and a checklist for older clubs whose members might wonder how they ever missed that one.

Bring out the towering questions, dial your discussion to Jumbotron and prepare for some big ideas.

The Twenty Indispensable Titles

■ ■ ■

The Amazing Adventures of Kavalier & Clay
(2000) by Michael Chabon

An epic tale of dizzying scope and ambition, Michael Chabon's Pulitzer Prize–winning novel takes us to New York on the eve of World War II. Everyone is smoking in a dreamy, art moderne city when Sammy Clay and his cousin Josef Kavalier—who is newly escaped from Prague—scale the fantastic wall of the comic book business. The dynamic duo create the most daring crime fighter in tights, the Escapist, who fights against evil and fascism in a world that needs saving.

Although each character has different reasons to escape, Harry Houdini-worshipper Kavalier is the truest escape artist of them all, leaving Europe in a coffin with the mythic clay Golem itself. He awaits word of his family left behind—especially his beloved brother—after the "tumblers of a great iron lock" have clicked into place. It is the eve of the Holocaust, and this heartbreak gives the novel its emotional resonance.

Clubs have been enthralled by Chabon's mix of the hard-boiled comic book world with dazzling fantasy elements of illusionists' tricks. Historical figures such as Orson Welles and Al Smith make happy appearances. But it is the haunting, funny and realistic friendship between Sammy and Joe that is the emotional center of *The Amazing Adventures of Kavalier & Clay*. The secondary characters are also first-rate, including ace Golem wrangler Kornblum, impresario Longman Harkoo and swashbuckling radio star Tracy Bacon. Don't miss the scene where Salvador Dali is rescued by Joe at a surrealist party in Greenwich Village.

Discussion questions, Picador: Too many questions are crammed into each of six sections, primarily centered on the book's major themes of escape. An interesting question about the book's footnotes touches on how the author creates his world, interspersing real-life events.

Furthermore: An opportunity to discuss comic books and show the latest examples torn from the hands of actual teenagers doesn't come up too often. Look for Art Spiegelman's two-page book review of the novel, inked as a graphic novel called *The Escapist!* (The New Yorker, October 30, 2000).

Selling *The Amazing Adventures of Kavalier & Clay* to the club: As contemporary as it is, this novel personalizes but never trivializes the Holocaust. So many authors try it and fail—discuss why this one succeeds so brilliantly.

■■■

Bel Canto
(2001) by Ann Patchett

Roxane Coss, world famous lyric soprano who makes Callas look like a spear carrier by comparison, is the evening's entertainment for Japanese businessman Mr. Hosokawa and the other guests of the Vice President in an unnamed South American country. Then the lights go out. All are taken hostage by a band of terrorists and the story begins. Roxane is at first a valuable hostage/commodity and then becomes the besieged mansion's lovely epicenter. She reigns by music.

But there are puzzlements. The mansion becomes an almost utopian community of music and shared responsibilities. It is also a setting of love for two unlikely couples. These shifting allegiances cause our greatest confusion—and is the source of *Bel Canto*'s power. Are our thoughts aligned with those of Mr. Hosokawa, who is gaining his heart's desire? And what are we to make of the terrorists, whose demands are both grandiose and vague as they, too, settle into a routine domesticity. What kind of transformative role does Gen the translator perform for the characters and for the author? What is really happening here? Is *Bel Canto* a tribute to the sustaining power of music (See "A Bel Canto Evening,")

Discussion questions, Harper Perennial: The introduction offers a succinct summary of the novel, the action and the issues that arise within. The discussion questions are good, especially those relating to Mr. Hosokawa, but there is a spoiler midway through the list. See chapter 9 for an interview with Ann Patchett.

Audio alert: Anna Fields narrates with clarity, authority and with a hint of anxiety in this superlative audio from HarperAudio.

■ ■ ■

Breakfast at Tiffany's
(1958) by Truman Capote

Here we meet Holly Golightly for the first, but not the last time. Her iconographic status as a devil-may-care, elegant party girl who dresses in slim, cool black dresses, wears dark glasses and a pearl choker, and drinks a lot of martinis is only partially the case. In *Breakfast at Tiffany's*, Truman Capote's masterpiece of short fiction, both Holly and the story itself are tougher than their movie-version counterparts.

The story is told as reminiscence about Manhattan in the years of World War II—a big surprise to many new readers who assume the story takes place in the 1950s because of the 1961 movie. The narrator and Holly are apartment mates in an East Side brownstone. At first he is mystified by Holly, then obsessed. They become fast friends, have a bitter falling-out and then a reunion before Holly disappears, apparently forever. But what a swell time! Holly's wild parties are depicted with precision and are beguilingly offset by her confessions of suffering from "the mean reds." Her ever-endearing solution is to head to Tiffany's where "nothing very bad could happen to you there."

Is Holly a phony but "a real phony," as her Hollywood agent suggests? Is she the prototype for today's aspiring starlet, or is she a product of her time and place, the last of a breed? Holly Golightly is one of the great characters in literature and her short life continues to be discussed avidly.

Furthermore: Truman Capote was a wildly ambitious writer whose career spawned a cottage industry for journalists and critics. Look for the article "The Truman Show," (the *New York Times Book Review*, December 5, 2004) or ask your librarian to print out the Gale Literary Database entry on Capote.

Cocktails: Triple martinis, something called a "white angel" concocted by barkeep Joe Bell, bourbon nightcaps and champagne cocktails on the house.

Take-home cookie: In honor of Cat, the kitty with no name, see Cats' Tongues recipe, chapter 1.

Fun fact: *Breakfast at Tiffany's* was a selection of the George Costanza book club, though George never actually read the book. This is the *Seinfeld* episode where George insisted on watching the tape with a video renter and his daughter in their apartment—spilling grape juice on their couch in the process.

Dressing thematically: Vintage Givenchy, though Holly herself had a single Mainbocher (look for one in a museum). By all means, treat the 1961 movie starring Audrey Hepburn and George Peppard as a parallel discussion exercise. The novella and the movie have their significant differences, as George Costanza learned the hard way. But as a movie about style, it is almost without parallel. The costumes by Givenchy could be worn today—just ask Sarah Jessica Parker. Compare and contrast Johnny Mercer's "Moon River" lyrics to the song Holly sings as she strums her guitar.

■ ■ ■

Crossing to Safety

(1987) by Wallace Stegner

What do clubs like best about discussing *Crossing to Safety*? Unquestionably, it is the searing analysis of one couple by another. Wallace Stegner's depiction of the enchantment four people feel when they fall in love with each other and the ambiguity of the relationship that follows is something altogether different than friendship. Or is it?

It is the Depression and our narrator Larry Morgan and his wife Sally move to the University of Wisconsin to begin teaching a term in literature. There they meet the couple who will change their lives, Sid and Charity Lang. The Langs are people of great refinement, humor and warmth, and the two couples become inseparable in a world of literature, young married fun, picnics and trips to Battell Pond, the Langs' edenic Vermont compound. Meanwhile, the serpent shows itself the garden. And it's not what you think.

All eyes are on bossy boots Charity Lang who gives new meaning to the concept "control freak." Yet, she is a woman of action and results, a kind friend and an enthusiastic wife. There must be a reason the author named her "Charity," isn't there? And what do you make of her "constructive daydreaming"? You will also want to discuss the epigraph, a Robert Frost poem, which is the source of the title.

Cocktails: Sherry on the porch, at six-thirty.

Entertaining thematically: The standard Lang picnic transported in Adirondack hampers includes "bags of sweet corn . . . boxes of crackers, chunks of aged Cabot cheddar . . . bowls of salad ready for dressing . . . Sara Lee cakes thawing . . . whatever fruits of the season" and dozens of steaks.

Furthermore: Stegner won a Pulitzer Prize in 1971 for *Angle of Repose*, one of the best books about the West, its history and topography (geology is also a minor theme in *Crossing to Safety*). And, like *Crossing to Safety*, it is about the marriage of Susan Burling and Oliver Ward, who move to the new Western frontier after the Civil War. Stegner is almost without peer in writing about the big subjects and landscapes in such an intimate style.

Selling *Crossing to Safety* **to the club**: It encompasses all of our subjects: love, friendship, books and the odyssey of life. Superbly written, *Crossing to Safety* will quickly become a club favorite.

■ ■ ■

The Dive from Clausen's Pier
(2002) by Ann Packer

On a Memorial Day weekend in Madison, Wisconsin, twenty-three-year-old Carrie Bell sets off for Clausen's Reservoir with her fiancé, Mike. Here, he takes the unfortunate shallow dive of the title, becoming paralyzed from the neck down. It's especially unfortunate for Carrie who had become disenchanted with this long-standing boyfriend well before the accident.

Carrie spends the rest of the novel in a quandary, and her talent for sewing becomes a metaphor for her life as well as a tantalizing avenue for professional advancement. The fabrics, the construction of the clothes she imagines and then actually sews, the identities she tries and moves beyond are artfully rendered by Ann Packer. New York City and Madison are persuasively described and form complementary backdrops for Carrie as she enters a particularly tortured postcollege phase in life. Club members will line up to support or disparage Carrie, and they love to dissect Kilroy, the attractive, intelligent but emotionally insecure new boyfriend who also happens to be forty years old. You will be discussing the next chapter long after the author has left the stage.

Discussion questions, Vintage Books: Excellent, engenders long and meaningful discussions. Is Carrie the heroine of her own book or does she fall way short? Equally provocative: Imagine an inverted version of *The Dive from Clausen's Pier* where Carrie is the one to have the accident.

Dressing thematically: The Carrie Bell Collection is a complete wardrobe for daytime (fluid pantsuit of black, red and gold print—don't forget the black camisole underneath) to early evening (pale gold lounging pj's) to evening (the dark green velvet dress) to really late night (the sensuous negligee and peignoir of silk). Or be as witty as you want to be, Carrie artschool style.

Selling *The Dive from Clausen's Pier* to the club: Love, fate, friendship and loyalty, plus all the possibilities that a trip to a shop might offer. An ideal first book if you are starting a book club.

■ ■ ■

Empire Falls
(2001) by Richard Russo

Working-class philosopher Miles Roby is leading exactly the life his mother warned him against. Her dying wish was that he never return to Empire Falls, a fading Maine mill town presided over by imperious moneybags, Mrs. Whiting. Guess what? He quits college, runs the down-on-its-luck Empire Grill and watches as his life alternates between disintegration and a kind of strained hope. Especially wonderful is the huge cast of secondary characters including Miles's wisecracking father, Max, his soon to be ex-wife Janine (at the center of many hilarious scenes), and in shades of sepia, memories of his doomed mother and her lover, Charlie. Barflies abound and who doesn't love tough but kind ex-mother-in-law Bea Majeski and the Silver Fox, who is a lot older than Janine thinks.

Empire Falls is a catalogue of failed marriages as well as a sharp socialscape of a diminishing place whose slogan might be "No trespassing without permission." Consider whether Mrs. Whiting, with her "dear boys" and life-destroying strategies, is worthy of any sympathy. Richard Russo brings all of his themes together in this Pulitzer Prize–winning novel.

Discussion questions, Vintage Books: Excellent. The questions are filled with depth and meaning and range from the major relationships (Miles and his daughter Tick, Miles and his mother) and the three families of Empire Falls: the Whitings, the Robys and the Mintys.

Cocktails: Though Mrs. Whiting never granted Miles and his brother David a liquor license, Bea was more than happy to pour brewskis, old-fashioneds and sidecars for the denizens of Empire Towers senior housing.

DVD alert: Ed Harris, Joanne Woodward and Paul Newman star in the HBO movie available on DVD. Perfection.

■ ■ ■

Girl with a Pearl Earring
(2000) by Tracy Chevalier

As composed as a Dutch still-life, as measured in its depictions of day-to-day tasks as the illustrations on a delft tile, *Girl with a Pearl Earring* is a novel about artistry and craft. Its spare writing style and its lovely teenage narrator who becomes a maid and eventually a model in the great painter Johannes Vermeer's household, satisfyingly invokes the period.

There are only thirty-five (possibly thirty-six) known works of the master. Vermeer's *Girl with a Pearl Earring* is thought to have been painted in 1665, and this is where our story is firmly placed. Griet is from a Protestant family and is faced with strange Catholic customs and unfriendly mistresses. Despite her trials, she is recognized by Vermeer as a person of delicacy and intelligence. Griet grinds the paints for him and observes the way he applies his paint, uses the camera-obscura and manipulates the sitter. She also knows she must live by her wits in a household riddled with financial woe, many children, a jealous wife and a fearsome mother-in-law. Maria Thins is beloved by clubs for her discussion potential. Griet's considerable pluck may be deemed anachronistic by some members.

Pondering the known Vermeers from books is a wonderful way to spend time at the club—you did bring them, didn't you? Each is filled with mystery and intimate luxury, and it's not difficult to imagine what inspired Chevalier.

Penguin Reading Group Guide: The questions themselves are basic, mostly concerning Griet's choices. But the guide contains an in-depth description of Vermeer's world and an excellent interview with Tracy Chevalier in which she explains the historic influences on the fictional story.

Colin Firth alert: Scarlett Johansson and Colin Firth faithfully inhabit the roles of Griet and Vermeer in this 2003 film version. Firth exhibits several moody Mr. Darcy-esque looks, especially when he magically appears in his studio to observe dreamy, wide-eyed Griet. Each scene and costume is an homage to the great painter.

Furthermore: For more information about Vermeer and his works, check out the exhaustive site http://essentialvermeer.20m.com. It offers complete information about each painting and clarifies scholars' positions on the possible thirty-sixth Vermeer.

■ ■ ■

The Hours
(1998) by Michael Cunningham
and
Mrs. Dalloway
(1925) by Virginia Woolf

Michael Cunningham's ingenious Pulitzer Prize–winning novel *The Hours* is a meditation on the classic work of modern literature, *Mrs. Dalloway*. In the latter novel, Virginia Woolf writes about a single day in the life of Clarissa Dalloway as she prepares for a party. It is famously interspersed with Clarissa's interior monologues about her present life and thoughts about her past loves. *The Hours* interweaves the themes in *Mrs. Dalloway* with portraits of three women: Virginia Woolf herself, who wends her way to her last crisis; New Yorker Clarissa Vaughn, who, like Mrs. Dalloway, is preparing a party amid thoughts of the past; and Laura Brown, who faces another kind of crisis in 1949 Los Angeles.

Clubs love discussing the roles of the women in both novels, especially the relationship between Clarissa Dalloway and Sally Seton in *Mrs. Dalloway* and their own lost loves and roads not taken. If you are rereading *The Hours*, reconsider the Mrs. Brown chapters as perhaps the strongest and most poignant, especially as a precursor to what happens to Richard, the honoree of the party who is dying of AIDS.

The passage of time, lost love and lively social portraits amid intensely personal crisis are ripe for exploration, and there is a twist at the end of *The Hours*. Don't miss the scene in Cunningham's novel when Virginia Woolf's sister, Vanessa, comes for tea with her children ("Hello, changelings") and a funeral is held for a thrush. It is a beautiful illustration of how differently the two sisters deal with life.

Discussion questions, *The Hours*, Picador: Excellent. The questions are abundant and thorough, serving as a guide to the intersecting stories and the links to Virginia Woolf's novel.

Discussion questions, *Mrs. Dalloway*, Harcourt: Very good. Questions concentrate on the characters' shifting points of view, Virginia Woolf's masterful interior and exterior descriptions, and the relationships of the female characters. The questions about the passing of time and the book's symbolism are covered deftly.

Furthermore: A growing cottage industry of companion books to *Mrs. Dalloway* include *Mrs. Dalloway's Party*, a collection of the original seven stories that were the basis for *Mrs. Dalloway* and *The Mrs. Dalloway Reader*. It features a fascinating collection of essays about Virginia Woolf and her books, and a selection of Woolf's journal entries and sketches.

■ ■ ■

The Killer Angels
(1974) by Michael Shaara

What is a hero? It is perhaps the most indispensable discussion question, maybe because the answer so often eludes us. The question comes into focus most vividly in *The Killer Angels*, Michael Shaara's elegiac, Pulitzer Prize–winning novel about the battle of Gettysburg. A palpable recreation of the greatest battle of the Civil War—and on the North American continent—the novel is a collection of vivid character studies made intimate by the protagonists' arresting interior monologues. All of the great warriors, including Robert E. Lee, James Longstreet and Joshua Lawrence Chamberlain, are present as they face the existential dilemmas of the battle ahead and war itself. "Never, forever, never, forever," is one of Chamberlain's dreamlike ruminations.

Did Lee fail because his ambitions were Napoleonic? Is personality destiny? Who is the true conscience of this book? *The Killer Angels* can be discussed in so many ways, from each side's reasons for fighting the war to the mistakes made and the opportunities exploited. Shaara approaches the Pennsylvania countryside in two different styles: genre painting and heroic mural. But both styles depict a kind of heaven and a piteous hell. Don't miss the observations of the Englishman Fremantle as he predicts a southern victory, worships Lee and calls slavery "a bit embarrassing."

Furthermore: *The Killer Angels* will send you scurrying to the library for books about the Civil War. Begin with *The Civil War: An Illustrated History* by Geoffrey C. Ward with Ric Burns and Ken Burns. It is the companion book to the PBS miniseries and concisely describes each battle, and includes a complete chronology of the war.

Doctorow alert: The long-awaited return of E. L. Doctorow has ended with *The March: A Novel of the Civil War*, which takes place during William Tecumseh Sherman's march through the Carolinas and Georgia less than two years after Gettysburg. Doctorow's trademark cast of characters from different walks of life appear in the historical setting.

Selling *The Killer Angels* to the club: When was the last time you read anything with battle maps? It's different, historical and unforgettable.

■ ■ ■

The Known World

(2003) by Edward P. Jones

As spare and elegant as a wanted poster, as stately as a tombstone, *The Known World* tells the story of Henry Townsend, a slave who becomes the protégé of his white master, William Robbins, and eventually becomes a slave owner himself. In *The Known World*, Edward P. Jones describes the complex, ever-alarming system of slavery. This is a genre-busting novel that can at times read like a Western or a detective story, a saga or an enigmatic epic poem.

Jones is a MacArthur fellow and won the Pulitzer Prize for this book. He has written an instant classic that plants us firmly in antebellum Virginia. The narrator is hyper-omniscient: he can see well into the future—into our own time, in fact, to trace ancestors in fascinating, seemingly historically accurate asides—or are they? Who among the characters seem to be favored in this perverse world and who, like the slave Moses, had their own peculiar destiny? What do the cryptic headlines that begin each chapter tell us and how do they serve the persistent, overarching theme of slavery? Jones is masterful in weaving the interior and exterior lives of Henry, his family and his slaves into the larger world that slavery created: everything and everyone has a price.

Don't miss the magical songs and incisive rantings of the wandering slave Alice Night ("I met a dead man layin in Massa lane; Ask that dead man what his name"). What role does she play in *The Known World*, and how many other subtle ways do the slaves revolt? The letters exchanged among the characters educated by Fern Elston are beautifully written and cloaked in the strange.

Discussion questions, Amistad: The paperback edition features an interview with the author, who describes the influences behind his fictional world and the dramatis personae of *The Known World*. It also includes his short story, "The Girl Who Raised Pigeons," which won the PEN/Hemingway award. The questions themselves are basic, though the significance of the title must be discussed.

Furthermore: A theme of folk art runs through *The Known World*. Discuss the creativity of the characters and the objects that they made—especially the carved walking sticks.

Selling *The Known World* to the club: Surprising and original, alive yet historic, it's an important book. Your discussions are sure to reflect all of the tensions contained within.

Life of Pi

(2001) by Yann Martel

A compulsively readable meditation and an adventure story about faith and loneliness, *Life of Pi* is a survivor's tale. Pi Patel, adrift on his raft, is more than up to the challenging task before him. Pi's father owned a zoo in Pondicherry, India, and this singular background is seamlessly woven throughout the narrative: Pi's fellow passenger, ward and companion turns out to be a Bengal tiger named Richard Parker.

Winner of the Booker Prize, *Life of Pi* works up to several dramatic points, with informative asides on a wide array of topics. Pi's enlightening meditations on religion (he is a combination Hindu, Muslim and Christian and is mockingly called "Swami Jesus"), animals and their personality-based behavior, how to serve sea turtle (first, catch one) and the finer points of tiger training are tantalizingly described. Pi Patel is an optimistic and cheerful fellow throughout his travails, and he has charmed and entertained book clubs since he made his appearance.

You will want to discuss the stunning twist right away, but while you are heading there, you might examine Pi's resourcefulness, whether he is taunting us by telling us this is a story that will "make you believe in God," and his extraordinary relationship with Richard Parker.

Discussion questions, Harcourt: Very good. Especially effective is the question about Pi's name and his debate with all of his spiritual advisors. Exactly what kind of book is this? A tragedy, romance, comedy or a little bit of everything? Spoiler alert: The questions about the ending are essential, but if you have not yet read the book, avoid reading through the questions.

Entertaining thematically: Pi's imagined banquet includes potato masala, cabbage *vadai*, masala *dosai*, spicy lentil *ransam*, coconut chutney, mint chutney, the usual nans, *popadoms*, *parathas* and *puris*, plus a variety of salads such as mango curd and fresh cucumber. Almond payasam and coconut burfi are among his desserts. Clubs may refer to the take-out menu.

Selling *Life of Pi* to the club: A unique opportunity to have a far-reaching discussion on life, love and survival, you can be as discursive as you want to be.

■ ■ ■

The Lovely Bones
(2002) by Alice Sebold

Susie is worried about the penguin in a snow globe on her father's desk—he seems to be a lonely figure. Her father tells her: "Don't worry, Susie; he has a nice life. He's trapped in a perfect word." Alice Sebold's poignant but often tough, even lurid, novel describes the short, but eternal life of a fourteen-year-old girl who is raped and murdered by a neighbor, Mr. Harvey. In this book we discover that everyone has his or her own version of heaven, but it is Susie's that has our complete attention. It is the source of one of the greatest book club discussions: What is your concept of heaven and will you be reunited with your pets?

Many club members have an affinity to members of Susie's grieving family—her father who almost falls apart but gathers all the inner strength to ultimately keep the family together; tough-cookie, ultrasmart sister Lindsey; and Susie's mother, whose actions are a source of big talk. This is one of Sebold's great achievements; she shows us the drama that happens after the crime, teenage love that grows, adult relationships that fall apart—all taking place well after the investigators have left the crime scene.

Discussion questions, Little, Brown: Excellent. The questions range from the rules of Susie's heaven, the role of her friend Ruth, whose body becomes the most controversial plot point, Mr. Harvey's childhood and Sebold's ultimate message.

Audio alert: Alyssa Bresnahan, the signature voice of the searching female protagonist, narrates *The Lovely Bones* (Recorded Books). Listen for her pointed pauses after the "she said." In the pauses and the dropped registers, she creates the spooky but realistic atmosphere the author intended.

Furthermore: Before *The Lovely Bones*, Sebold wrote *Lucky*, a memoir that described her rape as an 18-year-old college freshman. In the same tunnel, another girl has not been so lucky—she was raped, murdered and dismembered. Many clubs have compared the emotional centers of *Lucky* and *The Lovely Bones*, and how Sebold has created literature from life experience.

■ ■ ■

Middlesex
(2002) by Jeffrey Eugenides

This Pulitzer Prize–winning novel is everyone's favorite coming-of-age story about a Michigan hermaphrodite. Calliope Stephanides was raised a girl and she was quite successful at being one. She excelled at classic literature at the Grosse Pointe all-girl's prep school. ("Forget *Love Story*. Harvard couldn't match Troy as a setting, and in Segal's whole novel only one person died.") But our narrator has always been frank with us. He decides to become a man and has told us all along there is a genetic mutation in the ancestral pool, helped along by the big family secret. Cal tries to make sense of his world, observing "living sends a person not into the future but back into the past, to childhood and before birth, finally, to commune with the dead."

The premise is unique, the Greek American characters are loveable but never cloying, and the book is alternatively hilarious, sad and hopeful. *Middlesex* is an immigrant saga set against the background of world events such as the burning of Smyrna, the great Atlantic crossing and the Detroit race riots. But Jeffrey Eugenides made a sprawling multigenerational family story as personal and intimate as a teardrop.

You will be dissecting Cal's decisions on gender throughout the discussion, as well as the immigrant experience and the almost too-reliable narrator and his obsession with the Obscure Object of Desire ("the Object"). There are so many Greek Americans—grandparents Desdemona and Lefty; Cadillac-loving father, Milton; Jimmy Zizmo and the rest of the family—*Middlesex* makes *My Big Fat Greek Wedding* look like Masterpiece Theater. No detail is too small for this mini-epic, especially the wild twist near the end.

Discussion questions, Picador: Excellent and to the point, and there are a lot to choose from.

Dressing thematically: Charm bracelets in honor of the famous clique at Calliope's prep school, Baker & Inglis.

Selling *Middlesex* to the club: Genuinely funny, brimming with humanity, and it's even scientifically fascinating for all members who think they are scientists and doctors.

■ ■ ■

Midwives
(1997) by Chris Bohjalian

Midwives hails from the first, most classic era of Oprah's Book Club when carefully selected "book club" participants met in Oprah's faux living room to discuss the book, moving on to a faux dining room for an elegant, mystery meal served by silent, uniformed waitstaff. (Plead all you want; Oprah will never bring back this tableau.)

Midwives is a supreme example of the Book Club Classic. It's a suspenseful story where lives are turned upside down by a single night and one decision—a big one. Connie Danforth was fourteen years old when her mother, Sibyl, set out one icy night to "catch" a baby, just another night's work for a midwife. But that night, Sibyl had to perform an emergency cesarean section on a woman she thought was dead. Or was she still alive? And why is the book called *Midwives* when there is only one central character answering to that job description?

Connie narrates the story as a thirty-year-old, and it is a wise choice by Chris Bohjalian. The narrator can be omniscient and sympathetic, especially during her mother's trial, which Connie describes with maturity while remembering her teenage angst. Was the trial a contemporary witch hunt? Did the prosecution have some good points? Sibyl Danforth's notebook selections are provocative and crucial to the plot, ripe for discussion. *Midwives* is a chilling story that also incorporates a poignant coming-of-age theme.

Discussion questions, Vintage Books: Very good. Questions are posed about Sibyl's hippie past and how it affects her present predicament, the medical and legal establishments, and Sibyl's relationships with her husband and her lawyer. In the end, the discussion comes down to one issue: did Sibyl behave responsibly?

Selling *Midwives* to the club: Glaciers have slid, planets have been discovered and new clubs have formed since Oprah selected this novel. Has your present club had its home-birth discussion yet?

■■■

The Other Boleyn Girl
(2001) by Philippa Gregory

A smart bodice ripper, *The Other Boleyn Girl* is a compulsively readable, behind-the-scenes account of Henry VIII's court. Philippa Gregory's great gift to book clubs is a literate narrative with plausible historical characters whose ambitions and psychological motivations are set against sumptuous Tudor backgrounds. Gregory manages a quasi-feminist case for the two Boleyn girls as pawns of their family's grab for power. A study in sexual competition, the dialogue is costume-drama pitch-perfect. (" 'Suffolk acknowledged you,' she whispered.")

Mary Boleyn is the "other Boleyn" girl of the title. When she comes to court, she is a fourteen-year-old girl who attracts the notorious king, becoming his mistress. But not for long. He is soon beyond dazzled by Anne, and the descriptions of her stratagems to win him is just one of the glories of Gregory's narrative. Although we know the story, the reasons behind it becomes tragically clear. Clubs have especially relished discussing the relatives' role in the family business of putting girls into the king's bed. And Gregory has skillfully created a new literary type—a Boleyn girl. Her choice of letting the minor characters take center stage is effective and original.

Discussion guide, Touchstone: Excellent, proving that a first-rate guide does not have to be based on a classic work of fiction or a Pulitzer Prize—

winning book. This guide is fun and provocative in its own right, and has contributed to the book's popularity in clubs. Questions about brother George and his homosexual circle are especially provocative. Don't miss the interview with Philippa Gregory, which gives the historical background and is also a fascinating look at the writing process. Gregory cites her source material. A parallel reading experience for clubs.

Selling *The Other Boleyn Girl* to the club: Hold on to your bodices and join the bawdy, treacherous traveling court.

■ ■ ■

The Red Tent
(1997) by Anita Diamant

The novel is told by Dinah, daughter of Jacob and Leah in the book of Genesis. *The Red Tent* is a bold re-imagining because the biblical Dinah is merely mentioned. But she and the other women are front and center in Dinah's story, which begins before her birth and takes us through the flight to Egypt. Though Dinah's real mother is the capable Leah, her "aunts"—the other wives of Jacob—were her other mothers. The beautiful Rachel, quick Zilpah, the silent, tiny and dark Bilhah are all components of a female tribe. "Like any sisters who live together and share a husband, my mother and aunties spun a sticky web of loyalties and grudges."

But it wasn't all tension and jealousy. The women have a refuge in the red tent where they retreat for their monthly cycles to talk, sing songs and tell stories in a strong bid to be remembered. Giving birth is life and death as Inna, Rachel and Dinah become known throughout the lands for their skills as midwives. There are so many new, aromatic potions and mint-scented oils introduced by these healers, it was as if they were running a biblical spa.

Book clubs adore *The Red Tent* and talk about it all the time. They love the story of women in a violent society rent with revenge and retribution, the novel's irresistible storytelling that is essentially a recalling of a world of our mothers, and the evocation of a plausible Bible-era landscape where "in the red tent, the truth is known."

Discussion guide, Picador: Basic. There is a helpful, short explanation by the author about how she came to write *The Red Tent* and how she fleshed out the images of the Bible. She also offers a short explanation of "midrash" and the relationship among the sisters and Jacob. Many clubs have invited experts such as clergy, biblical experts and librarians to amplify the discussion.

The power of a cover: The crimson, pre-Raphaelite-style image of a woman in biblical robes is one of the very best. Can you think of other covers that have communicated a book's theme as vividly as this one?

■ ■ ■

The Shadow of the Wind
(2004) by Carlos Ruiz Zafon, translated by Lucia Graves

Barcelona, with its crumbling palaces, bloodstained pavement, cafes and old bookstores is a major character in this ripping thriller about a mysterious novel with a long, dark history. Young Daniel Sempere is taken by his father, a bookseller, to the Cemetery of Forgotten Books. He is allowed to choose one book from the incredible labyrinth of crammed bookshelves; The book is *The Shadow of the Wind* by an obscure author, Julian Carax. It is a choice that shapes Daniel's destiny in this magical, spellbound city.

Although he has been warned about the potential dangers of owning this book, how could he resist unraveling the mysteries wrapped in mysteries? There are many plot twists, and clubs have fallen in love with bawdy, wise and eloquent sidekick Fermin, who whistles boleros. Daniel asks Fermin if he could tell him something that has been on his mind. Fermin's reply? "But of course. Anything. Especially if it's shocking and concerns this yummy maiden." Several femmes fatales meet up with our heroes and the evil villain aptly named Fumero, who has an exquisitely psychopathic pedigree.

Discussions center on Daniel's reasons for risking all to discover the history of this accursed book and the intricate plotting set against a time of civil war and fascism. Are we given the right information at the right time? Order a cup of hot chocolate with sponge fingers and Serrano ham sandwiches at Els Quatre Gats and discuss.

Penguin Reading Group Guides: Very good, recalling many of the captivating lines throughout the book ("There are worse prisons than words") that drive the plot and comment on it at the same time. Don't miss the interview with Zafon.

Selling *The Shadow of the Wind* to the club: "Well, this is a story about books," Daniel tells Bea, and it is for bibliophiles everywhere. Fans of old fashioned thrillers set in evocative places, especially in the years before and after World War II, will also succumb to its charms.

■■■

The Sparrow
(1996) by Mary Doria Russell

An intense, suspenseful, emotionally resonant "historical" novel set in the future, *The Sparrow* has moved from cult favorite to must-discuss. The novel has everything a club could want: strong, believable characters, not one but two alternate universes and a plot that revolves around the characters' relationships with God after they are lured to another planet by mysterious singing.

Father Emilio Sandoz, a gifted linguist and a Jesuit priest, convinces a multitalented crew that they must explore the source of the beautiful extraterrestrial voices. Rome backs him up and an intergalactic expedition is arranged: these unearthly singers could be proof that "God had other children." Along this epic journey, the characters' faith in God and science is consistently tested. Was the mission really just a big misunderstanding? Do you approve of the author's use of foreshadowing? Can one be drunk on God? Everyone comes to adore tough doctor and fabulous cook, the witty Anne Edwards. She becomes a kind of Wendy to the crew of questioners and seekers. Mary Doria Russell is so convincing in her description of Rakhat, you will really miss Earth.

Discussion questions, Ballantine Reader's Circle: Excellent, a parallel reading experience. Questions concern the situation on Earth, where futures brokers look for brain talent to exploit; the Rakhat scientific mission; and the relationship between this brainy crew and past explorers like Columbus, Magellan and Cortez. What do you think will become of Sandoz? Even *Star Trek*'s most casual acquaintances will appreciate the brief references to the series, and there is even a question about the prime directive.

Entertaining thematically: Anne Edwards loves to plan menus and give dinners. In Puerto Rico, she and Emilio plan a feast of *bacalaitos*, *asopao* with *tostones* and tembleque. The cocktail of choice: Bacardi *anejo*.

Furthermore: It's official: Mary Doria Russell Mania has arrived with the best-selling *Thread of Grace*. It is a historical novel that takes place on the Ligurian coast of Italy at the end of World War II. Many clubs have also read *The Sparrow*'s sequel, *Children of God*.

Selling *The Sparrow* to the club: Antlers will lock over this one. Haunting and exciting, at times lurid, the novel is not overly science-fictiony and offers at least two great twist.

■ ■ ■

The Time Traveler's Wife
(2003) by Audrey Niffenegger

Trippy, romantic, pseudoscientific, *The Time Traveler's Wife* will provide many hours of discussion based on how many in your club buy into the sci-fi premise. Clare Abshire is six and Henry DeTamble is thirty-six when they first meet in back of Clare's parents' Michigan house. Throughout this adventurous romance set mostly in Chicago and alternately narrated by Clare and Henry, each struggle to live in the few years of "the present." But this proves to be difficult: Henry suffers from a genetic disease called Chrono-Impairment that causes him to time travel, visiting Clare throughout her life but in the here and now only briefly.

Time travel as plot and metaphor is an oldie but goodie, and one of the delights of this book is the strict way in which it cleaves to the stringent rules of engagement the author sets up between the two protagonists. Each section helpfully gives us the date and ages of the characters—"Saturday,

October 27, 1984 (Clare is 13, Henry is 43)." The two have a life and friends, including that affable Chicago anarchist Gomez ("My kittens, I have brought you a new toy"), and Henry even manages to hang on to his job as a librarian while quoting Rilke and waking up somewhere, anywhere, having been involved in a violent episode. But it is the mournful, romantic spaces in between the time travel that makes this novel a meditation on love.

Discussion questions, Harcourt: Excellent, a parallel reading experience. The questions take the reader from the concept of Clare spending so much of the book waiting, through Henry's condition and personality, to issues of time and the self.

The Time Traveler's Wife **download:** From opera to punk, the novel references a breathtaking range of musical allusions. Henry's mother was a famous singer whose death cut short a brilliant career (this is a pivotal plot point). She sang *Aida*, *Carmen*, *Madama Butterfly*, and Kurt Weill and Schubert *lieder*. Contrast with favorites of Clare, Henry and the rest of the gang: Patty Smith, Violent Femmes, the Sex Pistols and Iggy Pop. The perfect download would mark both points of the time-traveling spectrum.

Selling *The Time Traveler's Wife* **to the club:** A plot-driven romance played against a startling premise, it will engage and provoke.

■ ■ ■

Zorro
(2005) by Isabel Allende, translated by Margaret Sayers Peden

In this back story of the fictional hero Zorro, Isabel Allende has transformed what could have been a hokey tale of an early superhero into a rollicking historical romance, complete with fainting maidens, sweeping backdrops and duels of varying lengths and weaponry. But there is but one winning caballero. What's in it for us? It's an action-packed read from one of our favorite writers, who brings humanity and a sense of humor to this story of dual identities—fop versus fox. Begin your discussion with the classic question: What is a hero? Is the masked caballero any less of one because he is also a movie and TV star?

Diego de la Vega was born in southern California in the late eighteenth century, an outpost of the vast Spanish empire. His father was a Spanish aristocrat who fell madly in love with a beautiful, Shoshone warrioresse. Diego's unusual background combined with the violence around him—especially as perpetrated against Native Americans—has made him sensitive to injustices. The book shifts from colonial California to Barcelona, where Diego is sent to further his education along with his "milk brother," Bernardo. His character is further honed by the sweep of history that includes the Napoleonic wars, pirates (Jean Lafitte, but of course!), the chocolate and slave trades, and the perils of ship travel aboard the Madre de Dios. Details build, the era emerges and so does a sworn enemy: Moncada. Did you guess the identity of our narrator?

Dressing thematically: It's a real costume party: from simple linen pants of the neophyte with a sash around the waist (in winter, a striped serape) to the complete Zorro look by way of the elegant Jean Lafitte (all in black with a yellow silk sash, high boots and gold buckles) and, of course, the cape and mask.

Fun fact: According to the *Wall Street Journal*, Zorro Productions asked the author to develop this early story of our hero. At first she said no but then agreed—lucky for us. Look for a new musical with the Gipsy Kings.

Furthermore: Since *The House of the Spirits* (1987), Allende's works have been can't-miss selection for clubs. The author was born in Peru, raised in Chile and now lives in California. Her work has often combined magic with realism in the classic, Latin American literary sense. *Daughter of Fortune* (1999) and *Portrait in Sepia* (2001) will always be in book club rotation for their renderings of fragile, vanished worlds filled with family secrets. But the selections of true cognoscenti return to Allende's story collection *The Stories of Eva Luna* (1989), where the title character functions as a Latin Scheherazade, narrating twenty-three different stories of unlikely lovers.

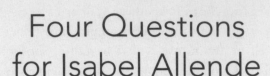

Four Questions
for Isabel Allende

Zorro *is an unusual novel in that it crosses genre lines and is a sweeping, historical romance. The pirates do not disappoint. How should book clubs approach the discussion of a book like* **Zorro***?*

It would be fun to watch some of the *Zorro* movies, either recent or old ones. The theme is always justice. *Zorro* is the romantic masked avenger who fights for the underdog. He is not violent; he prefers to humiliate the villain, not to kill him. He is athletic debonair, funny, lighthearted. He is not a tragic character. Yet he is the perfect hero.

How did you research **Zorro***?*

I read novels about the historical period. I went to all the places mentioned in the book including Barcelona, Panama and New Orleans. I took a couple of fencing lessons and studied about fencing and the choreography of sword fights in movies.I studied every aspect of the novel, from Catalan cuisine to Gypsies and secret societies. I love history because for me, it's very inspiring. Things have happened (and are happening) in the world that I could never imagine. The cliché that reality is richer than fantasy is absolutely true.

Have you ever been in a book club?

I have never belonged to a book club, not for lack of enthusiasm but for lack of time.

I heard of a book club that once a year chooses a scene from their favorite book and puts on a play. They write the dialogue and improvise costumes. They invite their friends and family, perform the play and then have a sumptuous dinner. Often, the food is inspired in the book. A club told me that they had Latin food when they chose a scene from *Eva Luna*.

Another good idea is what I saw in Australia: a walking book club. They meet in a park, they discuss the book walking for an hour and then they all have coffee in a lovely Italian place.

What are your beloved books?
My beloved books are so many that I couldn't possible make a list. Instead, I can offer a short list of a few books that I have read recently that are just perfect for a book club: *Peace Like a River* by Leif Enger; *The Kite Runner* by Khaled Hosseini; *Three Day Road* by Joseph Boyden; *The Painted Drum* by Louise Erdrich; *Snow Flower and the Secret Fan* by Lisa See; *Misfortune* by Wesley Stace; *Empire Falls* by Richard Russo; *House of Sand and Fog* by Andre Dubus; *The Wild Girl: The Notebooks of Ned Giles, 1932* by Jim Fergus; *Gonzalez and Daughter Trucking Co.* by María Escandón; *Shadow of the Wind* by Carlos Zafon.

No Leader, No Problem: Your Next Book

When you are proposing a book, don't resort to the filibuster or special pleading—though you may always keep these strategies in reserve. The club is not a stage for your every whim, but if you are ready to invest your social capital in a specific book, go to the mat. Just follow these rules:

- **Visualize the response**. You propose your usual list: Kingsley Amis, *Uncle Tom's Cabin*, middle-period Jackie Collins. They snicker. What went wrong? You need to think about the club's successes and find a book that you want to read within that wide parameter.

- **Prepare for the smack-down**. You may not feel the love just by mentioning the title, so make a case for it by bringing the book itself, along with reviews from newspapers, magazines and the Internet. Your own talking points for selling the book and reasons it would be a good idea for the club is the most important factor of all. Communicate the "why" with confidence.

- **Come armed with a Hollywood pitch**. "It's *The Nanny Diaries* meets *Cry the Beloved Country*." "It's a mix of Oprah, Orwell and *People* magazine." "I've heard it's Hillary Clinton's favorite book." This is where name dropping and mixed metaphors are a must. Even if it bombs, your club will enjoy the hype.

- **Be specific about word-of-mouth recommendations**. Use the exact quote about the book from a person you know—or better, someone everyone knows whose tips have panned out. Soon, with the words "Peaches recommends" you need not go further: Sold!

- **Remember variety counts**. Think of your recent reads. Is this selection different enough to provide much-needed variety? Is your club challenged enough with past selections? Push the envelope.

- **Visualize your book club shelf**. Can you see the selection among the greats and the against-all-odds favorites? Or is it filler that will just make club members mad?

- **Think ahead**. Are you prepared to take on the discussion duties? Even more important, are you looking forward to leading the discussion? Will you come armed with your own discussion questions in addition to the publisher's questions? It isn't fair to throw a book out and let it sink. Think ahead to the discussion and whether you are willing to create three to five discussion points. It's important that your friends are delighted and challenged, but only if you can give them the tools.

- **Plan before tackling tomes**. They can be very long, and reading time is not abundantly available. Make it easy on everyone and establish a time for each section of the book, Oprah-style (all summer for *Anna Karenina*, anyone?). Suggest a reading time spread out across one, two but no more than three months. Intersperse with DVD nights (and gentle reminders) and the promise of a big celebration at the end. Soon, this will become a custom of your club.

- **Sweeten the deal**. If you know it will be a challenging book, offer to make something everyone will like. It's funny how the maniacal laughter ceases after a slice of your famous chocolate raspberry torte.

- **Call to order**. Many clubs enjoy the free-for-all discussion about the next book. But if this system is not working consider these classic strategies:

The next host chooses the book.
Vote with ballots, using as many rounds as you wish at the club.
Solicit suggestions online, and have the next host either choose or
    conduct an online vote.

Club Rules: E-mail Stylings

When it is your turn to host and send out your first e-mail notice, you must minimally include:

- The name of the book
- The date of the next meeting
- The time (and note in caps if this is a new time)
- The address, phone numbers and directions
- A one-paragraph summary of the book.

You must also send a reminder a day or two before the meeting.

For skyrocketing attendance: Just add—and, of course, deliver—these lines:

Cocktails will be served.
Elaborate desserts to follow the discussion.
Take-home cookies

RSVP: If it's the style of your club to RSVP, note this in a prominent place, even the subject line. Most clubs do need an attendance count for meals, and if you are the lucky coordinator, type your RSVP line in ALL CAPS and include a reply-before date. Don't make the host come after you: she's busy and probably annoyed though she will never show it.

After the club: Send the recipe that everyone loved via e-mail within a week of the last club. Save one for your club scrapbook. And if it was an especially great event or holiday party, take it upon yourself to write up the menu, choose a great typeface, attach and send to everyone.

When Pets Misbehave: Baddest Kitty

One of Miles Roby's chief nemeses in *Empire Falls* happens to be the most vicious: Timmy the Cat. The kitty's crimes? A demonic nature; an irrefutable reputation as Mrs. Whiting's familiar; sudden spooky appearances; bloody-fanged, head-curling escapes; upholstery shedding; screenrenting; screaming. And of course she has at least nine lives. When Timmy sees Miles, she pulls back her lips to reveal her razor-sharp teeth, and her fur stands on end as she arches her back, hisses and spits. All in a day's work in the Whiting household.

Timmy's method acting may have also been fueled by the fact that the Whitings, who probably took her in more as an act of symbolism than anything else, referred to her as a male though she was always a female.

Not all pets are as bad as Timmy and not all owners are Mrs. Whitings, but a pet's bad behavior is often indulged by its owner. And as a guest, you certainly do not want to speak ill of a Timmy's or Tabitha's homeschooling. So what do you do when the evil one perches on the coach right next to you? You have been warned against petting ("she hisses and bites"). And you can never depend on the host to notice—he often has his own hosting chores, not to mention an indulgent agenda.

"The biggest issue is keeping cats out of food and drink and off of seating areas," says veterinarian Dr. Merry Crimi. "[These are] basic house manners that all cat owners should be working on. All cats are capable of learning that some areas are taboo. The often-used excuse that 'cats have a mind of their own' isn't a valid reason for not training a cat in the basics."

It's important for cats to have a quiet place they can retreat to, or even a separate room. When pet trainer William Berloni has guests, he puts his cats in a separate room with a sign, "Please Do Not Disturb—Cats Sleeping." Says Berloni, "Cats are solitary, but if you train them right, they can be part of the party."

Book Club Style:
Flowers from *The Hours* and
Mrs. Dalloway's Hothouse

Michael Cunningham and Virginia Woolf employed flowers as symbols and dramatic devices to advance their stories and develop the characters. In *Mrs. Dalloway*, Sally Seton picked hollyhocks and dahlias, cut off their heads and "made them swim on top of water in bowls." This display scandalized aunts in both books. And did you note how often roses were employed in *The Hours* and *Mrs. Dalloway*?

Bunches of lilacs, hollyhocks, dahlias, delphiniums, irises, dark and prim carnations, sweet peas, roses ("after a superb summer's day," red, white and even made of frosting in *The Hours*), hyacinth, blue hydrangea, and orchids are prominently mentioned, especially in *Mrs. Dalloway*.

Fieldtrip: Have a special club to honor the flowers in both books. You will buy the flowers yourself. Clubs love to meet in smaller groups to buy flowers at the local green market, garden-club sale or other field-trip-worthy destinations. Green markets are excellent places to find whole branches of flowering blossoms in season and fruits and vegetables with stems intact.

Best time of year to hold this club: April through June for flowers; summer for dahlias, sweet peas.

Vases and containers: You may not have a silver collection of Mrs. Dalloway proportions, but you can buy inexpensive small jars and containers for club display or for take home bouquets. *Best practice*: In tiny glass vases or jars, pack your flowers in tight bouquets, enough for every member. Place bouquets around the meeting place and give to each person as they leave. Inexpensive vases can often be found at Pier 1, Target and Big Lots, for instance. *Traveling tip*: Place each little jar in flat box and distribute at the club.

Put your collections to use: Silver trophy cups, especially from the Mrs. Dalloway era, are nostalgic and useful. White roses bunched tightly is a classic.

Bouquets and take-home branches: You can arrange flowers by type or color, or mix them up. Any blooming flowers from the garden bunched together in tight bouquets will work. Large branches (lilacs work especially well) loosely arranged in a tall container communicate to club members this is a special event. Depending on the time of year and your region, consider almond, apple, pistachio, dogwood, pear, peach, lilac, cotton and pussy willow branches.

Take home blooms: As each member leaves, wrap a bouquet or branch in florist paper or tissue. Tie with a ribbon or raffia.

Planning tip: Many flower sellers and nurseries have a wide range of papers for a minimal cost or free. Ask for the latest in ribbons and raffia for easy bows.

A garden meeting: Members love meeting in a garden, surrounded by anything you can actually grow. Take your cake stand and teacup collection outside for an instant garden book club. At the end of the club, let members take their own cuttings, or cut the plants for them. Have pruning shears and small containers or wrapping paper ready for take-home bouquets.

The Costume Drama

THE NOVELS

The Birth of Venus★
  by Sarah Dunant

The Borgia Bride
  by Jeanne Kalogridis

Captain Alatriste
  by Arturo Perez-Reverte

Casanova in Bolzano
  by Sandor Marai

The Crimson Petal and the White★
  by Michel Faber

A Factory of Cunning★
  by Philippa Stockley

Fingersmith★ by Sarah Waters

The Intelligencer★
  by Leslie Silbert

Jamaica Inn
  by Daphne du Maurier

The Lady and the Unicorn★
  by Tracy Chevalier

Life Mask★
  by Emma Donoghue

The Mists of Avalon★
  by Marion Zimmer Bradley

*The Secret History of the
  Pink Carnation*
  by Lauren Willig

Slammerkin★
  by Emma Donoghue

Tipping the Velvet
  by Sarah Waters

THE SERIES

Dorothy Dunnett
  The Lymond Chronicles★
  Ringed Castle★
  Pawn in Frankincense

Philippa Gregory
  The Queen's Fool★
  The Other Boleyn Girl★
  The Virgin's Lover
  The Wideacre Trilogy

Pamela Kaufman
  The Book of Eleanor★
  Shield of Three Liones★

Robin Maxwell
  *The Secret Diary of Anne
    Boleyn*
  Virgin: Prelude to the Throne★
  The Wild Irish
  The Queen's Bastard

★*Publisher includes discussion questions.*

Rosalind Miles
  I, Elizabeth★
  The Child of the Holy Grail★
  The Knight of the Sacred
    Lake★
  Guenever, Queen of the Summer
    Country★
  Tristan and Isolde Trilogy★
Sharon Kay Penman
  The Queen's Man★
  Cruel as the Grave★
  Dragon's Lair★
  Time and Chance★
  The Reckoning
Jean Plaidy
  Queen of This Realm
  The Rose without a Thorn★
  Mary Queen of France★
  The Lady in the Tower

The Thistle and the Rose★
In the Shadow of the Crown★
Anya Seton
  Katherine
  Dragonwyck
  Green Darkness
David Starkey
  Six Wives
  Elizabeth: The Struggle for the Throne
Alison Weir
  Mary, Queen of Scots
  Henry VIII The King and His
    Court★
  The Life of Elizabeth I★
  Six Wives of Henry VIII
  The Princes in the Tower
  Children of Henry VIII
  Eleanor of Aquitane: A Life★
  The War of the Roses

NONFICTION

Elizabeth and Mary: Cousins, Rivals and Queens by Jane Dunn
Marie Antoinette by Antonia Fraser★
Perdita by Paula Byrne
Georgiana: Duchess of Devonshire by Amanda Foreman★
A Venetian Affair by Andrea di Robilant★

The Bell Jar by Sylvia Plath: An Appreciation

"The floor seemed wonderfully solid. It was comforting to know I had fallen and could fall no farther."
—*The Bell Jar*

What can you say about a girl who is in love with death? At the hands of author Sylvia Plath, fictional Esther Greenwood turns us into all-ears confidants to her suicidal distress, while retaining its power to shock. *The Bell Jar*'s twin reputations as a thinly veiled fictional account of Plath's own descent into mental illness and as one of the first feminist books in an age that was quite specific about what young women should be doing to ensnare a husband, has insured its position as a Book Club Classic.

The novel begins in that "queer, sultry summer, the summer they electrocuted the Rosenbergs" and the electroshock theme does not waver. Nineteen-year-old Esther has been selected as a college guest editor for a New York women's magazine, just one of the many prizes, scholarships and accolades Esther—as well as the real Sylvia—wins. Esther casts a satiric eye on her friends with funny, raucous scenes of bad dates and first jobs ("and then we saw the girls from the magazine moving off in a row, one cab after another, like a wedding party with nothing but bridesmaids"). We think: she's so young, so brilliant, so jaded and so poisoned by crabmeat salad stuffed in an avocado pear.

After the editorship ends, Esther returns home to live with her mother in Massachusetts. Here, she slides into mental illness, is given shock therapy, attempts suicide and is almost successful. Esther makes a somewhat fragile recovery as the novel ends, though we are just getting started.

The bell jar is Esther's metaphor for a life of "stifling distortions"—and she fears it would envelop her again. For Sylvia Plath it does. After winning yet another scholarship, this time a Fulbright, Plath met the British poet Ted Hughes, married him, had two children and continued to write poetry up to the end. In 1963, a month after *The Bell Jar* was published in London under the pseudonym Victoria Lucas, Plath committed suicide. She was thirty years old.

The twentieth anniversary edition of *The Bell Jar*, published in 1996, is the indispensable edition. Its foreward describes the often torturous but fascinating publication history of the book, detailing how Plath's mother fought against its publication in the United States. The edition includes detailed biographical information about Plath, as well as eight drawings Plath sketched in New England.

For the real dissection of the Plath legend, the indispensable companion book is Janet Malcom's *The Silent Woman: Sylvia Plath and Ted Hughes*. Originally a 1994 article in *The New Yorker*, Malcolm exhumes the Plath–Hughes marriage, takes us through the major poems of our "suicidal poetess" and examines some of the events depicted in *The Bell Jar*. Readers will soon learn that Malcolm is the real-life Thursday Next as her literary sleuthing leads her into hidden archives and dark recesses Officer Next could only imagine.

In honor of Esther's New York pal Doreen (whose college was so fashion conscious, "all the girls had pocketbook covers made out the same material as their dresses"), mix up a batch of old-fashioneds and begin your discussion of the *The Bell Jar* as well as its literary descendants. Without it, would there be *Love Story*, *Bridget Jones's Diary*, *Girl Interrupted*, *The Lovely Bones*, or *Virgin Suicides*? Like hell, there would. But save enough time— and strength—for Plath's poems. In an electrifying audio, *The Voice of the Poet: Sylvia Plath* (Random House Audio Publishing), the poet herself reads from *The Colossus and Other Poems*, and her last, dazzling, famously fraught, collection, *Ariel*.

The Tween Book Club 101

Anne of Green Gables by Lucy Maud Montgomery

Bad Boy: A Memoir by Walter Dean Myers

Because of Winn Dixie by Kate DiCamillo

Black Beauty by Anna Sewell

The Bridge to Terabithia by Katherine Patterson

Bud, Not Buddy by Christopher Paul Curtis

Caddie Woodlawn by Carol Ryrie Brink

Charlie and the Chocolate Factory by Roald Dahl

Charlotte's Web by E. B. White

Chasing Vermeer by Blue Balliett

Chinese Cinderella: True Story of an Unwanted Daughter by Adeline Yen Mah

The Chronicles of Narnia by C. S. Lewis

Dealing with Dragons: The Enchanted Forest Chronicles by Patricia C. Wrede

The Diary of a Young Girl by Anne Frank

Everything on a Waffle by Polly Horvath

Fever 1793 by Laurie Halse Anderson

Forest of the Pygmies by Isabel Allende

Foretelling by Alice Hoffman

47 by Walter Mosley

From the Mixed-Up Files of Mrs. Basil E. Frankweiler by E. L. Konigsburg

The Giver by Lois Lowry

Half Magic by Edward Eager 265.

Harry Potter Paperback Box Set (Books 1–5) by J. K. Rowling

Hatchet by Gary Paulsen

Heidi by Johanna Spyri

Holes by Louis Sachar

Hoot by Carl Hiaasen

Island of the Blue Dolphins by Scott O'Dell

Journey to the River Sea by Eva Ibbotson

Kira-Kira by Cynthia Kadohata

Letters from Camp by Kate Klise

Lily's Crossing by Patricia Reilly Giff

Little Women by Louisa May Alcott

A Long Way from Chicago by Richard Peck

Monster by Walter Dean Myers

My Father's Dragon by Ruth Stiles Gannett

My Louisiana Sky by Kimberly Willis Holt

Number the Stars by Lois Lowry

Out of the Dust by Karen Hesse

The Phantom Tollbooth by Norton Juster

Pippi Longstocking by Astrid Lindgren

Princess Academy by Shannon Hale

The Princess Diaries by Meg Cabot

Roll of Thunder, Hear My Cry by Mildred D. Taylor

Ruby Holler by Sharon Creech

Sarah, Plain and Tall by Patricia MacLachlan

The School Story by Andrew Clements

The Secret Garden by Frances Hodgson Burnett

Shiloh by Phyllis Reynolds Naylor

The Sisterhood of the Traveling Pants by Ann Brashares

Sounder by William H. Armstrong

Stuart Little by E. B. White

The Tale of Despereaux by Kate DiCamillo

Treasure Island by Robert Louis Stevenson

Tuck Everlasting by Natalie Babbitt

Understood Betsy by Dorothy Canfield Fisher

The View from Saturday by E. L. Konigsburg

Where the Red Fern Grows by Wilson Rawls

The Witch of Blackbird Pond by Elizabeth George Speare

The Witches by Roald Dahl

A Wrinkle in Time by Madeleine L'Engle

A Bel Canto Evening

Plan a musical evening that will delight Roxane Coss and your entire club. You will assign one group to the music, another group to the food and beverages, and a lucky individual—you know who—is assigned all crafts.

Bel canto selections are widely available from personal collections, on-line or at your library. But you can begin with these. Check with your local librarians or opera aficionados for CD and download suggestions.

Renee Fleming: *Renee Fleming* (Decca); *Bel Canto* (Decca); *Signatures—Great Opera Scenes* (Decca)

Maria Callas: *La Divina Complete* (EMI); *La Sonnambula* (EMI)

Lesley Garrett: *Diva* (Silva America)

Renata Tebaldi: *Grandi Voci* (Decca)

Joan Sutherland: *La Stupenda: The Supreme Voice of Joan Sutherland* (Decca)

Marian Anderson: *Marian Anderson Sings Bach, Brahms, Schubert* (RCA)

TAKE-HOME PROGRAMS

Printer-friendly decorative papers are widely available, and you might even find a package of twenty-five sheets for $1. Look for packages or single sheets everywhere from CVS and the supermarket to your favorite craft and art supply store. Collect them for upcoming book club events and invitations, especially seasonal papers or those illustrating a theme from a book you have read and loved.

Have fun with typefaces, but decide if you want it to be readable or an interesting artifact. A bold headline typeface combined with an italic body copy makes an impressive presentation and take-home program.

Sample program (see page 88):
  Headline: Copperplate Gothic, 18-point boldface
  Subhead: Copperplate Gothic, 14-point, all small caps
  Body typeface: Blackadder ITC, 14 point

Print out a program for each member and invited guest, with extras for last-minute guests. Don't forget to insert a program in your club scrapbook or club portfolio.

Other ideas: If you want to go to another level, you can buy an ecru imprintable program (crane.com, $35), which includes cards, sheets and matching ribbons.

Special thanks to Randolph Blakeman and Ann Patchett for music selections for Bel Canto program.

A BEL CANTO EVENING
PROGRAM

"Ah! Non Giunge Uman Pensiero" from La Sonnambula by Vincenzo Bellini, performed by Maria Callas

"Song to the Moon" from Rusalka by Antonin Dvorak, performed by Renee Fleming

Quando m'en vo' soletta "Musetta's Waltz" from La Boheme by Giacomo Puccini, performed by Renee Fleming

"Ebben? . . . Ne andro lontana" from La Wally by Alfredo Catalini, performed by Renata Tebaldi

"O mio babbino caro" from Gianni Schicci by Giacomo Puccini, performed by the London Philharmonic, with Lesley Garrett

"Casta diva" from Norma by Vincenzo Bellini, performed by Joan Sutherland

"Suicidio!" from La Gioconda by Amilcare Ponchielli, performed by Maria Callas

"Un bel di vedremo" from Madama Butterfly by Giacomo Puccini, performed by Renee Fleming

Ave Maria composed by Franz Schubert, performed by Marian Anderson

BEL CANTO MENU

White Peach Bellinis

Smoked Salmon Canapés Buffet

Smoked salmon slices
Buttered black bread
Capers, lemons, freshly ground pepper
Chopped eggs

Chocolate Cake with Strawberries

Fresh White Peach Bellinis

The summer is the best time to make these peach beauties. But out of season, you can substitute peach juice or nectar, or frozen peaches. If you must, Bellini mix is available at liquor and gourmet stores.

5–6 large white peaches, peeled, to yield about 2 cups of peach puree
8 ounces peach liquor
2 bottles chilled Presecco
Chilled flutes

In a blender, puree the peach slices until the mixture is thick. Strain through a sieve into a small bowl.

Spoon 2 ounces of the puree and 1 ounce of the peach liquor into each chilled flute. While stirring with a spoon, slowly add the chilled Prosecco until it reaches the top of the glass

Serve immediately. Keep Prosecco chilled in an ice bucket.

Hoskins Smith's Almost-Flourless Chocolate Cake

SERVES 12

This recipe came from Hoskins Smith, who became inspired by the food blog Chocolate & Zucchini. Hoskins developed this recipe and served the rich, delicious cake at her book club. Her two secrets? President's brand butter and the Trader Joe's brand Pound Plus, a dark chocolate bar.

1 10-ounce dark chocolate bar

1 teaspoon vanilla

A pinch cinnamon

2 sticks butter at room temperature

1¼ cups sugar

5 eggs

1 tablespoon flour

Preheat oven to 350 degrees.

Butter the bottom of an 8-inch springform pan. Line the bottom of the pan with a fitted piece of buttered parchment paper.

Melt the chocolate over low heat or over a double boiler, stirring constantly, until it is smooth. Remove from heat and let cool.

Add the vanilla and cinnamon to the chocolate.

In a separate bowl, cream butter with the sugar while adding eggs one at a time.

After the chocolate has cooled, temper with the butter and egg mixture, ½ cup at a time. When the mixture is smooth, add the flour and continue to mix until a smooth batter forms.

Pour batter into the springform pan and bake for 45 minutes. When the top of the cake feels slightly firm to the touch, remove from oven and let cool for at least 30 minutes.

When ready to serve, slide a thin, sharp knife around the sides of the pan to loosen the cake from the pan. Invert pan on a serving plate to release the cake. Discard the parchment paper.

Garnish with strawberries or raspberries, and serve with whipped cream.

If You Were in a
1930s Book Club

1930

The Apes of God by Wyndham Lewis

As I Lay Dying by William Faulkner

The Bridge by Hart Crane

Cakes and Ale
    by W. Somerset Maugham

Cimarron by Edna Ferber

The Maltese Falcon
    by Dashiell Hammett

Poems by W. H. Auden

Vile Bodies by Evelyn Waugh

1931

The Glass Key by Dashiell Hammett

The Good Earth by Pearl S. Buck

Grand Hotel by Vicki Baum

Guys and Dolls by Damon Runyon

Sanctuary by William Faulkner

Shadows on the Rock by Willa Cather

Strong Poison by Dorothy L. Sayers

The Waves by Virginia Woolf

1932

Black Mischief by Evelyn Waugh

Brave New World by Aldous Huxley

Cold Comfort Farm
    by Stella Gibbons

Light in August by William Faulkner

Magnificent Obsession
    by Lloyd C. Douglas

One Way to Heaven
    by Countee Cullen

The Seal in the Bedroom and Other
    Predicaments by James Thurber

The Sheltered Life by Ellen Glasgow

The Story of My Life
    by Clarence Darrow

Tobacco Road by Erskine Caldwell

1933

Anthony Adverse by Hervey Allen

The Autobiography of Alice B. Toklas
    by Gertrude Stein

The Case of the Sulky Girl
    by Erle Stanley Gardner

It Was the Nightingale
    by Ford Maddox Ford

Miss Lonelyhearts by Nathanael West

1934

Appointment in Samarra
    by John O'Hara

Good-bye, Mr. Chips by James Hilton

A Handful of Dust by Evelyn Waugh

Heaven's My Destination
    by Thornton Wilder

I, Claudius by Robert Graves

Lust for Life by Irving Stone

Murder on the Orient Express
    by Agatha Christie

The Postman Always Rings Twice
    by James M. Cain

Tender is the Night
    by F. Scott Fitzgerald

1935

Butterfield 8 by John O'Hara
Green Hills of Africa
    by Ernest Hemingway
The House in Paris by Elizabeth Bowen
It Can't Happen Here by Sinclair Lewis
Life with Father by Clarence Day
Lost Horizon by James Hilton
Lucy Gayheart by Willa Cather
Mapp and Lucia by E. F. Benson
National Velvet by Enid Bagnold
North to the Orient
    by Anne Morrow Lindbergh
Of Time and the River
    by Thomas Wolfe
Personal History by Vincent Sheean
Seven Pillars of Wisdom
    by T. E. Lawrence
Studs Lonigan by James T. Farrell
They Shoot Horses Don't They?
    by Horace McCoy
Vein of Iron by Ellen Glasgow

1936

Absalom, Absalom! by William Faulkner
Eyeless in Gaza by Aldous Huxley
Gone with the Wind
    by Margaret Mitchell
The Thinking Reed by Rebecca West

1937

The Citadel by A. J. Cronin
The Hobbit by J. R. R. Tolkien
The Late George Apley
    by John Phillips Marquand
Of Mice and Men by John Steinbeck
The Years by Virginia Woolf

1938

Brighton Rock by Graham Greene
The Death of the Heart
    by Elizabeth Bowen
Listen! The Wind
    by Anne Morrow Lindbergh
Madame Curie by Eve Curie
My Sister Eileen by Ruth McKenney
Rebecca by Daphne du Maurier
Scoop by Evelyn Waugh
The U.S.A. trilogy: The 42nd Parallel,
    1919, The Big Money
    by John Dos Passos
The Yearling
    by Marjorie Kinnan Rawlings

1939

And Then There Were None
    by Agatha Christie
The Big Sleep by Raymond Chandler
Black Narcissus by Rumer Godden
The Day of the Locust
    by Nathanael West
Goodbye to Berlin
    by Christopher Isherwood
The Grapes of Wrath
    by John Steinbeck
Johnny Got His Gun by Dalton Trumbo
Not Peace but a Sword
    by Vincent Sheean
Pale Horse, Pale Rider
    by Katherine Anne Porter
Rogue Male by Geoffrey Household
The Sword in the Stone by T. H. White
Wind, Sand and Stars
    by Antoine de St.-Exupery

3

CLASSIC FICTION

"... well, let us not gossip about the past."
—Charlotte Haze in a letter to Humbert Humbert, *Lolita*

They have been described as "permanent master-pieces" by Professor Vladimir Nabokov, but you can call them the evening's snack. And here's another thing you can count on: the characters of classic fiction never learn that they should never, ever, ever go to the ball, the carnival, the street demonstration, the sea voyage or the agricultural fair. These festivals are merely precursors and portents, omens and symbols. For our characters are often heading straight for hell, no matter what you tell them. They are not listening to you.

Bad luck for them, good luck for us. Nabokov describes the situation: a real, historic figure Count Friedrich Ferdinand von Beust (1809–1886) is mentioned in passing by Tolstoy in *Anna Karenina*. The count lived, wrote memoirs, had a career. Who cares? It is the characters Tolstoy created who will live forever and that is what we are here to discuss. These are our very own fairy tales after all, and though they offer wildly different versions of enchantments, Miss Havisham, Emma Bovary and Anna Karenina may be under the same spell.

Has a day gone by when you haven't seen or heard a reference to *The Great Gatsby*, *Heart of Darkness*, *Nineteen Eighty-Four* or *The Grapes of Wrath*? Journalists, commentators and your friends are not *always* making literary references to impress. These classics really mean something to us—Fitzgerald, Conrad, Orwell or Steinbeck are guides to the present and signposts for the road ahead.

Winston Smith, in the inner sanctum of the inner party, makes a sad toast: "To the past." Famously, Jay Gatsby wanted to recapture the past. For Winston Smith and Gatsby, nothing turned out as planned. They could not know what we do: the books of classic fiction are truly alive, and vibrantly present tense.

The Twenty-one
Indispensable Titles

■ ■ ■

The Age of Innocence
(1920) by Edith Wharton

Edith Wharton loathed the strictly codified society of her upper-class youth in 1870s New York, so when she later took up her pen, the result was a heady mixture of social satire, nostalgia and an exacting portrait of a dilettante. *The Age of Innocence* is the story of Newland Archer, who strays from his intended, the attractive but conventional May Welland, and is pulled toward the enigmatic, semi-outcast Countess Olenska, otherwise known as "poor Ellen." Venerable ancestress Mrs. Manson Mingott, drowning in flesh, casts an amused eye on the scene over which she presides, and she is just one of the many characters that uphold the social order. All of New York society behaves as a "tribe," and Newland Archer eventually succumbs to its will.

Wharton give us the full Gilded Age treatment with a spring wedding in Old New York, mandatory opera attendance and trips to posh late nineteenth century watering holes from St. Augustine to Newport, where Newland pursues Ellen. Wharton's attention to the smallest detail of the courtship rituals and the questioning of those values make *The Age of Innocence* resonate to this day. Is Wharton's book as much, if not more, about maturity and satisfaction than about love? Can you find examples of innocence amid the finery? Don't miss the farewell dinner in honor of Ellen Olenska where those who are trained to conceal are in defining form. Wharton won a Pulitzer Prize for *The Age of Innocence*, the first woman to do so.

Dressing thematically: Faded sables, yellowing ermines, towering ostrich feathers and family diamonds. Don't forget your best betrothal sapphire and the diamond-tipped arrow pin you won at the archery contest.

Editions that make a difference: The Norton Critical Edition has the fascinating annotated text. Explanations abound on everything from the language of flowers to the promotion of St. Augustine as a tourist destination—in an essay by Harriet Beecher Stowe!

For further discussion: The newspaper series that everyone is talking about, "Class Matters," appeared in the *New York Times* in 2005. The series details personal, contemporary stories about class and money in America and each story has relevance to almost every book we read and discuss. Available at nytimes.com; a fee may be required.

■ ■ ■

Anna Karenina
(1877) by Leo Tolstoy

The greatest, darkest love story of all time, *Anna Karenina* is also an historical epic set in a vanished society—late-nineteenth-century, artistocratic Russia. The seven major characters here are linked by family, society and ongoing courtship, but the odd number of major characters mean there is always a man or woman on the outs. Disastrous consequences ensue and the fate of Count Leo Tolstoy's heroine still retains its shock value.

Anna is married to severe bureaucrat Karenin, but courted by Count Vronsky, the character about whom the word "dashing" could have been invented. The pair begins an open, obsessive, adulterous affair that horrifies members of society (there are rules for this kind of thing), and the tragic conclusion serves as counterpoint to the endearing love story between the spiritual Konstantin Levin and young, beautiful princess Kitty. But all eyes are on the title character. Did Anna ruin everything with her overly passionate nature? Is she an archaic type? Begin your discussion here.

Oprah picked the Richard Pevear and Larissa Volokhonsky translation for her summer book club. She loved the character of Levin most of all, relating to his ever-seeking life philosophy and his love of Kitty. You will have your own pets, and if you are reading *Anna Karenina* a second time, you might take up the true connoisseur's favorite: Anna's brother and Dolly's husband, Prince Stepan Arkadyich Oblonsky. He's called "Stiva" in the Pevear/Volokhonsky translation and Steve, by Nabokov in his lectures. This good-hearted bon vivant, living beyond his means and never deterred from the next lavish meal or vodka bar, aspires to a cushy position. More important, he brings each set of characters together throughout the book. Stiva does get a cushy job at the end as a reward "for services rendered to the author," according to Nabokov.

Don't miss: The scene at the skating rink between Levin and Kitty; the cinematic ball scene where Anna and Vronsky make their debut; and the calamitous horse race, a little microcosm of this dying world and of each character's fate.

Edition that makes a difference: The Penguin edition Oprah chose is easy to read and ingeniously constructed. The footnotes are a treat (tip: don't flip back after each note, but after each chapter), and the best discussion ideas could be drawn from the Pevear/Volokhonsky introduction. These include the themes of city and country life, and the variations of love, family and happiness played out among the Magnificent Seven.

Dressing thematically: A corsage of fresh violets.

Selling *Anna Karenina* to the club: You will be able to say, with complete authority: "Oh, he's a real Count Vronsky type." You will allow two to three months reading time.

Beloved
(1987) by Toni Morrison

The Nobel laureate takes us to school. Her curriculum? Defiant structure; suspense mixed with gorgeous and harrowing imagery; poignant, strong and eerie characters. And it's a ghost story. The haunting is Toni Morrison's metaphor for the horrors, murder, dislocations and loneliness of slavery. Her style has been described as magic realism, but this does not go nearly far enough to describe the world of *Beloved*, where the lunatic asylum might be considered a safe haven.

Sethe, a former slave, and her daughter Denver live at 124 Bluestone Road after the Civil War. Paul D, an old friend, arrives at the house to court Sethe but is driven away by a new arrival found at the carnival: Beloved. Who is she? She is known to everyone and not known. Morrison leaves plenty of clues along the way, shrouded in evocative language, moving forward and backward in time. Descriptions of the natural world with its chokecherry trees commingle with everyday life and the beyond.

Your discussions will center on the haunting by Beloved, Denver's role in the story and the way in which Morrison uses the ghost story to illuminate the biggest ghost story of them all. You will talk about the supernatural and the natural, and whether there are magical properties to the more earthbound characters such as Paul D. and Sethe's mother-in-law Baby Suggs.

Morrison's themes are further encapsulated by the dedication, the epigraph and her complete authority over both sides of the spirit world.

Audio alert: Don't miss the author's reading of this work (Random House Audio), a spellbinding masterpiece in its own right.

Fun Fact: To promote the movie of *Beloved*, in which she produced and starred, Oprah modeled for the October 1998 cover of *Vogue*.

Furthermore: From *The Bluest Eye* to *Sula*, *Song of Solomon*, *Tar Baby*, *Jazz* and *Paradise*, the maestro takes us on the literary ride of our lives.

■ ■ ■

A Fine Balance
(1996) by Rohinton Mistry

Compared to Dickens and Balzac, chosen by Oprah, *A Fine Balance* is that rare contemporary novel that is immediately recognized as one of the enduring great books of literature. But don't let that scare you. In this masterpiece, Rohinton Mistry interweaves the lives of four characters while he accomplishes something exquisite: he jauntily mixes sadness and cruelty with mischief and survival. After all, it's only a small obstacle.

It is 1975 during India's state of emergency in a city by the sea, easily recognizable as Bombay. But the political backdrop of corruption and social upheaval is merely what happens to our towering ordinary people—tailors Ishvar and Om, the student Maneck and the youngish widow Dina, who decides to live a life of self-reliance instead of marrying a suitor her brother Nusswan finds ("But which raja's son are you waiting for?"). Improbably, the four from two different classes live in a tiny apartment, becoming for a brief time a small family within chaos.

A Fine Balance is filled with warmth, humor and observations about the human condition. Each character is a kind of philosopher, but Ishvar truly is one. " 'Special government diet,' " Ishvar tells the cashier-cum-waiter at the Vishram Vegetarian Hotel after he notices Ishvar and Om have lost weight. Did you find all the references to balance and how difficult it is to maintain? The shocking events of this big but compulsively readable story will keep you chattering for many sessions to come.

Discussion questions, Vintage Books: Thorough. Especially good are the questions about the book's symbols, the importance of the chess set to Maneck, the caste system and the birth-control program. How, indeed, might you even begin to approach Beggarmaster—ruthless, freakish, kindly or something else altogether, especially as he philosophizes about humanity and his employees—"my beggars."

Selling *A Fine Balance* to the club: Big events played out on smaller stages, and that might just be the definition of a modern classic. Exhuberant dialogue combines an ingenious sprinkling of Indian words with customized English expressions ("Okayji," "the whole jing-bang trio," "Bash the rascal"), the characters are unforgettable, and the settings range from the Venus Beauty Salon to forced labor camps, to that world within a world, Dinabai's verandah.

■ ■ ■

Frankenstein, or the Modern Prometheus

(1818) by Mary Wollstonecraft Shelley

Here you will learn, as we all must, that Frankenstein is the *doctor* and the monster is simply called Monster or less formally, the daemon. In this "strange and terrific story," university student Victor Frankenstein becomes obsessed with the idea of animating a creature based on the theory of galvanism. It was a semiscientific notion at the time Shelley wrote this gothic tale—and invented the science fiction genre while she was at it.

Frankenstein raids the charnel houses, dissecting rooms and slaughterhouses for body parts, creates his monster and then rejects it as hideous, the project a catastrophe. Friendless and dejected, the Monster tries to understand the life he was brought into and his choice of reading material is excellent: *Paradise Lost* becomes his bible in reverse—he begins to identify with Satan and becomes a killing machine (" 'Accursed creator!' "). His victims are Frankenstein's loved ones and when he tells his creator, cinematically, "I will be with you on your wedding-night," you know he means what he says.

Discussions center on our shifting sympathies for the Monster. His part of the tale is so earnest and emotionally resonant ("I learned from your papers that you were my father, my creator") while Frankenstein's is so self-serving and witless, it's no wonder we have little loyalty to the author of such a dismal catalogue of failure. Discussions about contemporary versions of the Frankenstein story involving the Creator and his creation, false science and playing God will abound. The Monster even poses his own discussion questions: "Am I to be thought the only criminal, when all humankind sinned against me?"

Edition that makes a difference: The introduction to the perfectly sized Everyman's Library edition has a complete recounting of Mrs. Shelley's life as the daughter of famous eighteenth-century radicals and the wife of the romantic poet Percy Shelley, as well as succinct interpretations of the story. Don't miss the literary chronology of Mary Shelley's life and times ("1811, Jane Austen: *Sense and Sensibility*; George III declared insane . . .").

Furthermore: The Frankenstein story took on a life of its own with the invention of movies, and scholars have said they were made for each other. Screen Frankenstein movies from the early sound period up through Mel Brooks' still-hilarious *Young Frankenstein*.

■ ■ ■

The Grapes of Wrath
(1939) by John Steinbeck

Newly released from prison after killing a man in self-defense ("anybody would" is the consensus), Tom Joad goes home to find the Dust Bowl and the Great Depression have taken the family farm. Famously, the Joads are loading up the ancient Hudson for a trip out of the desert into the supposed promised land of California along with so many other Oklahoma families. The journey is filled with abject hardship and humiliation as the Joads are forced to live in Hoovervilles while desperately looking for work.

You will be deeply involved with this family, especially the relationship between Tom and Ma Joad as they face a life-and-death-struggle. *The Grapes of Wrath* is packed with plain speaking and symbolism, hand-painted signs along the road and journalistic interludes about Route 66, a turtle moving across a highway and California itself. But it is the depiction of the Joad family's plight and Tom Joad's empowering speech ("I'll be ever'where—wherever you look. Whenever they's a fight so hungry people can eat, I'll be there.") that make *The Grapes of Wrath* transcend its own time.

Penguin Reading Group Guide: The introduction is very good and describes the reasons *The Grapes of Wrath* is considered a naturalistic epic. The family, and the roles of former preacher Jim Casy as a martyr and Ma Joad as "the citadel of the family" are also explored. Watch out for spoilers at the beginning of the questions.

DVD alert: The 1940 John Ford movie starring Henry Fonda is Hollywood at its most socially conscious. And the DVD version includes Movietone newsreels about the Dust Bowl with expert commentators.

Selling *The Grapes of Wrath* to the club: The title is taken from "The Battle Hymn of the Republic," and the evening's simple task is to decide whether it is *the* or even *a* great American novel.

■ ■ ■

Great Expectations
(1860–1861) by Charles Dickens

When were you last reunited with Pip, Miss Havisham, Estella, Magwitch, wise Biddy and good, dear Joe? Once you begin rereading Charles Dickens's masterwork, you will realize how much you missed them. You will even enjoying hissing at the minor characters like Estella's betrothed, the egregious Bentley Drummle, and weep over almost every scene between Pip and Joe ("Pip, dear old chap, life is made of ever so many partings welded together").

We find Pip being "brought up by hand" by his sister and her kind husband, blacksmith Joe Gargery ("What larks!"). Early in the book, Pip helps the convict Magwitch by bringing him food and a file, a foreshadowing incident. Pip pursues the life of a nascent gentleman and a young man of great expectations, having assumed his benefactor to be the doomed, jilted bride, Miss Havisham. Estella, who was the ward of that faded spectre in the chair, has been trained to hate men and so rejects Pip. But it is Pip's growth as man and accepting of his family and fate that makes *Great Expectations* the ultimate coming-of-age novel.

Penguin Reading Group Guide: An excellent introduction that interweaves Dickens's life with that of one of his greatest heroes, Pip. The questions discuss Dickens multiple styles of social commentary, the industrial world versus the characters and the central mystery. The idea posed about things not being what they seem will be central to your conversation.

Furthermore: Many scholars feel that Dickens's big three, written in succession, were *A Tale of Two Cities* (1859), *Great Expectations* (1860–1861) and *Our Mutual Friend* (1864–1865). Plan to add Dickens's masterworks to your schedule and see if you agree.

Selling *Great Expectations* to the club: Imagine how much more you have to bring to the story of this young man's rise in the world at each stage of his great expectations than you did when you were Pip's age. Enjoy tracing the modern equivalents on film to the source masterpiece. You will allow a reading period of at least two months, with a DVD night in between. Best practice: A holiday-time discussion.

■ ■ ■

The Great Gatsby
(1925) by F. Scott Fitzgerald

Our greatest American folktale, *The Great Gatsby* begins with Nick Carraway's reminiscence of his midwestern past. It is elegiac and cautionary, and we come to identify with our narrator as an observer and outsider. Carraway's story centers on the rise and fall of the mysterious, fantastical Jay Gatsby. A self-made man whose fortune is of dubious origin, Gatsby is a dreamer who insists he can repeat the past and claim once again the love of the beautiful, married Daisy Buchanan ("Can't repeat the past? . . . Why of course you can!" he famously tells Nick). Mythically, he ends up a victim of his own delusions.

Again and again, Fitzgerald returns to his theme of the American dream—and the moral emptiness of the careless rich who desperately try to manage their boredom. We know the geography and symbolism well: East Egg; the boozy parties; the ghostly, all-seeing billboard; the green light at the end of the dock; the too-fast, deadly cars. But the power of *The Great Gatsby* is that on subsequent readings, you will still hope it ends differently this time. It does not.

Editions that make a difference: The Scribner seventy-fifth Anniversary Edition includes the authorized text and concise biographical notes about the history of *The Great Gatsby* and of F. Scott Fitzgerald. The novel was virtually forgotten in the author's time, only to return with a vengeance starting almost immediately after Fitzgerald's death in 1940. It's all part of the legend of this great American novel that you, old sport, will need to talk about and toast.

Discussion question: Daisy Buchanan or Jordan Baker?

Cocktails: It's the Jazz Age, named by Fitzgerald and embodied by this book. At the Plaza Hotel (also a setting in *The Great Gatsby*), he and his wife Zelda enjoyed orange blossoms with bootleg gin. Gatsby served champagne in "glasses bigger than finger bowls" and "floating rounds of cocktails." Tom, Daisy and Jordan Baker variously quaff highballs, gin rickeys, and mint juleps. Watch out for Miss Baedeker—after five or six cocktails she always starts screaming.

Dressing thematically: About Gatsby's shirts, Fitzgerald was very specific. The shirts were of "stripes and scrolls and plaids in coral and apple green and lavender and faint orange with monograms of Indian blue." Daisy cried over them stormily.

■ ■ ■

Heart of Darkness
(1902) by Joseph Conrad

In the interior you will no doubt meet Mr. Kurtz, and while you are at it, consider how hard it is to understate the influence of Joseph Conrad's short novel. Recollecting with an eerie clarity, our narrator, Marlow, makes a stop in the sepulchral city where he receives his contract. But he is really on his way to hell. What he finds in the colonial outpost of the Belgian Congo is a native population dying, the colonial accountants at their ledgers and the rumor of a "universal genius" and a great ivory hunter named Kurtz. When Marlow pilots up the river to find and capture him, he is face to face with the devil-god himself.

Begin at the end with the famous last lines of Kurtz's, " 'The horror! The horror!' " How many horrors does Conrad recount? What are we to think of Marlow after his return from the heart of darkness? The novel is filled with metaphor, symbolism and alluring description (Kurtz in his lair of grubbed ivory is described as "an enchanted princess sleeping in a fabulous castle"), and it should be your calling to find specific language that reflects Marlow's murderous journey. The author's use of the climate and geography of the "center of the earth" where Marlow is told, "Anything—anything can be done in this country" adds to the legend and influence of *Heart of Darkness*. Marlow attempts to answer the questions about humanity's immorality and lack of principles. Does he succeed in his mission?

Maps for everyone: When Marlow was "a little chap," he had a passion for maps and was especially obsessed with that one river—the Congo. His boyhood obsession becomes his metaphoric journey and ours. The Norton Critical Edition has a map of the Congo Free State 1890, among other valuable support texts.

Furthermore: Readers and writers often turn to Conrad when world events get the better of them. He never fails. Especially valued are Conrad's masterworks *The Secret Agent, Lord Jim* and *Nostromo*, and the short story *The Secret Sharer*. The epigraph of TS Eliot's "The Hollow Men" is from *Heart of Darkness*: "Mistah Kurtz—he dead"; it would make a good companion discussion. It has often been noted that Conrad, born to a Polish noble family, learned English only after he became a seaman on a British merchant ship.

DVD alert: As a metaphor for evil and horror, *Heart of Darkness* was also the basis of *Apocalypse Now*, Francis Ford Coppola's fever-dream film about Vietnam.

■ ■ ■

Invisible Man
(1952) by Ralph Ellison

Out of the fire, into the melting pot, *Invisible Man* is a scary and funny nightscape of race and society, each episode told seamlessly by the invisible man. You find out why the novel is an acknowledge masterpiece on the first page when our narrator, never named, stakes out his territory as an invisible man. His journey begins when he is expelled from a Negro college in the South ("It was a beautiful college"), and a cruel joke by college president Dr. Bledsoe takes him to New York City. Our identification with his plight increases as he meets the Brotherhood, a group of rich Communists who further use the invisible man for their own ends.

The invisible man gets a job at Liberty Paints, whose slogan is "If It's Optic White, It's the Right White." Further, the line was proudly written by a black man, a longtime employee. A fallen comrade sells dancing Sambo dolls on a busy New York street. The vast secondary cast—Dr. Bledsoe, Tod Clifton, Brother Jack, Mary, Ras the Exhorter, even the mythical shape-changer Rinehart—support the theme. The encapsulating scene at the Golden Day is a tour de force of hallucinatory realism.

Does the cloak of invisibility still apply today? Why does Ellison continually return to the deathbed speech of the invisible man's grandfather? And don't you think *Invisible Man* is the opposite of *Great Expectations*?

Discussion questions, Vintage Books: Good, as the questions speak to the "paranoid style of American literature." Topics such as the role of the white "benefactors" and the multi-episodic style will get you started.

Audio alert: Joe Morton narrates *Invisible Man* (Random House Audio) with actorly precision, allowing the listener to inhabit the space of every character—male and female, black and white, rich and poor.

■ ■ ■

Lolita
(1955) by Vladimir Nabokov

You may know the story of this sinister memoir: European emigre Humbert Humbert settles in America with his erudition, book learnin' and his obsession for young girls he calls nymphets. In a series of darkly humorous episodes, HH marries Lolita's mother Charlotte Haze, who dies a timely death at the hands of McFate. It is just one of the many neologisms Vladimir Nabokov invents in *Lolita*, as Humbert becomes Lolita's stepfather and captor.

A perverse fairy tale, a nutty detective story, a travelogue of mid-twentieth-century America or a biting parody of the age of psychoanalysis? You decide. *Lolita* has engendered controversy since the moment it was almost not published. It was only after Graham Greene named it one of the best books of 1955 (*Lolita* had been published by the tiny Olympia Press in France) that its sensational world-wide publishing history began.

Professor Azar Nafisi named her own book after *Lolita*, so you won't want to wait another month to get into the discussion. After all, this cruel, crisp comic-tragedy will tear your club to pieces. The antler locking will begin and end over Humbert, one of the most unreliable narrators in all of literature. You will argue over his crimes, his pleas for understanding, his sad strategies, our complicity in hearing him out. What does Humbert mean when he says, "I have only words to play with"? Are Humbert and Lolita each captors of the other? Is Clare Quilty the real villain or just a figment of Humbert's imagination? Is gum-chewing, comic-book reader Lolita a full-fledged character? Would you let that mediocre mermaid Charlotte Haze into your book club?

Don't miss: Charlotte's near rendezvous with destiny at Hour Glass Lake one tropical Tuesday morning; Quilty's rambling monologue as he pleads for his life ("A thing or two I know about the chief of police makes him my slave . . . You may use my wardrobe"). For those reading *Lolita* for the second or third time, note the many clues for the clueless Humbert in the "detective story."

Discussion questions, Vintage Books: If you were wondering what a perfect set of discussion questions look like, here it is. They rely heavily on the annotated version but the questions are deep, thorough and provocative, involving the games, the clues and the pathos.

Edition that makes a difference: *The Annotated Lolita* by Alfred Appel. After reading this edition—Professor Nafisi's students in Tehran demanded it— you will wish *every* book was annotated. A masterpiece unto itself, this version translates Humbert's French and cites every reference from the Greeks to Edgar Allan Poe to Gene Autry. It is absolutely essential in following the trail of each enchanted hunter.

DVD and audio alert: There have been two major movies based on *Lolita*: one from 1962 directed by Stanley Kubrick with bits of the original screenplay by Nabokov. A 1997 version starred Jeremy Irons, who also reads *Lolita* in a superb audio book from Random House Audio Publishing.

Cocktail: "Pony upon pony of gin." Or Humbert's Ramsdale favorite, pineapple juice and gin.

Selling *Lolita* to the club: Ladies and gentlemen of the jury, the discussion will be the tussle of your lives.

■ ■ ■

Madame Bovary
(1856) by Gustave Flaubert

Notorious daydreamer and adulteress Emma Bovary consumes novels like an addict, filling her head with romantic notions and ideals that drive her to destruction. She subscribes to women's magazine, "devoured every word of every account of a first night . . . she knew the latest fashions . . . she pored over the interior decorating details in the novels . . . she brought her book with her even to meals." Sound familiar? Among the many other greatnesses of *Madame Bovary*, it is a snapshot of mid-nineteenth-century bourgeois life in all its striving and hypocrisy.

Country doctor Charles Bovary is clearly not up to the task of husband, according to Emma ("What exasperated her was Charles's total unawareness of her ordeal"). She takes up with local aristocrat Rodolphe, and after he grows bored with her, Rodolphe packs his break-up letter in a basket underneath freshly picked apricots and has his plough boy deliver it directly to Madame B. That's cold, but there's worse to come. Emma's next liaison is with the dull and unworthy Leon with whom she has the famous, endless carriage ride of doom in Rouen. Debts pile up as anticipated by the evil Lheureux, and Madame Bovary does the one last thing.

Clubs will want to discuss that superb tragedian Emma Bovary, her career and her demise. How did Emma become Madame Bovary? Was she an ordinary women with extraordinary dreams? Is reading to blame? Flaubert was a famous perfectionist, often taking a day to find *le mot juste* and a week to write a paragraph. Don't miss Emma's first assignation, her walk across the fields and the heartbreaking clubfoot operation. Save time to discuss the secondary, counterpoint character Homais, the ever-punctual pharmacist and up-and-coming man of the new age.

Selling *Madame Bovary* to the club: A selection of the Wisteria Lane Book Club, at least one desperate housewife found it "inspirational." But you will actually read the book. Don't forget to tag your favorite descriptive passage of field, flower or fair and read aloud.

Gemma Bovary: Here's a medium that won't be going away: graphic novels that draw on classic fiction. Even the Hardy Boys and Nancy Drew have their own dark versions in graphic novel form.

For a clever updating of the *Madame Bovary* story, bring the graphic novel *Gemma Bovary* by Posy Simmonds to the club. Gemma is a contemporary Londoner who marries Charlie Bovary, moves to Normandy and shares many of Emma's delusions and shopping habits. Gemma Bovary works best as a satire of British versus French culture, and everyone will love the graphics.

■ ■ ■

Moby Dick
(1851) by Herman Melville

Don't you be rolling your eyes. *Moby Dick* is a maximum thriller, a dangerous adventure brimming with meaning. The writing is, modern and magical. Can you think of a better time to meet that famous monomaniac Captain Ahab on his final, fateful *Pequod* voyage seeking the white whale? Our narrator and star witness is Ishmael, but you will also be formally introduced to a bevy of celebrity seamen including tattooed pagan Queequeg and first mate Starbuck, a good Quaker who is unheeded in the looming disaster.

Is this a book without a hero or would that be Captain Ahab, fatal flaw and all? Is it an epic poem or a novel? Why is Ishmael so lonely and why does Melville keep him alive? Snack on the many instances of foreshadowing, symbolism (hint: coffins are everywhere) and approaching horror.

When the *Pequod* meets and sails away from the *Bachelor*, a ship brimming with wealth, good fortune and pennants, you know it is heading back to Nantucket while the *Pequod* is heading to hell—with us on board!

It's historical, it's biblical and many scholars love to describe the American-ness of the novel. Melville chronicles the ships the *Pequod* meets, and it's social satire at its best: "The English whalers sometimes affect a kind of metropolitan superiority over the American whalers; regarding the long, lean Nantucketer, with his nondescript provincialisms, as a sort of sea-peasant."

Penguin Reading Group Guide: The introduction is excellent, bringing out the discussion themes of whiteness, the void, Ahab versus Ishmael and the idea that a discussion will inevitably head to zero and infinite conclusions.

Quote to impress: The first line ("Call me Ishmael") is quoted so often, it has become an annoying cliché. A better choice is found further down the page: "whenever it is a damp, drizzly November in my soul."

Furthermore: *Ahab's Wife, or, The Star-Gazer* (1999) by Sena Jeter Naslund is based on the one line in *Moby Dick* when Captain Ahab mentions his young wife. Book clubs have loved this story of Una Spenser, who grew up in Kentucky but soon escapes to a New England lighthouse and has her own sailing and romantic adventures while getting to meet the major literary stars of the era. *Ahab's Wife* is beautifully illustrated by Christopher Wormell.

Nonfiction alert: Nathaniel Philbrick's *In the Heart of the Sea: The Tragedy of Whaleship Essex* tells the story that inspired *Moby Dick*. The *Essex* left Nantucket in 1819 and was torn to pieces by the sperm whale it was hunting. The survivors drifted in the South Pacific, ultimately resorting to cannibalism to survive. The *Essex* tragedy was the *Titanic* of its day.

Selling *Moby Dick* to the club: Fire up the tryworks, and don't look back.

1984

(1949) by George Orwell

Have you ever considered *1984* as a brisk tale of espionage? A love story about two doomed idealists? A concise history of the Nazi and Stalin regimes? A pop masterpiece featuring a codefied language that we use every day? Consider these questions and other thought crimes when reading and discussing George Orwell's eternal dystopia.

Winston Smith begins to have a lot of questions on the job at the Ministry of Truth. He is a minor party functionary, participates in the charming festival of Hate Week, fears the constant surveillance ("Big Brother is Watching You"), but has bought an illegal diary to record his real thoughts about Big Brother: he loathes him. Winston then meets Julia, the girl from the Fiction Department, with whom he begins an illicit affair. Inevitably, they are apprehended and Winston finds himself in Room 101. His torturer knows a thing or two about how to conduct an interrogation dripping with sarcasm and tautology. ("The object of persecution is persecution. The object of torture is torture.") Does Winston truly become "the last man"? If war is peace and ignorance is slavery, does it still apply to present-day humanity and politics? Consult *1984*'s Appendix for clues.

Penguin Reading Group Guide: Excellent, a parallel reading experience. The question topics range from O'Brien's roles, Winston Smith's dreams and whether Winston can be considered an heroic character. The introduction is to the point, and there is a good biography of George Orwell.

Cocktails: Victory Gin at the Chestnut Tree Cafe, a thought criminal's last stop. And though *1984* has been made into an opera, it's only a matter of time before some enterprising hipster puts the song Winston hears at the cafe to music: "Under the spreading chestnut tree, I sold you and you sold me."

The father of Newspeak: Eric Arthur Blair was born in British-ruled India in 1903. In 1933 he used "George Orwell" as a pen name for the first time when his book of essays, *Down and Out in Paris and London*, was published. In addition to a large body of work, the author has bequeathed us the incessantly used adjective "Orwellian." How did he know?

Audio alert: Richard Brown (Blackstone Audio Book) and Richard Matthews (Books on Tape) are first rate narrators for different editions of this perfect "radio drama."

Nonfiction alert: *Finding George Orwell in Burma* (2005) by Emma Larkin centers on the 1920s when Eric Blair was an intelligence agent for the British Empire—an experience Orwell recounted in *Burmese Days* (1934). The author visits the current Myanmar and finds the whole place Orwellian.

Selling *1984* to the club: Freshly chilling and utterly suspenseful, it will be a revelation.

■ ■ ■

One Hundred Years of Solitude
(1967) by Gabriel Garcia Marquez, translated by Gregory Rabassa (1970)

The Nobel laureate takes us on a nonstop tour of the human condition in this hallucinatory, fabulous nightmare. The town of Macondo may be mythical, but the hundred-year family saga of the Buendias reads just like fresh parchment—and the lusty, dreamy hellscape Gabriel Garcia Marquez has created will always be part of our secret history.

Jose Arcadio Buendia and his wife Ursula are from the founding families of the cursed town where solitude and nostalgia are not just metaphors, but everyday experiences. Throughout the chronicle of life and death foretold, Colonel Aureliano Buendia, who famously faced the firing squad and remembered the afternoon his father took him to discover ice, has led thirty-two fruitless civil wars. Suitors are spurned; industrial progress in the form of a mechanical ballerina, the cinema, the railroad and the velocipede arrive, advance the plot and leave in a haze of nostalgia and death. Meanwhile, matriarch Ursula makes and sells animal candies in the shape of little roosters and fish to keep the family going through the insomnia plague, the civil wars and the rains.

The detailed, everyday life is contrasted matter of factly with the fantastical. Readers who are coming to *One Hundred Years of Solitude* a second time may note how terrifying the realism has become, dominating the magic. Begin your discussion here.

Discussion questions, Harper Perennial: Basic. There are sixteen questions, so you are bound to find several to get the discussion started.

Discussion sourcing: For an in-depth and fascinating guide to *One Hundred Years of Solitude*, go to oprah.com and read the notes from Marquez biographer Gene H. Bell-Villada. He discusses the book's major themes, including human isolation and Marquez's use of time, humor and politics. The biographical notes about the master are fascinating: did you know that Marquez's grandmother supported the family by making candy animals? The site includes additional discussion questions for each section of the book.

Furthermore: Marquez has had a long and illustrious literary career, and clubs have embraced many of his great works: *The Autumn of the Patriarch, Chronicle of a Death Foretold, Love in the Time of Cholera, The General in His Labyrinth*.

■■■

Palace Walk
(1956) by Naguib Mahfouz,
translated by William H. Hutchins and Olive E. Kenny (1989)

Nobel Prize winner *Palace Walk* begins as World War I is coming to a close. Tyrant of his household and loveable bon vivant in the lively, sensual Cairo society of parties and women, al-Sayyid Ahmad tightly controls his two worlds. His wife and daughters can never leave the house, as taught by a strict interpretation of Qur'an. His three sons, however, often have the run of the city as nationalism grips Egypt; though they all defy—and fear—

their father, Yasin, Fahmy and Kamal, the youngest, are very different from one another. Yet, we are in familiar territory. This family is bound together by love and faith, but challenged by al-Sayyid Ahmad's intense anger and imperious dictates. "He's more than a father," Yasin tells Fahmy. "He's the ultimate."

You will not stop talking about al-Sayyid Ahmad, utterly recognizable in his dual roles as puritanical pater familias and man about town. Is he a figure of pure hypocrisy? Do we recoil from the delight we take in his fabulous interior monologues and find them poignant as well as repugnant? A great deal of the discussion will center on his wife, the religious Amina, and how much complicity she has in the way she is treated by her husband—as a humbled servant. Or is she courageous, forging her own world with the well-loved family coffee hour, filled with daily chat and a fortune reading by the sisters? This home is "the world of the emotions" that al-Sayyid Ahmad reviles. A family saga with a plot that incorporates the sweep of history, *Palace Walk* also has the enchanting intimacy of a small coffeehouse in Cairo.

Discussion questions, Anchor Books: Excellent, a parallel reading experience. Many of the questions contrast a Western reader's insight with Mahfouz's descriptions of Egyptian society and universal themes.

Furthermore: *Palace Walk* was the first book in Mahfouz's acclaimed *Cairo Trilogy*. You won't want to stop until you find out what happens to the family (*Sugar Street* and *Palace of Desire* complete the trilogy). *The Map of Love*, a romance that tells the story of two Western women in Egypt across the twentieth century, has also become a club favorite.

■ ■ ■

Sister Carrie
(1900) by Theodore Dreiser

Theodore Dreiser's novel of success and degradation set in the 1880s and 1890s will strike modern readers as completely contemporary. It is the story of large-eyed Carrie Meeber who arrives in Chicago only to be buffeted by poverty and the prevailing forces of industrial capitalism. But soon she is in a love triangle with traveling salesman Charles Drouet and married, wealthy burgher George Hurstwood. Carrie is then on her way in a world of acquisitions and stardom as the narrative moves from Chicago to New York. Readers might be surprised to see the words "celebrity" and "idol" used throughout the book, and their meanings have barely changed today.

Dreiser was a newspaper reporter and the editor of women's fashion magazines. He describes how the whole society works, from its dumbwaiters to its starched collars and strikebreakers, and sprinkles real celebrities like John L. Sullivan throughout. "A woman should some day write the complete philosophy of clothes," Dreiser tells us in the beginning, but it is he who tells all not only about clothes, but also about the décor, the restaurants, the first phone booths and theaters of the moment. Each gilded object and fashion show is juxtaposed with the urban jungle that swallows Hurstwood whole.

Symbolism (the rocking chair, the leaves in the storm, the snow and the cold), natural selection, chance and real events of the time often contribute to a far-reaching discussion. Is each of the characters unsympathetic and amoral in some way? What do you make of the one character—Drouet—who does not change? And what about that groovy slang ("a fine stepper" and even "out o' sight!")?

Dressing thematically: Be-ringed and be–scarf-pinned, the characters revel in the material world—on their way up, that is.

DVD alert: *A Place in the Sun* (1951) starring Elizabeth Taylor and Montgomery Clift is based on Dreiser's other great work, *An American Tragedy*. Clift plays a poor worker who kills his fiancée (Shelley Winters) to court the wealthy and beautiful Taylor.

Selling *Sister Carrie* to the club: Melodrama in the best sense of the word, it's as if you found a fashion magazine from the 1890s—with life-and-death labor struggles and compelling melodrama as the articles. Hurstwood's double crime is said to be based on the true story of Dreiser's sister.

The Sun Also Rises

(1926) by Ernest Hemingway

It's the 1920s and a group of expatriates, still reeling from World War I, are adrift and drinking up a storm in Paris. Jake Barnes is famously wounded and this is an ever-present undercurrent throughout the novel. Brett, Lady Ashley, a woman of the world who eventually leaves her many suitors for a famous bullfighter after the gang arrives in Pamplona for a seven-day bullfighting fiesta, is the love interest of one and all. In the Hemingway universe, *The Sun Also Rises* is a book about behavior: who responds well and honorably and who does not. Do the old rules still apply? This is the signature novel about the "lost generation," a phrase attributed to Gertrude Stein.

How do we discuss this widely imitated and satirized book, renowned for its world-weary dialogue that is alternatively pugnacious or dead-on? (Brett on her martini: "It's good. Isn't it a nice bar?" Jake: "They're all nice bars.") The anti-Semitism leveled against group outcast Robert Cohn and the vivid bullfighting scenes are equally good entry points for discussion. Start off with Hemingway's writing, especially in the way he creates atmosphere in at least three major settings. And consider what literature was like before *The Sun Also Rises*.

Discussion questions, Scribner: Especially provocative is the question about the epigraph from Ecclesiastes that contains the title phrase and how it is relevant to the disaffected cast.

A Moveable Feast: Considered a companion book to *A Sun Also Rises*, *A Moveable Feast* was written in the late 1950s and published posthumously in 1964. This book has had incredible staying power, as have its many tropes: being young and in love in Paris, writing in cafés from dawn to dusk, drinking at seductively named expatriate hangouts (see "The Many Favorites of Ernest Hemingway," page 130). Hemingway's views on F. Scott Fitzgerald and Gertrude Stein detailed in *A Moveable Feast* are still debated, while a droll conversation between Hemingway and Ford Maddox Ford about what constitutes a gentleman continues to amuse.

Furthermore: *A Farewell to Arms* (1929), the great romance of World War I, and *For Whom the Bell Tolls* (1940), Hemingway's novel of the Spanish Civil War, are continually in the mix of club selections. Though Hemingway won a Pulitzer Prize for *The Old Man and the Sea* (1952) and won the Nobel Prize in 1954, he was plagued by alcoholism and ill health. He shot himself in 1961.

■ ■ ■

Vanity Fair
(1848) by William Makepeace Thackeray

Money is worshipped to death, celebrity can be had at a price, there is a big battle in the east and careers rise and crash to earth. Though *Vanity Fair* was written in 1848, the story was ripped from a timeless newspaper. Considered the greatest of all Victorian novels, it is a world that you will recognize at once. William Thackeray's depiction of success, failure and power is set in England during the Napoleanic Wars—Waterloo is the big battle, and all the characters go off to see it as if it is a big holiday. By now, you know this kind of thing never ends well.

But Thackeray's greatest creation is Becky Sharp. Is she a lovely Beelzebub or a superior bad angel who redeems herself? Your discussion will begin and end here, for *Vanity Fair* wraps around Becky like a cashmere shawl sent on the latest boat from that outpost of Empire, India. Our little adventurer claws her way to the top of English society, using her considerable brains, beauty, charm, great writing skills and an incomparable singing voice. It's not enough. The artful little minx was born to an opera dancer and no one can forget it. She is one of the worst mothers in all of literature, but you will be captivated and appalled by her stratagems in a society that offered women next to nothing.

Our nosy and tireless narrator describes Vanity Fair as "a very vain, wicked, foolish place, full of all sorts of humbugs and falsenesses and pretensions." Maybe that's why the book is subtitled "A novel without a hero." Though Becky's hapless husband Rawdon Crawley was a gambler, he did have his sympathetic side, while William Dobbin, who loves the dull Amelia Sedley, behaves honorably and sees right through Becky. And yet, he is no Mr. Darcy, and you will want to further analyze his role and those of the rest of the non-heroes. Thackeray poses his own excellent discussion questions at the end of the novel.

Penguin Reading Group Guide: Very good, especially the questions about those flip sides, Becky and Amelia. You will be anxious to talk about other novels in comparison to *Vanity Fair*, such as *Madame Bovary* and *Gone with the Wind*.

Editions that make a difference: Look for any edition with the strange and wonderful illustrations drawn by Thackeray himself.

Dressing thematically: Haul out your ermine tippet or the large combs like tortoiseshell shovels for your hair.

DVD alert: The latest movie version starring Reese Witherspoon as Becky and directed by Mira Nair (*Monsoon Wedding*) provides fodder for a mini-discussion. Don't miss Becky's Bollywood style dance at the Marquess of Steyne's notorious soire.

Selling *Vanity Fair* to the club: Absorbing and addicting, it's a cornerstone book. You will permit a reading period of two or three months, interspersed with DVD nights.

■ ■ ■

Washington Square
(1881) by Henry James
and
The Master
(2004) by Colm Toibin

A classic portrait study, *Washington Square* is the story of a society doctor, Dr. Austin Sloper, who is a widower and man of science and irony. He lives with his only daughter, Catherine, in the house on Washington Square. Sloper considers Catherine dull and naïve, so when the penniless but handsome Morris Townsend comes to ask for her, the doctor is blunt in his dismissal. But Catherine loves the selfish young man and persists in keeping the suit alive. The fate of these three characters play out in a Jamesian world of society, money and thwarted desire.

Clubs will want to dissect the choices of the three characters, especially Catherine's, and how the house in Washington Square serves James's purpose. Is Dr. Sloper a monster or a protector? Which characters leave the stage with dignity? Does your opinion of "poor Catherine" change? Who exactly has won the battle? How do today's fortune hunters play the game?

An indispensable companion novel to the work of Henry James is *The Master*, an ingenious, intensely beautiful meditation about James's interior and public life. It offers superb, lifelike portraits of the family and the friends James treasured, dissected and often put off-limits throughout his life. Best of all, Colm Toibin subtly relates how James's work and his life intersect, illuminating the masterworks while still shrouding the master in privacy.

Chief among the mysteries is James's loneliness and unresolved sexual identity, and both are deftly explored by Toibin. Especially illuminating is the portrait of the James family at the center of a New England in the midst of intense intellectual flowering that ended with the Civil War. This is a book for everyone who has had a crush on the James family, especially that "independent republic," Alice.

Henry James's teen book club: For an entire summer before they entered Harvard, James and his fellow teen Thomas "Sargy" Perry read and reread all of Nathaniel Hawthorne and met to discuss his work. One of their favorite book club discussions was about *The Scarlet Letter*. Scholars will see the influence of the earlier master in *Washington Square*.

Dressing thematically: You may not come to the costume ball as Daisy Miller, per Lady Wolseley's instructions in *The Master*. You must be a Gainsborough, a Romney or a Sir Joshua.

Furthermore: *The Master* will leave you desperate for more Henry James. *Portrait of a Lady, The Aspern Papers, The Wings of the Dove, The Ambassadors, The Golden Bowl* and the short stories, especially *The Beast in the Jungle*, could fill out years worth of club selections.

What Is a Classic?

In *Why Read the Classics?*, the writer and critic Italo Calvino offers several definitions of a classic book. "A classic is a book which has never exhausted all it has to say to its readers" is one of his definitions. And here's another: " 'Your' classic is a book to which you cannot remain indifferent, and which helps you define yourself in relation or even in opposition to it."

There are many definitions of a classic book, and your club can develop its own definition for the club's collective classics list or a book considered by scholars to be in the pantheon. Try out these criteria on a new or old book club favorite:

- It can be read, reread, and read again.

- You are unafraid to bring it up to the club.

- It can be read aloud without the slightest bit of embarrassment.

- You will find new things in it every time.

- It improves, even on brief review.

- It withstands the test of time, fads and fashion.

- It is made better and deeper in almost every medium: miniseries, movie or audio version.

- It can speak to you at different times of your life—or reinforce the things it has always said so eloquently.

- It is its own world.

- Its themes are often, but not always, big ones—courtship, love, marriage, war, death, friendship.

- It is one of a kind, or first of its kind.

- You feel lucky to be able to enter the mind of the author, whose ideas will surprise you even the second time around.

Club Rules: How True!
Mark Up Your Book
without Mercy

How best to add your two centimes to the discussion and sound authoritative and confident while you are at it? Everyone else has brought the publishers' discussion questions, but only you have read actively. Because as you have read—pencil in hand, stickies at the ready and your book a masterpiece of your luminous thoughts and incisive perceptions—you have instinctively followed the dictates of Mortimer Adler, founder of the Great Books of the Western World.

In his famous essay about how to really own a book, Adler says you don't own a book unless you have scribbled all over it, writing in the margins. Your interaction with the book is active, your mind alive with ideas you can share at your next club.

An annotated system devised by you for you could soon be in reach. Motivate yourself with hieroglyphics only you understand: fanciful ribboned bows, primitive fish, elegant checks, inverted beach umbrellas—only you will know what you are talking about. If you are marking a paragraph and a mere underlining of words won't do, try these secret symbols—and the inventive scribbling will really get their attention on club night.

Some readers like to annotate the inside covers with mini character descriptions, themes, plots and other notes. Others scribble over a pad or a separate piece of paper, listing the characters and their traits. And for those of us who cannot mark a book? Stickies, Post-its, reading notebooks and pads are our friends.

For maximum effect, don't forget to review your notes right before the club.

MASTER CLASS

- Create a character list inside the book or on a separate piece of paper, even in a Word or Excel file. Include the name of the character, relation to other characters, function in the novel and quotes.

- Jot down your changing thoughts and perceptions about the story, characters and narrator—especially the unreliable and unlikable kind—to really put your annotation system in overdrive.

- Include words and phrases that you would like to discuss with the group.

- Create a color-coding system devised by you—colors for specific characters, themes, or other ongoing plot issues you have identified.

And don't even *think* of lending out your copy of *Plutarch's Lives*, Shakespeare's works or *The Federalist Papers*. These books, according to Adler, "are as much a part of you as your head or your heart."

When Pets Go Missing

Though Ernest Hemingway and his wife employed their cat F. Puss as a babysitter when they were out on the town in Paris—and in *A Moveable Feast* the author described those who repeated tales of cats smothering babies as "ignorant and prejudiced"—sometimes our pets need their own babysitter.

Consider the case of black standard poodles Max and Abner, visiting littermates playing in the backyard. The host is so busy with preparations, she hasn't noticed they've escaped. Bad Abner—he is so always in trouble, leading Max astray, opening the gate himself! By the time the guests arrive, a search party throughout the neighborhood is already in progress. The dogs are found—a mile away and attending another party—and are rescued by the host. But by that time, the spirit has been torn out of the event.

A club host can have many duties, and pets are often last on the list, sometimes with disastrous results. "There are no quick fixes, but a little planning goes a long way," says celebrity pet trainer William Berloni.

If you are hosting for the first time, or if the holiday bash is at your house and you have many tasks, consider the use of a predesignated "sitter." A responsible pet lover in the neighborhood can play with and supervise your animal and any visiting animals in an area separate from the meeting. And a supervised "doggie party" may be just the thing.

PETS' NIGHT OUT

- Make arrangements for a dog sitter or a friendly placement at a neighbor's if you are consumed by hosting chores.

- Keep guests' pets from minimum to nil while you are preparing.

- Assign your child or neighbor to supervise the pet or pets who arrive at the club or club party.

- Allow your pet to make an entrance at the time you and his minder designate.

- Make sure your pet is in a safe, enclosed place so it will not escape during the many comings and goings of members.

- Prepare as much as you can in advance so that you are calm and relaxed and your pet is either in a safe place or can be trusted to not exhibit undesirable behaviors. Or escape.

- Make sure all pets are fed, walked and ministered to before the club arrives. The last thing you want to do on a special book club night is make an emergency visit to the vet or pin your pet's mug shot on trees.

The Tween Book Club:
The Lion, the Witch and the Wardrobe
by C. S. Lewis

". . . and whether it was more like playing with a thunderstorm or playing with a kitten Lucy could never make up her mind."
—The Lion, the Witch and the Wardrobe

What would it be like to return to Narnia? But this time, you are accompanied by a few fellow travelers on the road that leads to C. S. Lewis's magical kingdom. *The Chronicles of Narnia* consists of seven books, with *The Lion, the Witch and the Wardrobe* the second. It's a world imbued with a philosophical dark beauty, and it is in a constant state of rediscovery, especially in light of the recent big-screen epic.

The Lion, the Witch and the Wardrobe begins like so many adventure tales, in the real world. In the time of the air raids, Lucy, Peter, Susan and Edmund Pevensie are sent to the house of a professor in the country, and the atmosphere is rife for even stranger events. One rainy day, Lucy, who loves the smell and feel of fur in the old wardrobe, stumbles on a new world. She meets a faun, Mr. Tumnus, who tells her about this world, Narnia. The news is not good. The White Witch has made the land into a frozen wasteland that is "always winter and never Christmas."

No one believes her, but Edmund is next through the wardrobe and he is not so lucky: he meets the dreaded witch and becomes addicted to her Turkish delight. Soon, the rest of the children are deeply involved in Narnia, where they meet the great lord and king, the lion Aslan. Together, they set out to save Edmund, now the witch's prisoner. A great battle takes place and a prophesy comes true: the four children occupy the four thrones in Cair Paravel. As this is a British fairy tale, they also return punctually—presumably for tea—to the professor's house, where no time has elapsed.

The Chronicles of Narnia are usually seen as a Christian allegory, with Aslan the Christ figure. Clubs often talk about faith, loyalty, time and deep magic. The talking animals are the most noble creatures, while the Sons of Adam and the Daughters of Eve must learn hard lessons. It is a magical story filled with meaning and love. Especially moving is the comfort Susan and Lucy give a sad and lonely Aslan, burying their "cold hands in the beautiful sea of fur." The girls shed tears all night as Aslan moves to his likely destruction. After the tears, there is only quiet and "you feel as if nothing was ever going to happen again."

The charming illustrations in many editions of *The Lion, the Witch and the Wardrobe* are by Pauline Baynes: the girls are dressed in 1950 style frocks and Edmund is in short pants as they cope with the ever-changing Narnia landscape. But don't miss Lewis's dedication to goddaughter Lucy Barfield; this elegiac meditation on childhood and the inevitability of growing up is worthy of many conversations.

Scholars say Lewis wrote the books in the Narnia series in the 1950s as an affirmation of his faith—and the last word in a real philosophical debate about the existence of God that took place at Oxford's Socratic Society in 1948. Lewis's real life adversary was Elizabeth Anscombe, professor of philosophy at Cambridge. Though she squashed him at the debating society, Lewis, indeed, has had the last word.

With Lewis's reputation continually enhanced by *The Chronicles of Narnia* (though his friend J.R.R. Tolkien is said to have intensely disliked the stories), his books about Christianity are receiving renewed attention. There is even a series of little gift books under the titles *What Christians Believe, Made for Heaven, Virtue and Vice* and *Paved with Good Intentions*. His other works include *The Problem of Pain* (1940) and *The Screwtape Letters* (1942). *A Year with C. S. Lewis: Daily Reading from His Classic Works* is a day-by-day inspirational book with headings for each day of the year, including "Understanding Evil," "Forget Yourself" and "The Thrill Is Gone." *The Screwtape Letters* and *Mere Christianity* are sources for many of the selections.

The Many Favorites of Ernest Hemingway

LOCATION	WATERING HOLE	COCKTAILS/DRINKS	FUN FACT
Key West	Sloppy Joe's	Mojitos	The bar opened the day after Prohibition was repealed, Dec. 5, 1933. Hemingway was a frequent fixture.
Havana	El Floridita	Daiquiris	The bartender and owner of the El Floridita Hotel dubbed Hemingway's favorite daiquiri "the Papa Doble."
Paris	Café des Deux Magots, Closerie des Lilas, Brasserie Lipp, The Dingo, Harry's New York Bar, Le Dome, Café des Amateurs, Hotel Ritz, Café Rotonde, The Select, The Falstaff Bar, The Crillon, Prunier, Le Trou dans le Mur	Dry sherry with James Joyce, café crème, beer, vermouth cassis, whiskey and soda, champagne, scotch and a half lime, *une demi-blonde*, Bloody Marys, brandy, Sancerre, seventy-three dry martinis	At the front during World War II, Hemingway filled his water bottles with gin and cognac. But while liberating Paris, he—and everyone—drank dry martinis at the Hotel Ritz.
Paris	At Gertrude Stein's, 27 rue de Fleurus	Distilled liqueurs from purple and yellow plums or wild raspberries served from cut-glass carafes	Stein's advice to Hemingway: "You should only read what is truly good or what is frankly bad."
Lyon to Paris	Road trip with F. Scott Fitzgerald	Whiskey and Perrier after breakfast, white Macon, two citron presse and two double whiskeys to make whiskey sours	According to Hemingway, Fitzgerald thought he was gravely ill on this trip and took asprin with his whiskey sours.
Venice	The Gritti Palace	Daiquiris, scotch, bourbon, tequila, and vermouthless martinis	Hemingway started the day with three bottles of Valpolicella.

Classic Fiction
Anniversary Party

"But that's the aim of civilization: to make everything an enjoyment."
—*Stepan Arkadyich,* Anna Karenina

You are celebrating a significant milestone of your club—the first, fifth, tenth or twentieth year of continuous meeting. Or your twentieth member has just joined the club. Or you have successfully completed all of Proust, Dickens or *Madame Bovary*—in French. Commemorate your accomplishment with ideas torn from the pages of your favorite books.

In *The Age of Innocence*, Edith Wharton was quite specific about a Gilded Age dinner of "velvety oyster soup, shad and cucumbers, then a young broiled turkey with corn fritters, followed by a canvas-back with currant jelly and celery mayonnaise." And don't forget that Gilded Age favorite, turtle soup. In *The Great Gatsby*, Fitzgerald was equally specific describing a magical buffet of "glistening hors d'oeuvres, spiced hams crowded against salads of harlequin designs and pastry pigs and turkeys bewitched to a dark gold."

Gatsby had a corps of caterers at his disposal in his glory days, but you, too, have a team. For special events, many clubs assign one dish per person with one member—usually the host—coordinating assignments. Others use gourmet groceries to prepare the main course, and the members are responsible for bringing the rest.

No matter what you decide, our classic authors do not disappoint in the specifics. And planning the event will allow you to connect with their writing in different ways.

At the end of the party, add a sample of your souvenir menus, recipes, pressed flowers and photos to your club scrapbook. And begin planning next year's gala.

MENU NOTES

Champagne cocktail bar: Designate a bar area either in the kitchen or living room—one that Nick Carraway wouldn't mind slinking off to in his white flannels. You will need champagne flutes, ice buckets and bar linens. And consider hiring a young adult in the house or in the neighborhood to bartend, just to make the whole party more authentic.

Look for Schramsberg or Scharffenberger champagne as the best brands for the money. Or, if you really want to see some reaction, serve pink champagne; it looks beautiful and may summarize your celebration best of all.

Serve the champagne straight up or as a cocktail, but keep it in the refrigerator until one hour before you are ready to serve it. Then move the champagne to ice buckets in the designated bar area.

Oysters: With enough notice, many fish stores and supermarkets will shell the oysters for you and pack them on rock salt. This should be your last stop before the event: oysters should be placed on crushed ice immediately and served.

Fruit platters Madame Bovary: Greengages are greenish yellow plums that Emma arranged when a neighbor came for Sunday dinner. And at the marquis' chateau, there were pyramids of greengages on a bed of vine leaves. Look for greengages or plums at the green market, but you can substitute any fresh fruit in season.

Cheese Oblonsky: Stepan Arkadyich requested his parmesan from the Tartar waiter who remembered, too late, that Stehan did not like the naming of dishes in French. Cheese selections to end a meal are limitless—and it is the easiest assignment for one lucky member.

Animal candies Ursula: This is a job for the candy maker in the club or the person who is a whiz at finding things on the Internet. Candy molds of every type of animal—including those in *One Hundred Years of Solitude*—are readily available. The tamest way to approach this is to identify the animals you are looking for and begin your search. Confectioners often have marzipan animals, and you know who in your group will appreciate the road-kill gummies you can find in the supermarket.

MUSICAL SELECTIONS

In the famous *Great Gatsby* party scene, a piece is played at the request of Gatsby, "Vladimir Tostoff's Jazz History of the World." It hypnotized the swinging party and made girls swoon.

"The Jazz History of the World," which the conductor related had recently been played at Carnegie Hall, could only be the work of the thinly disguised George Gershwin. To make your guests swoon, choose from a wide array of the jazz age maestro. On the CD *George Gershwin: Greatest Hits* (Sony), Leonard Bernstein plays "Rhapsody in Blue," Yo-Yo Ma accompanies conductor John Williams on "Preludes for Piano" and Sarah Vaughan sings "Summertime" from *Porgy and Bess*, accompanied by the Los Angeles Philharmonic.

As for the yellow cocktail music described by Fitzgerald, it's freestyle.

NOTES ON DÉCOR

Take advantage of Flaubert's exquisite language in *Madame Bovary* and listen to his suggestions. As Emma and Charles drive up to the marquis' chateau, they see "tufts of shrubbery—rhododendrons, syringas and snowballs" lining the graveled drive. When they enter the chateau, "candle flames cast long gleams on rounded silver dish-covers." And on the table, "oversized fruit is piled up on moss in openwork baskets." "On the wide-bordered plates the napkins stood like bishops' mitres," and a row of bouquets lined the length of the table. Note, as well, the flowers that made up the coiffure of the ladies: forget-me-nots, jasmine, pomegranate blossoms, wheat sprays and cornflowers. The formidable dowagers wore red headdresses like turbans.

Less formally—and in honor of Anna Karenina—place small vases of fresh violets around the room and table. You will remember she wore them at the ball when she danced the night away with Count Vronsky.

An epergne is an ornate eighteenth- or nineteenth-century centerpiece that holds little dishes or candles or a combination of these. They were often made in silver or gold and could be the owner's prize possession and a symbol of arriving in the world.

Miss Havisham had one, described as "a center-piece of some kind" covered in cobwebs, decorating a table filled with the decaying remnants of the wedding feast. Like the ragged wedding gown Miss Havisham wears and the bridal flowers in her hair, the room and its accessories are all symbols of her fate and part of the set décor in the moldering mansion. If you check around, you might have an epergne, too. Haul it out and show it to the gang, adding any bits of family history or historical facts that you can know or can find out.

CRAFT: SOUVENIR MENU HOW-TO

For a smashing menu design right from your computer, incorporate a simple, elegant typeface on ivory or white paper with a gold border. Print out the menu on as heavy stock as you wish. Print extras for last-minute guests and for your club scrapbook.

For an extra layer of souvenir protection, add a sheet of vellum on top of the menu and tie with ribbons.

Sample menu:

Headline: Edwardian Script ITC, 24-point

Each menu item: Edwardian Script ITC, 22-point

Best printer-ready paper stock: The Paper Company, 8.5 × 11-inch, Ivory

Classic Fiction Anniversary Party Menu

Iced Champagne Cocktail Bar Gatsby

Oysters Oblonsky
Soupe Printaniere
"Canvasback" Edith Wharton
Heirloom Tomato Platter

Fruit Baskets Madame Bovary
Cherries, pineapple, greengages, pomegranates
Cheeses Oblonsky

Sticky Toffee Pudding and
Toffee Sauce Charles Dickens
Animal Candies Ursula

Champagne Cocktail

MAKES 8 DRINKS

8 sugar cubes
Dashes Angostura bitters
8 ounces brandy
Chilled champagne

In each flute, place a sugar cube, add the bitters to coat. Slowly add brandy and then the champagne, filling the flute to the top of the glass.

Adeline Penberthy's Vegetable Soup with Pistou

SERVES 8

This soup can be enjoyed by Prince Oblonsky as just a minor part of a meal or by everyone else as an entire meal with bread and salad on a regular book club night.

2 cups onions, diced

2 leeks, sliced, white only (use the whole bunch if they are small)

12 cups beef broth

2 cups canned tomatoes, cut in half and drained

2 cups fresh green beans, ends split off and halved

2½ cups diced potatoes

2 teaspoons salt

2 teaspoons pepper

1½ cups angel hair pasta, broken into 1-inch lengths

4 cloves garlic

4 teaspoon freshly chopped basil

1 teaspoon dried or fresh sage

2 teaspoons dried or fresh thyme

4 egg yolks

½ cup extra virgin olive oil

4 tablespoons tomato paste

4 tablespoons grated Parmesan

1. Saute onion and leeks until tender. In a large pot, combine the onion and leeks with the broth, tomatoes, green beans and potatoes. Cover and

heat until boiling. Then simmer for 30 minutes. Add salt, pepper and pasta. Cook for another 15 minutes.

2. In a separate bowl, mash garlic, basil, sage, thyme and egg yolks. Gradually add olive oil, tomato paste and Parmesan. Add a little hot soup to this mixture and then add the mixture to the pot. Heat and serve with grated cheese.

Travel tip: Prepare Step 1 in advance and make Step 2 at the club, alerting your host about the number of eggs you will need. Allow about 30 minutes for on-site preparation.

"Canvasback": Duck Breasts with Boysenberry Sauce

SERVES 8

Though canvasback was de rigueur in the days of Edith Wharton's youth, you can find duck breasts in many supermarkets. You can also substitute Cornish game hens or chicken for the duck breasts—just roast, cut into quarters and serve. Almost any berry preserve can be substituted for boysenberry.

For the duck:
6 boneless duck breasts
6 tablespoons extra virgin olive oil

For the sauce:
2 cups red wine, Pinot noir for example
1⅔ cups chicken broth, preferably organic
1⅔ cups beef broth
2 tablespoons fresh orange juice
½ teaspoon dried rosemary
1 bay leaf
1½ teaspoons butter at room temperature
1½ teaspoons all-purpose flour
½ cup boysenberry preserves

For the duck: Salt and pepper each duck breast. In a large nonstick skillet, heat 6 tablespoons of extra virgin olive oil. Sear duck breasts, about 4–5 minutes on each side. Cut each duck on the diagonal as thinly as possible, and place on a bed of wild rice. Time saving tip: Look for wild rice that can be microwaved.

For the sauce: In a large saucepan, combine wine, broths, orange juice, rosemary and bay leaf. Bring to a boil and continue boiling over low heat until the sauce is reduced, about 30 minutes. Combine butter and flour and whisk with simmering liquids in the saucepan. When the mixture has thickened, add the boysenberry preserves and simmer. Remove the bay leaf and strain the sauce for seeds into a medium bowl.

Travel tip: You can make the sauce one day in advance and refrigerate. Heat the sauce before serving.

Heirloom Tomato Platter

SERVES 8

This is an easy platter to prepare and the secret is a trip to the green market or well-stocked grocery. At the market, look for a variety of heirlooms, which might include:

Black Prince	Brandywine
Purple Cherokee	Uglyripe
Aunt Ruby	Green Zebra
Red Vine	Local (native) beefsteak
Striped German	Mini heirlooms
Gold Yellow	

For the table:

Extra virgin olive oil	Plate of lemon quarters
Balsamic vinegar	Salt and pepper
Sherry vinegar	

Preparation: Slice tomatoes and mix and match the colors and varieties. Garnish with whole basil leaves.

Field trip: A club trip to the green market, especially at a time when you are planning a special event or hosting, is always fun and productive. Establish a budget, and set off to the market.

Markets often have the freshest produce as well as bunches of herbs, baked goods, heirloom eggs and poultry, jams, chutneys, and native cheeses. If it is tomato season, try to find varieties you haven't tasted before, get the full produce profile from the producer and bring back the information to the club. Don't forget your camera—many of the stands list the varieties of the day on a blackboard, so take photos and add them to your club scrapbook or portfolio.

Sticky Toffee Pudding and Toffee Sauce Charles Dickens

SERVES 6

This pudding from Charlaine Fontelieu's recipe was served to her in a London hotel. She refused to leave the premises without the recipe.

For the pudding:
1 cup boiling water
¾ cup dates, pitted and chopped
1 teaspoon baking soda
1 stick and 2 tablespoons unsalted butter, softened
¾ cup sugar
2 eggs
1 teaspoon vanilla
¾ cup all-purpose flour

For the toffee sauce:
¾ cup sugar
¾ stick unsalted butter
1 cup heavy whipping cream

Preheat the oven to 350 degrees.

In a medium bowl pour boiling water over chopped dates. Add the baking soda, stir and set aside to cool.

In a separate bowl, cream the butter with the sugar. Add the eggs, one at a time, and beat into mixture. Add the vanilla. Fold in flour. Add the date mixture and stir until smooth.

Pour the batter into an 8 × 8-inch greased pan or oven-to-table casserole dish. Place in center of the oven and bake for 1 hour.

About 15 minutes before the pudding comes out of the oven, prepare the sauce: In a saucepan, combine the sugar and butter with half the cream and cook over medium heat. Boil until golden brown, about 12 minutes. Cool slightly and whisk in the remaining cream.

When pudding is springy to the touch, remove it from the oven. Pour the warm toffee sauce over it and return it to the oven for an additional 10 minutes. The crust should be slightly browned. Cool slightly; serve warm with whipped cream or Devon cream.

4

BRIT LIT 101

"Good night. Sleep innocently."
—Anthony Blanche to Charles Ryder, *Brideshead Revisited*

Here, the elegant master storytellers are at work. The English tradition of social satire, quirkiness, and narrative invention mixed with scarily brilliant dialogue is a pleasure to read and dramatic to discuss. The world-weary antiheroes of Waugh or Greene constitute the best kind of theater. And our idea of a good time is to have a pitched battle about Ian McEwan's *Atonement*: Dazzling conceit or a work of genius? When we gather, we all become "mordant analysts," just one of the superior social commentaries in Alan Hollinghurst's *The Line of Beauty*.

The authors of Brit Lit continually create new character types in settings of moody enchantment and at times, harrowing immediacy. It's a level playing field for all books once they reach the living room. Helen Fielding cleverly tweaks Jane Austen's *Pride and Prejudice* in her own masterly satire, *Bridget Jones's Diary*. But there is still no denying the force of the original and the idea that a book written in 1813 is more alive today than ever before.

Fielding, like so many others before her and after her, focused on the exquisite romantic missteps between Mr. Darcy and Elizabeth Bennet. But after a session on our couches and comfy chairs, we can discuss the Great One as well as any pretender, imitator and homagist.

And that goes for you too, Flora Poste. You may have channeled Austen's superpower of observation and unleashed it on your vole-worshipping relatives at Cold Comfort Farm, but to us it's business as usual.

Lay in your gin-and-tonic supply, fire up the DVD player for parallel viewing nights and consider these gimlet-eyed assessments of two world wars, Empire and the mopping-up operations after the sun has set. Most of these immortals have received or are about to receive the full movie-star treatment. But no one knows the backstory better than we do.

The Ten Indispensable Titles

■ ■ ■

Atonement
(2001) by Ian McEwan

A ripping psychological drama and a historical romance, *Atonement* boasts two endings and one of the greatest characters in literature, Briony Tallis. Ian McEwan uses the tormented but supremely observant and possibly talented Briony as the instigator of wrenching events that take place before World War II. And then all roads lead to the disaster at Dunkirk.

Discussions of the book center around the shifting role Briony plays in the drama in which she, the precocious little sister, spies on everyone. But when Briony turns her spying arts on older sister Cecilia and her lover Robbie Turner, we see how sexual jealousy becomes a motivating spirit. McEwan's unique brand of psychological suspense where "the truth had become as ghostly as invention" has us gripping the edge of the old diving pool. The author also keeps us busy with bitter irony, symbolism, foreshadowing, weather metaphors and satire. What exactly did cousin Lola do and with whom on that fateful night? Who was eventually punished for which crimes? Does Briony ever forgive herself? Do we forgive her? Ultimately, *Atonement* can be seen as Briony's "gift" to Cecilia and Robbie, but it is a paltry one. Don't miss the scene in the library between the lovers, a fleeting moment of happiness.

Discussion questions, Anchor Books: Superb. The questions concentrate on Briony's actions, her life as a playwright and her role in the family. Class and its importance in *Atonement* are treated significantly, and there is a question citing the epigraph from Jane Austen's *Northanger Abbey* and why McEwan chose it.

Cocktails: Just before the airless dinner, cocktails were served. "Despite the late addition of chopped fresh mint to a blend of melted chocolate, egg yolk, coconut milk, rum, gin, crushed banana and icing sugar, the cocktail was not particularly refreshing." Wonder why. Clubs will want to consider Cecilia's favorite: gin and tonic.

Furthermore: Before *Atonement*, clubs read *Enduring Love* and *Amsterdam* (winner of the Booker Prize). But the publication of McEwan's latest novel, *Saturday*, was considered a true literary event. London neurosurgeon Henry Perowne is faced with a series of unexpected events on a single Saturday in London. The prepared discussion questions are excellent, and readers have had gripping conversations about a post-9/11 world. Those in the know read *Saturday* along with the insider guidebook, *London A–Z*.

Selling *Atonement* to the club: Historic sweep, a true romance, superb writing by a master at the top of his form, those two endings. *Atonement* actually delivers what so many books claim: it's a contemporary novel that stands with giants. And many will disagree.

■ ■ ■

Behind the Scenes at the Museum
(1995) by Kate Atkinson

In one of the only instances of sarcastic magic realism, Kate Atkinson creates a lower-middle-class family saga of dark humor, biting wit and redemption you don't even mind. Our narrator Ruby Lennox never waivers: "It's Christmas Eve when Gillian pays the price of all those golden-blond curls." Ruby's description of family life above the pet shop is poignantly funny and deeply moving.

Not even the Lennox ancestors are safe from Ruby's withering descriptions, and a major theme emerges: why are so many characters living the wrong life? *Behind the Scenes at the Museum* has a wonderful twist at the end and lots of clues along the way. Did you guess? Reading this novel is one of those experiences when you say to yourself, "That's me!" or "That's my family!" Start admitting it and see where the conversation leads.

Discussion questions, Picador: Basic, though there is a fascinating question about the book's reception in England where a critic called it "anti-family." Fun fact: Atkinson cites Jane Austen and Kurt Vonnegut as most influential.

Bake-off: Ruby's mother Bunty, a teeming brew of fastidious frustration, always insisted on homemade birthday cakes, "their defects smothered by buttercream and stuck with candles like martyred hedgehogs." But one year she was traumatized enough to buy a bakery cake that was "exquisite—crisp, swan white icing that's been sculpted into scrolls and waves and plumes of snow." Organize a small bake-off, with one member assigned to buy a snowy bakery cake, another to bake a buttercream cake, martyred hedgehogs optional. After all, isn't it *always* someone's birthday?

■ ■ ■

Birdsong
(1993) by Sebastian Faulks

We all know what happened on the killing fields of World War I. It is a testament to Sebastian Faulks's taut and suspenseful writing that we hope against hope it all turns out differently this time. Englishman Stephen Wraysford is an orphan given Dickensian opportunities. He grows up to be a recognizable twentieth-century type: a brooding, impetuous young man left by the woman he loves and soon embroiled in an endless, horrific war. Bogart would play him. *Birdsong* moves from 1910 France though World War I and intercuts a story set in England in the 1970s.

The author made an interesting choice of alternating the two worlds, and this would be a good place to start the discussion. When we are in the modern-day story, aren't we aching to be back in the trenches with the mud, rats and mates we have come to know? There is much that is shocking in this book, especially the fate of the war's victims, always at the mercy of "alive and dangerous currents."

Discussion questions, Vintage Books: Excellent. The nineteen questions are thorough and touch upon the many characters and the roles they play in this epic. Especially good are the questions about symbolism in the novel and the reactions of soldiers and civilians to the incomprehensible destruction wrought by World War I.

Furthermore: Clubs embraced *Charlotte Gray* in droves, but consider *On Green Dolphin Street*, Faulks's underrated novel from 2001. It takes us to Washington in 1960 when British career diplomat Charlie van der Linden and his wife Mary are posted to Washington. A sizzling love affair ensues between Mary and journalist Frank Renzo as Vietnam is heating up. A highly charged ending will lead to drama for you and the club.

Selling *Birdsong* to the club: Members who automatically reject books with World War I subject matter must reconsider. Emphasize that this is a love story and a psychological thriller. The grim trench warfare scenes might even be described as exciting in the hands of this contemporary master.

■ ■ ■

Brideshead Revisited
(1945) by Evelyn Waugh

A masterpiece of memory and loss that Evelyn Waugh accurately described as his "magnum opus," *Brideshead Revisited* is a merciless depiction of an aristocratic Catholic family between the wars. It's also a story of at least two doomed love affairs. Charles Ryder, now an officer in World War II, is stationed at Brideshead and narrates: "My theme is memory, that winged host that soared about me one grey morning of war-time."

Although we want to start rereading the book as soon as we get to the final chapters, consider the discussion a second chance. The conversation often centers around each Marchmain in crisis and how the family's Catholicism affects the action. Charles and Sebastian, Charles and Julia, Sebastian and Lady Marchmain, Sebastian and Nanny Hawkins—the relationships provide endless themes. Why did Julia marry the energetic know-nothing Rex Mottram? Or was Rex, a man of the new age, one of Waugh's most inspired creations, along with man-about-Oxford Anthony Blanche?

Most readers remember Charles's and Sebastian's deliciously elliptical "languor of Youth" summer at Brideshead—another key discussion point. What may resonate now is the novel's glorious structure, the ever-present theme of death and the wrenching observations of the fabulous Anthony Blanche. Is he to be trusted? It may be hard for contemporary readers to understand the family's separateness from the rest of society, or even the triumph of faith in this multileveled work. Don't miss the often-heated argument about the deathbed scene and "a twitch upon the thread." Ashtrays will fly.

Audio alert: Jeremy Irons, who played Charles Ryder in the miniseries, narrates *Brideshead Revisited* (Caldman). It exists in its own universe, not better than reading the book, just different—and just as good.

***Brideshead Revisited*, the miniseries**: The 1981 Granada miniseries (the twentieth anniversary edition, available on DVD) was a cultural event when it aired and introduced new audiences to Waugh's book. It also made icons of Irons and Anthony Edwards as teddy-bear-clutching Sebastian. Of the latest movie treatments, we do not speak. If you screen the original miniseries during one of your club house parties, ask yourselves if it's a theme park of nostalgia or a classic work in its own right.

Dressing thematically: Current runway stylings that include sweaters, twenties- and thirties-style suits and cashmere coats. But vintage is better and inherited is best.

Drinking thematically: Alexander cocktails at the George Bar with Anthony Blanche, a bottle of 1906 Montrachet and a Clos de Bere, 1904, to get you through a meal with Rex Mottram in Paris.

Furthermore: *Scoop* (1938) was Waugh's incomparable newspaper satire, still avidly read today. William Boot, an innocent country essayist, is tapped by Fleet Street to cover a war in the fictional Ishmaelia. He returns as a star reporter for *The Daily Beast*, touted as "Boot of the Beast," a pawn in the vicious war with its rival, *The Daily Brute*.

Cold Comfort Farm

(1932) by Stella Gibbons

"I think I have much in common with Miss Austen," Flora Poste tells us with her usual modesty, early in the novel. "She liked everything to be tidy and pleasant and comfortable about her, and so do I." The recently orphaned Flora is daunted by absolutely nothing, even the laughable dreariness of Cold Comfort Farm. Settled in with her distant cousins, the Starkadders of Howling, Sussex, she hunkers down with the *Pensees* of Abbe Fausse-Maigre and the latest *Vogue* and sets right to improving the collection of untamed eccentrics.

Flora's arch observations and problem-solving techniques in the face of Great Aunt Ada Doom, the holy-rolling Bretheren and the hunting gentry embodied by the Hawk-Monitors makes her the CEO of Howling. Have a smashing good time chatting about the Starkadders, the bright young things and Flora's obsession with not only Miss Austen, but also all of the Brontës. She talks about these dead authors as if she saw them the day before at the New River Club, a club so haughty no member could be divorced!

Applaud Flora's greatest triumph—protégé Elfine's conquering appearance at the Hawk-Monitors' ball. Is Flora just a fabulist when comparing herself to Austen, or is it a dazzling foreshadowing of the Jane Austen industry to come? Is Flora a great character in her own right? Though *Cold Comfort Farm* is perfect in its way, is there is a kind of desperation on Flora's part to be bright and airy?

Cocktails: After a long evening at the dreaded annual "Counting," Aunt Ada Doom has rejected her usual immense breakfast in her darkened rooms and opted for a hell's angel. Flora mixed "an egg, two ounces of brandy, a teaspoon of cream and some chips of ice in a jam-jar," and it became a "foaming" concoction. Clearly, a hell's angel is shaken, not stirred.

Audio and DVD alert: The incomparable narrator Anna Massey reads *Cold Comfort Farm* (Sterling Audio). Her voicing of Urk, Seth, Amos, Mrs. Beetle and the rest of the Starkadders is a masterpiece of comic inflection. The 1995 movie starring Kate Beckinsale before she strapped on black leather to hunt vampires is perfect for DVD night.

■ ■ ■

The Golden Compass
(1996) by Philip Pullman

The first book in the trilogy *His Dark Materials*, *The Golden Compass* is for every club member who cannot abide Hobbits in the living room. Though he has created a dark fantasy world, Philip Pullman emphasizes the deep emotional life of the characters. The fantasy averse will also be relieved to know that there is another plucky heroine, Lyra Belacqua and her trusty daemon Pantalaimon in whom she confides and seeks comfort. Lyra meets a bedeviling assortment of armed polar bears, evil Gobblers and witches on the road to discovering the truth about her kidnapped friend Roger.

Begin your discussion with the concept of "daemons"—creatures that are a combination pet, familiar and companion. How do they help sort out who is to be trusted and when? What is the glamorous Mrs. Coulter's real story? Can you get a better education at Jordan College or at Hogwarts? What would your daemon—and that of your club—be like? But mostly, what happens next? This is a haunting, complex world but it is an important and rewarding one. The biggest surprise of all is Pullman's staunch antireligion point of view in this book and in the succeeding titles (*The Subtle Knife* and *The Amber Spyglass*).

Discussion questions, Random House Children's Books: Excellent. *His Dark Materials* has been described as John Milton's *Paradise Lost* for teens. In this guide, Pullman talks about *Paradise Lost* and what it means to him and his own tale. The other questions take us through the structure of a world run by the Church, Lyra's character, the relationship of Lord Asriel and Mrs. Coulter and those armored bears. Don't forget to discuss the binary imagery.

Selling *The Golden Compass* to the club: Variety, depth of reading list, your middle schooler read the entire trilogy last year.

The Line of Beauty
(2004) by Alan Hollinghurst

It's the early 1980s and Nick Guest, a budding Henry James scholar, leaves Oxford to become an almost accidental lodger with the wealthy Fedden family. Nick moves into a small room in their aesthetically fabulous Notting Hill house and circulates in their milieu. Gerald Fedden, a Tory MP, is at the epicenter of high Conservative society in the age of Margaret Thatcher ("the Lady"). Nick is gay and from a middle-class family, making him a double outsider—and ideal protagonist—in a story where the references to *Alice in Wonderland* underscore the portrait of this unreal, glittering looking-glass world.

Winner of the Man Booker prize, *The Line of Beauty* balances on the edge of two cultures: the opulent 1980s Thatcherite halls of power and the gay scene in London as the AIDS scourge begins. The beauty and occasional toughness of the language, the gradual unfolding of the relationships within Nick's adopted family and between Nick and his lovers makes *The Line of Beauty* both an elegy for and the crystalization of an era. Does Nick deserve our sympathy? Is he a pawn in a much larger game or does he have a hand in the events that unfold? Can you identify and describe the various meanings of "the line of beauty"? Don't miss the house party in France, the climactic anniversary scene featuring a visit from the PM and the sensational, pitch-perfect ending.

Cocktails: At six. Gin and tonic, champagne or a jug of Pimm's.

The Man Booker Prize: *The Line of Beauty* won this prize in 2004 and it is among the most prestigious in all of books, heralding authors for the ages. Keep your eye on *Never Let Me Go* by Kazuo Ishiguro (he won the prize in 1989 for *The Remains of the Day*), *The Accidental* by Ali Smith and *On Beauty* by Zadie Smith. These authors are Man Booker finalists and winner and have been avidly adapted by clubs. Zadie Smith (*White Teeth*) should get her vestments from the dry cleaner in preparation for her dizzying ascent.

DVD alert: Some of the characters in *The Line of Beauty* go to see *A Room with a View*. Revisit this Merchant Ivory classic and discuss what Hollinghurst meant by including it.

Selling *The Line of Beauty* to the club: The structure of *Brideshead Revisited* meets the 1980s scene of drugs, gay sex and Margaret Thatcher. It's a perfectly executed original.

■ ■ ■

Pride and Prejudice
(1813) by Jane Austen

You think you've read the godmother of all fiction because of the BBC adaptation we all saw and loved. Your club had perfect attendance when you went to see the Keira Knightley version. But be honest: no book club can have a real collective memory without *Pride and Prejudice*. While Austen wrote about a proscribed social world, her work is open and accessible to modern readers because she is unstinting about the truth—and she is bold and satiric. Can anyone resist her happy endings?

Everyone adores the proud, intelligent, psychologically astute but not infallible Elizabeth Bennet. She is one of five daughters—the ones whose eyes are trained on that single man in possession of a good fortune. The hunt is on as the sisters and their suitors choose, reject and pledge their love to each other, while Austen calculates each prospective husband's net worth. Austen forms a complicit bond with the reader, and that is just one of the reasons *Pride and Prejudice* seems so modern. We are part of the action, and more important, the gossip at Longbourn. Best of all, we are first to know about the unfolding love between Elizabeth and Mr. Darcy.

When does Elizabeth realize that she loves Darcy? How does Austen create the perfect romantic suspense? Is Elizabeth too acquisitive when she imagines herself as mistress of Darcy's estate, Pemberley? What are the modern equivalents of the dating rituals in the world of Jane Austen? These are irresistible and inexhaustible subjects. Don't miss the superb verbal catfight between Elizabeth Bennet and Lady Catherine de Bourgh.

Penguin Reading Group Guide: Excellent, a parallel reading experience. The introduction includes a biography of Jane Austen and her world and looks at her popular renaissance. The questions are very good and the topics include Mr. Bennet, the transformations of Elizabeth and Darcy, and the role of the secondary, comic characters—all are ripe for perpetual discussion.

Selling *Pride and Prejudice* to the club: They've faked reading it for so long, why start now? Because, you say, it is the basis for everything, they can now understand all the references to Mr. Darcy and Elizabeth Bennet, and they can even chortle at Mrs. Bennet. Still not buying it? Members may listen to one of several excellent, unabridged audio editions.

■ ■ ■

The Prime of Miss Jean Brodie
(1961) by Muriel Spark

She's mad, bad and dangerous to know. But Miss Jean Brodie is one of the greatest characters in literature and you really should meet her. Muriel Spark—she was Dame Muriel to you—has created a character for clubs to savor and analyze. And like all great books, *The Prime of Miss Jean Brodie* is a unique, fictive summation of time and place.

Miss Jean Brodie teaches at Edinburgh's Marcia Blaine School for Girls. It is the early 1930s, a time of widespread poverty and fascism, which Miss B. applauds. She is in her prime, an unironic phrase she continually impresses on her hand-chosen core of elite girls, the crème de la crème: Sandy, Jenny, Rose, Monica, Eunice—and for scapegoating purposes, the doomed Mary Macgregor. Miss Brodie shares with her set the fruits of her knowledge, which is clearly not part of the curriculum. Instead of arithmetic, she tells her students about her lover who "fell on Flanders Field," her trips to Italy and the columns of Black Shirts that so impress her. She controls, manipulates and rails against the school's "team spirit," and is a figure of intense romance and fascination for the girls of impressionable age. *The Prime of Miss Jean Brodie* has so many famous lines, you could have an entire meeting devoted to them.

Spark's narrative moves forward and back in time, contributing to the book's chilling atmosphere and its theme of betrayal. It's a technique you will want to add to your list of discussion themes.

Discussion questions, Harper Perennial: Very good. Questions center on Miss Jean Brodie's character, and Sandy's pivotal role.

DVD alert: If you ever wondered how Dame Maggie Smith got her Oscars, see this movie.

Master class: *Memento Mori*, *The Girls of Slender Means* and *Loitering with Intent* are among Spark's classic works of wit, elegance and unflinching style. Many critics cite Spark's novels as among the best ever written in English.

■ ■ ■

The Quiet American
(1955) by Graham Greene

British war correspondent Thomas Fowler—that old colonialist—is on the job in early 1950s Vietnam. The French face defeat at the hands of the Vietminh and a new power, the Americans, is sending advisors. Alden Pyle is the quiet American and Fowler's relationship with him, even after Pyle's death, is the political allegory everyone is talking about.

It is a deceptively simple book from the master. Graham Greene presents us with a flawed, morally conflicted Fowler in all of his forthright duplicity. Heated discussions center around Fowler, and minds can change in the course of the evening. "How many dead colonels justify a child's or a trishaw driver's death?" asks the increasingly agitated Fowler, who is faced with the dilemma of choosing sides. Or is this really a dilemma? *The Quiet American* is a historical snapshot, but timeless in the way the characters must deal with moral issues amid the bloodshed that they have a hand in creating.

The role of American force in the world is now Topic A. Greene is not above using symbolism and metaphor for Indochina and the oncoming hell, even more awful than the French colonial war that is raging in the book. Phuong, the beautiful young Vietnamese woman whose beauty has an acknowledged shelf life, is Fowler's mistress and may be betrothed to Pyle. Does she represent Vietnam? Is Pyle the innocent we imagine or something else entirely? Who is lying?

Edition that makes a difference: The Viking Critical Edition of *The Quiet American* includes the text, several critical essays by and about Greene and an invaluable chronology of Indochina history. Discussion questions and themes are helpfully outlined in four sections.

Furthermore: *Brighton Rock, Heart of the Matter, The Power and the Glory, The Third Man, The Ministry of Fear, The End of the Affair, Our Man in Havana.* Make it official: vow to read at least one Graham Greene book a year.

Cocktails: Vigot, the French officer who confirms Fowler's description of the recently deceased Pyle as "a very quiet American," seems as if he stepped right out of *Casablanca*. "He was murdered by the Communists. Perhaps the beginning of the campaign against American aid. But between you and me—listen, it's dry talking, what about a vermouth cassis around the corner?"

"Too early" was Fowler's reply.

Touring Thematically: Channeling Jane Austen

Jane Austen completed only six novels—*Sense and Sensibility*, *Pride and Prejudice*, *Mansfield Park*, *Emma*, *Northanger Abbey*, and *Persuasion*—and each is its own world. Even her uncompleted novel *Sanditon* is contemplated at the highest levels: it is considered her first "modern" work, a social satire about speculation at a fashionable seaside resort—and a precursor to the industrial world ahead.

For the author lived as one world was ending, and a new one of social upheaval was just beginning. But Austen could not know that she had spawned her own industrial revolution in books, movies and televisions, and will, no doubt, be included in technologies even we have yet to hear of. Meanwhile, fans may buy a mind-boggling array of products from a *Pride and Prejudice* board game to a sterling silver Jane Austen cuff bracelet described as "poesy jewelry."

We are currently in the high season of a Jane Austen revival, joyfully abetted by movies and television. Let's review the highlights reel. To date, there has been one superb miniseries (the BBC's *Pride and Prejudice* starring Colin Firth and Jennifer Ehle now available on a "special edition" DVD from A&E) and another wonderful, though less well-known, BBC version of *Emma* starring Kate Beckinsale (*Jane Austen's* Emma available on DVD from A&E). The now-classic Hollywood movie *Clueless* starring Alicia Silverstone is based on *Emma* (its "Whatever" edition is available in DVD), while the Gwyneth-Paltrow-as-Emma vehicle is available on DVD from Miramax.

The latest big-screen version of *Pride and Prejudice* starring the Oscar-nominated Keira Knightley as Elizabeth Bennet was a picturesque crowd-pleaser (MCA Home Video). Of course, we always return to *Sense and Sensibility* (Sony Pictures DVD), the much-honored Ang Lee film from

1995 starring Kate Winslet and Emma Thompson, who won an Oscar for the screenplay. Did the success of this movie launch our current Jane obsession? Please discuss.

There are countless books, in every genre—from mystery to romance to dating guides—that take off mostly from *Pride and Prejudice*.

But there is only one Jane Austen and she lived from 1775–1817. She was born in the small village of Steventon in Hampshire, the seventh of eight children. She never married and her inspiration came from her family and its small circle. Jane was very close to her only sister Cassandra: the author died in Cassandra's arms of what is now believed to be Addison's disease.

Literary tourism is booming and your club may even visit Chawton Cottage in Chawton, Hampshire. The cottage where Jane spent her last years with her mother and Cassandra was on part of an estate her brother Edward inherited. It is now a museum of Jane. The Jane Austen Society of the United Kingdom, which helps with the cottage's preservation, holds its annual meeting here, and if you visit, you might run into Margaret Drabble or P. D. James, who have been guest speakers.

And as any acolyte will tell you, Jane Austen lived in Bath for six years, and the Regency hot spot played a prominent role in *Persuasian*, *Mansfield Park* and *Northanger Abbey*. Austen avidly studied the hyper social scene at this former Roman spa, though according to contemporary reports, when she was told the family was moving to Bath, she fainted. The Bath Assembly Rooms are open for a visit, and clubs may meet in the Pump Room for coffee or tea, summoning the spirit of the author who actually lived in the neighborhood—at 27 Green Park Buildings, and later at the deeply unfashionable Trim Street.

Jane Austen is buried in Winchester Cathedral.

Meeting Thematically: Form a Spin-Off Literary Society

"But I don't want a job."
—*Bertie Wooster to Aunt Dahlia,* Right Ho, Jeeves

What ho! The eternally sunny Edwardian fantasy world of P. G. Wodehouse is taking on new life as the object of adoring societies and online enthusiasts. Best known for creating those tireless vaudevillians, the allknowing Jeeves and the clueless Bertie Wooster, Woodhouse is becoming more beloved all the time. Bertie's celebration of life—and avoidance of any actual work—is positively inspirational. He and his friends Gussie Fink-Nottle, Pongo Twistleton and Catsmeat Potter-Pirbright perfected cheerful idleness between the preluncheon snifter and a hard night at the Drones Club throwing cards into top hats. As for the women, stock characters include the perennially engaged Madeline Bassett and formidable aunts, Agatha and Dahlia.

Ok, you ask, what's in it for us? A great deal, it turns out. We share with such literary societies as the Baker Street Irregulars, the Jane Austen Society and the Trollope Society of America an unstinting admiration for favorite authors and the characters they created. Of course, the societies don't stop at merely discussing their favorites—they often impersonate them at banquets and annual gatherings that are "positively ill with atmosphere," according to Bertie.

Jazz-Age secret language, alternative geography, invented civilizations and a big annual banquet—you can't wait to get started. If you love J. K. Rowling, J.R.R. Tolkien, Terry Pratchett, Douglas Adams, Georgette Heyer, Anthony Powell, Patrick O'Brian, Rudyard Kipling, E. F. Benson, Anthony Trollope, Jane Austen or any Brontë, consider forming a separate society:

- Begin with your home book club and gauge interest in an author you want to spend more time reading and getting to know. The author's work should have deep or merry themes (the feudal spirit!) that lend themselves to special meetings.

- Be prepared to discuss the author's craft and the way he or she achieves magic. The deeper you go, the more that is revealed.

- Consult with a local authority such as a college professor or the retired head of the English department at your local high school. One of these experts could be your first guest speaker.

- Ask yourself: Will the characters' dialogue stand up in a banquet, a toast or a fancy-dress ball? Can it be savored over a luncheon or in a private room at your local library?

- Check out fan websites such as wodehouse.org and The Republic of Pemberley at pemberley.com. Be informed before you make your pitch to your book club or other friends and associates.

- Think about an annual gourmet book club. E. F. Benson's Mapp and Lucia series, for example, features whole menus of precise dishes.

- Report back to your base club and tell them about the balls, banquets and cricket matches you have organized. Don't be surprised if you get new recruits.

When Pets Preen

Is there a book club member who could resist a freshly groomed Bacchus, a newly clipped Terence or a just-coiffed Lambchop? What about the modest Sandy who sees all and says little from his tartan blanket? And we all look forward to catching a glimpse of that impeccable Persian, Zeus, who awaits her attendants on her high-back chair. We thrill to the joint appearance by superbly trained sibling black labs Mike and Pomeroy with double shining coats. Fergie, a small terrier, has superb timing and prances into the meeting at the precise moment for her close-up.

And the most memorable night at any club is when your host introduces the club to her newest puppy, the world's most adorable creature. You are quickly on the phone to Madison Square Garden to alert them.

Your pet's participation in the club is often a high point of the meeting, and you can show off your pet ownership skills as well. A trip to the pet spa might be an indulgence or just the thing when the club comes over. At the very least, dogs should be bathed, nails should be trimmed and coats should be groomed. Lisa Peterson of the American Kennel Club suggests a trip to the groomers a few days before the club meeting. "Dogs tend to shed a lot right after a bath, and you don't want all that fuzz in the book club," she says. "Daily brushing is the best grooming tip."

Make sure the meeting area is vacuumed of all shed hair well before club members show up. That includes the pet's favorite spots on the couch (and yes, under the couch), her favorite armchair and every single place food is served. It really ruins the effect of a wondrous book club when members leave with animal fur clinging to their clothes.

And never dismiss the possibility that pets can participate in dressing thematically. "If the group enjoys a theme night based on the current book they're reading and enjoys pets enough to play with costumes, it may afford a seriously pet-passionate group a fun way to enjoy an evening together," says vet Dr. Merry Crimi.

"The kerchief thing is simple—for instance, if you're reading about the Civil War, blue-and-gray theme is easy. Ribbons and bows are perfect because they're simple and not time consuming."

Before you start dressing your pet as if it stepped out of *Sense and Sensibility*, think about your pet first. "Keep it simple so that it doesn't absorb energy and time that will detract from your experience, and keep the dress up safe," says Dr. Crimi. "Consider that your pet or others might try to chew on or swallow things used for dress up."

PREENING CHECKLIST

- Complete brushing and removal of all dead hair
- A good bath and blow dry
- All nails trimmed and clipped
- A spray bottle filled with water to tame pooch's unmanageable curls
- A kerchief around the pet's neck to reduce shedding of hair and any dirt in the coat
- Mandatory flea and tick control
- Litter boxes at a distance and sparklingly cleaned

The Tween Book Club:
The Witches by Roald Dahl,
Illustrated by Quentin Blake

"We have a great task ahead of us! Thank heavens you are a mouse."
                                                            —*Grandmamma*

Though Roald Dahl tells us in the first line of *The Witches* that this is not a fairy tale, it really is one, don't you think? It is an exciting, devilishly funny modern tale of enchantment, discovery and adventure that may even make you tear up. And since we've all read and gone to see *Charlie and the Chocolate Factory*, *The Witches* is the next, most logical step.

Our intrepid young hero and narrator, orphaned when his parents die in a car accident, is sent to his grandmother in Norway. Grandmamma is kind and a little mischievous, and she soon sets him wise about the way of witches. She is an expert on the subject, after all. Puffing on a cigar, she describes the cold cases of missing children in the world-weary style of any detective who has seen it all. Witches don't wear silly black hats and cloaks or ride in broomsticks, the better to capture unsuspecting children. They look like regular people, and they have management meetings in elegant seaside hotels with strict annual goals as set forth by Her Grandness, the Grand High Witch. The witches' goal this year? To wipe out every child in England by taking over the best sweetshops and spiking the goodies with Formula 86 Delayed-Action Mouse-Maker that turns children into mice.

The battle is on and our young hero foils the witches with great ingenuity and at great personal risk to himself when he is transformed into a mouse by the potion. Luckily, he has a wonderful loving grandmother, who bears quite a resemblance to Winston Churchill in the sublime Quentin Blake illustrations. In fact, the battle doesn't end when the book does—the great task continues in boy mouse versus evil witches. What do you think happens after the book ends?

Sweets are a pivotal plot point here and of course in *Charlie and the Chocolate Factory*. Compare and contrast other Dahl stories as well as modern classics. *The Witches* was first published in 1983. What do you think Lemony Snicket and J. K. Rowling learned from Roald Dahl?

Many books, including this one, would not be as perfect without their heavenly illustrations. How do Quentin Blake's suit Dahl's suspenseful, offbeat fairy tale? After you have talked about it, commemorate the event by making *The Witches* bookmarks and devouring some chocolate mice.

The Tween Book Club Recipe: Chocolate Mice in Honor of *The Witches*

MAKES ABOUT 24 MICE

Preparing these chocolate treats can be a group project, or the adults can make them as a surprise for the younger members.

1 7 ounce package microwave dipping chocolate
1 13 ounce package Hershey's Kisses
1 10 ounce jar maraschino cherries with long stems attached
1 2.25 ounce package slivered almonds
White icing sold in tubes
Red sprinkles
Edible star decorations

Following package directions, melt the dipping chocolate in a microwave-safe bowl in the microwave.

Unwrap as many Hershey's Kisses as there are cherries.

On a large sheet of waxed paper, lay out the cherries and the Hershey's Kisses. For each mouse: Dip a cherry in the melted chocolate and quickly place the flat end of a Hershey's Kiss against the chocolate-covered cherry with the stem (or "tail") of the cherry placed in a horizontal direction. The point of the Hershey's Kiss will form the nose of the mouse.

Place 2 slivered almonds between the Hershey's Kiss and the cherry to form the ears.

Apply 2 dots of white icing on each Hershey's Kiss for the eyes. Use a moistened toothpick to apply a single red sprinkle at the center of each eye.

Using the white icing as glue, apply one star decoration for the nose.

After a few minutes, the chocolate will be set and the mice will be ready. Place the mice on a large serving plate, noses pointing to the center.

The Tween Book Club Craft: Bookmarks in Honor of *The Witches*

You will need:

Edition of *The Witches* with illustrations by Quentin Blake
Computer with scanner
Good-quality printer paper
Craft knife or scissors

A good sample layout would consist of the following elements:

- The title of the book
- An illustration from the book
- The name of the author
- The date your club met to discuss the book
- The name of your club

1. Each club member may pick one favorite illustration from *The Witches*. Have a vote and elect the image for the commemorative bookmark. (Hint: The smaller and more vertical the image the better.) Try, for instance, the illustration of our hero brushing his teeth in an eggcup.

2. Designate a producer who has good computer equipment, including a scanner.

3. Scan the chosen image. If you want to get extra fancy, you can also scan the decorative chapter marker found underneath each chapter title.

4. Size the illustration to fit within the borders of a uniform bookmark size, for example 7 × 1¾ inches. Choose a typeface for the title and author.

5. When you have completed your bookmark layout, copy and paste it to create enough images for everyone in the club, plus a few extras. As you copy and paste the image, make sure to leave enough space in between each bookmark (around ⅛ of an inch) for cutting. Paper should be printed in landscape mode.

6. Print out as many copies of the bookmark as you wish onto the heaviest, glossiest paper your printer can handle. Cut them out carefully.

7. Take your bookmarks to your local print shop and have each laminated.

8. Distribute at your next meeting—a keepsake of your club and memory of your reading.

P. G. Wodehouse 101

All pretty clear, what? P. G. Wodehouse is an acquired taste and may not be embraced by all fellow book club members. As for the characters' "choices," let's just say it's all preordained. But we love these books because they are so predictable, hilarious and timeless.

Aficionados will not touch any post-1940 Wodehouse. And though he wrote over 90 books over a long lifetime, 1920s and 1930s Wodehouse is the place to be. A compendium such as *Life with Jeeves*, which includes *The Inimitable Jeeves*, *Very Good, Jeeves!* and *Right Ho, Jeeves* is a good way to begin. *Blandings Castle*, *Uncle Fred in the Springtime*, *Psmith in the City* and *Leave it to Psmith* are considered the best of the non-Jeeves and Wooster. The maestro, Jonathan Cecil, narrates many audio versions of the Wodehouse canon and they are not to be missed.

Surprise! Though Wodehouse was worshipped by Evelyn Waugh, who called him "my revered master," he became an American citizen and was considered the father of the situation comedy. Wodehouse was a man of show business, having written the lyrics to many Broadway shows (*Anything Goes*, *Oh Kay!*) and even a few Fred Astaire movies in the 1930s. He was also a founding member of the Hollywood Cricket Club.

Rapper's delight: Gussie Fink-Nottle and Madeline Bassett ("The Bassett") exhibit the tender pash and Bertie Wooster prefers one does not "beat around the b." Circumstances become "circs." and a bath is a "splash in the old porcelain." Aunt Agatha or Aunt Dahlia is referred to as "the relative" or "the old flesh and blood."

Grand master P. G. was so ahead of his time, he might be considered old school. By creating his own language—Jazz Age slang interspersed with masterly dialogue ending with cunning but often show-bizzy jokes—the reader can completely lose himself or herself in this hectic social whirl.

Before we drop the subj., it must be said that for a sometimes befuddled layabout, Bertie has an impressive vocab. "I stake everything on propinquity, Jeeves," he tells the most famous gentleman's gentleman of all time.

Cocktails: Bertie and the gang like their martinis, but in *Uncle Fred in the Springtime*, there is a "beverage called May Queen." Its official title is several words long, but is constructed like this: "Its foundation is any good dry champagne, to which is added liqueur brandy, armagnac, kummel, yellow chartreuse, and old stout, to taste."

Jeeves famously concocted mysterious post-hangover drinks for Bertie called pick-me-ups or tissue restorers. But Bertie always appreciated a whiskey and soda served by the Incomparable One. Though he hated to admit it, even B. knew who was really in charge.

Whiskey Sours in Honor of P. G. Wodehouse

MAKES 8 DRINKS

2½ cups fresh orange juice

4 teaspoons granulated sugar

½ cup fresh lemon juice

1 cup bourbon or blended whiskey

Ice cubes

Red maraschino cherries and sliced orange for garnish

Mix together the orange juice, sugar and lemon juice in a pitcher. When ready to serve, add bourbon.

Transfer to Art Deco cocktail shaker, shake vigorously, adding ice to taste. Pour into matching silver cups. Garnish with maraschino cherry and orange slice.

Travel tip: Pour all ingredients except the bourbon into a large thermos. Add bourbon when you get to the club, shake vigorously and serve.

Luncheon at the Club:
Cucumber Tea Sandwiches
with Variations

MAKES 36 SANDWICHES

For guests at Longbourn, Howling or just in case a famous Edinburgh spinster drops by, you will want to serve a version of this classic sandwich. Prepare the listed variations for meetings in the garden or supper at the club.

1 cup Hellmann's mayonnaise

2 tablespoons light sour cream

2 teaspoons whole grain mustard

3 teaspoons fresh lemon juice

2 tablespoon grated lemon zest

Salt and pepper to taste

2 loaves of thinly sliced white, whole wheat or pumpernickel sandwich bread,
    Pepperidge Farm, for example

1–2 cucumbers, peeled and thinly sliced

Sprigs of watercress

Mix together mayonnaise, sour cream, mustard, lemon juice and lemon zest in a medium bowl until well blended. Salt and pepper mixture to taste.

Trim crusts off bread and arrange in pairs. For each sandwich, spread one slice of the bread with lemon mayonnaise. Place several pieces of cucumber on this slice and top with the other slice of bread, pressing sandwich together. Cut in half on the diagonal.

Place sandwiches on a linen-cloth-lined tray. If you are using the variations below, arrange the rows by fillings. Garnish with sprigs of watercress.

Variations: Add thinly sliced ham or turkey to the sandwiches. Replace cucumber with sprigs of watercress or radishes, sliced pears or sliced apples. Vary the breads and consider using a brioche or homemade white bread, adding fruit preserves and chutneys to thinly sliced prosciutto combinations.

Spring Salad Plate

SERVES 12

10–12 hard-boiled eggs, sliced
Red Bliss Potatoes with Dill Dressing (recipe follows)
Roasted Cherry Tomatoes (recipe follows)

Arrange egg slices, potatoes and cherry tomatoes on a serving platter, in roughly three sections.

Red Bliss Potatoes with Dill Dressing:
3 tablespoons Dijon mustard
2 tablespoons apple cider vinegar
⅓ cup and 1 tablespoon of extra virgin olive oil
2 tablespoons finely chopped fresh dill
Salt and pepper to taste
1 pound red bliss potatoes, cooked, cooled and quartered

For the dressing: Combine the mustard, vinegar and whisk until smooth. Slowly add the olive oil to the mixture. Add the dill. Salt and pepper to taste. In a separate bowl, gently toss the potatoes with dressing.

Roasted Cherry Tomatoes:
4 cups small to medium cherry tomatoes, stems removed
3 large cloves garlic, peeled
1½ teaspoons kosher salt
3 tablespoons extra virgin olive oil

Preheat oven to 450 degrees.
Place tomatoes in a single row in an ovenproof pan. Toss with garlic, salt

and oil, coating all of the tomatoes. Roast for 25–30 minutes, checking them from time to time and tossing. The tomatoes are done when they are slightly blackened.

The tomatoes can be made the night before and served cold.

If You Were in a
1940s Book Club

1940

The Crazy Hunter by Kay Boyle

Darkness at Noon by Arthur Koestler

For Whom the Bell Tolls
    by Ernest Hemingway

The Heart Is a Lonely Hunter
    by Carson McCullers

How Green Was My Valley
    by Richard Llewellyn

Kitty Foyle by Christopher Morley

Mrs. Miniver by Jan Struther

Native Son by Richard Wright

Portrait of the Artist as a Young Dog
    by Dylan Thomas

The Power and the Glory
    by Graham Greene

A Stricken Field by Martha Gellhorn

World's End by Upton Sinclair

1941

Berlin Diary by William L. Shirer

The Keys of the Kingdom
    by A. J. Cronin

The Last Tycoon by F. Scott Fitzgerald

Mildred Pierce by James M. Cain

Now, Voyager by Olive Higgins Prouty

What Makes Sammy Run?
    by Budd Schulberg

1942

Cross Creek
    by Marjorie Kinnan Rawlings

Dragon Seed by Pearl S. Buck

Dragon's Teeth by Upton Sinclair

The Last Time I Saw Paris by Elliot Paul

The Robe by Lloyd C. Douglas

The Song of Bernadette
    by Fran Werfel

The Stranger by Albert Camus

They Were Expendable by W. I. White

1943

The Fountainhead by Ayn Rand

Guadalcanal Diary by Richard Tregaskis

The Human Comedy
    by William Saroyan

Ministry of Fear by Graham Greene

One World by Wendell L. Willkie

Our Hearts Were Young and Gay
    by Cornelia Otis Skinner
    and Emily Kimbrough

A Tree Grows in Brooklyn
    by Betty Smith

The Walsh Girls by Elizabeth Janeway

1944

Anna and the King of Siam
    by Margaret Landon

A Bell for Adano by John Hersey

Green Dolphin Street
    by Elizabeth Goudge

The Lost Weekend by Charles Jackson

The Razor's Edge
    by W. Somerset Maugham

Yankee from Olympus
    by Catherine D. Bowen

1945

Animal Farm by George Orwell

Arch of Triumph
    by Erich Maria Remarque

Black Boy by Richard Wright

Brideshead Revisited
    by Evelyn Waugh

Cass Timberlane by Sinclair Lewis

The Crack-Up by F. Scott Fitzgerald

Daisy Kenyon by Elizabeth Janeway

The Egg and I by Betty MacDonald

Gigi by Colette

The Member of the Wedding
    by Carson McCullers

The Thurber Carnival
    by James Thurber

1946

All the King's Men
    by Robert Penn Warren

Delta Wedding by Eudora Welty

The Hucksters by Frederic Wakeman

Lord Weary's Castle by Robert Lowell

The River by Rumer Godden

The Stranger by Albert Camus

Zorba the Greek
    by Nikos Kazantzakis

1947

Doktor Faustus by Thomas Mann

East Side, West Side
    by Marcia Gluck Davenport

Gentleman's Agreement
    by Laura Z. Hobson

Lydia Bailey by Kenneth Roberts

The Pearl by John Steinbeck

Tales of the South Pacific
    by James Michener

Under the Volcano by Malcolm Lowry

1948

The Age of Anxiety by W. H. Auden

Cry, the Beloved Country
    by Alan Paton

Dinner at Antoine's
    by Frances Parkinson Keyes

The Heart of the Matter
    by Graham Greene

The Gathering Storm
    by Winston Churchill

Intruder in the Dust
    by William Faulkner

The Naked and the Dead
    by Norman Mailer

Other Voices, Other Rooms
    by Truman Capote

Pilgrim's Inn by Elizabeth Goudge

The Plague by Albert Camus

Raintree County
    by Ross Lockridge Jr.

Sexual Behavior in the Human Male
    by Alfred C. Kinsey

The Street by Ann Petry

The Young Lions by Irwin Shaw

1949

Cheaper by the Dozen
    by Frank B. Gilbreth Jr.
    and Ernestine Gilbreth Carey

Complete Poems by Robert Frost

The Egyptian by Mika Waltari

Father of the Bride
    by Edward Streeter

The Man with the Golden Arm
    by Nelson Algren

1984 by George Orwell

Point of No Return
    by John P. Marquand

A Rage to Live by John O'Hara

RED, WHITE
AND NOIR

The oleanders are in bloom and the detectives have a lot of questions. While the hunt is on for the perpetrators, our protagonists can hardly shake off their despair. Discordia, the goddess of marital strife in *The Corrections*, has paid her last visit. Anhedonia? That's what *every* morning is like. These are our grimmer fairy tales, made all the more potent by our dissections of life on a mean street or a bucolic, creepy college campus.

Fear is the theme. Claustrophobia is the sensation. Noir is the atmosphere. Some of these thrillers have uplifting moments. Some even have what passes for happy endings. But each is tough-minded, often violent, and provokes the most intense, hair-raising conversations. It's the age of anxiety where murder, suicide, domestic violence and dystopia keep us cowering. These are elegantly suspenseful novels where fear and paranoia are polished to a shiny, malevolent sheen.

Even as the midday sun blazes, the books in this chapter are autumnal and shadowy. The characters have seen more than is good for them, and something terrible is going to happen. Or the terrible thing has happened, and we are about to hear all about it. The authors who work this swanky crime beat create daymares and nightscapes that haunt and inspire—and they win a lot of literary prizes in the process. These books are so stylishly written, they are practically designed for all club members who "don't do bodies."

Mix a batch of stiff martinis, pack them in a thermos and summon the spirits of both Roosevelts and Walter Neff, dim the lights and prepare for a few great urban legends.

The Ten Indispensable Titles

The Alienist
(1994) by Caleb Carr

A Gilded Age *CSI*, with a long cameo by Police Commissioner Theodore Roosevelt, Caleb Carr's historical confection has retained its power and popularity. The cast of characters fascinated by the new scientific age comprise an unorthodox investigative unit who seek a serial killer preying on child prostitutes in the New York of 1896. John Schuyler Moore, a crime reporter for the *New York Times*, tells the story of this group led by Dr. Laszlo Kreizler, a type of psychologist then known as an "alienist." It is the pathological profile developed by the good doctor that leads the crew on the killer's trail.

Carr is especially adept at describing the period details of 1890s New York, from the sordid brothels and lurid crime scenes to the famous restaurant Delmonicos, where the group retires to quaff Madeira and rehash the particulars of the case. They are joined by Sara Howard, a police department secretary who has an important role to play.

Psychology and modern police methods with which we are now overly familiar were in their infancy, and the time period creates its own kind of suspense. How does Carr use the historical setting to advance the plot? How does corruption play its traditional role in this urban story? And how clever was the author to include a delightful, worshipful portrait of Teddy Roosevelt in the years before he became president? The story is told from the perspective of the future in 1919, another shrewd device.

Drinking thematically: Chateau Lagrange, morning coffee spiked with good French cognac after an all-nighter on the case and a foaming dark mug of Wurzburger at Brubacher's.

Selling *The Alienist* to the club: An always-welcome selection, the novel is for all members who like their historical fiction on the seamy side and their police procedurals concisely summarized, with the scientific banter neatly interspersed amid the ghoulish realism.

■ ■ ■

Black and Blue
(1998) by Anna Quindlen

It opens with a simple, declarative sentence: "The first time my husband hit me I was nineteen years old." In *Black and Blue*, Anna Quindlen precisely lays out the brutal trajectory of spousal abuse and its aftermath. Fran Benedetto is the mother of a ten-year-old son, a nurse and the wife of a New York City cop. She has been beaten one too many times. With her life in the balance, she relocates to Florida in a domestic violence version of the federal witness protection program.

Quindlen, who won a Pulitzer Prize for her *New York Times* column, returns to her reporter roots and the result is a compulsively readable, ripped-from-today's-headlines account of Fran's new life as Beth Crenshaw. She creates real characters in a sadly plausible situation where the relationship of victim and victimizer never goes away. *Black and Blue* is a real thriller, with a sense of menace—and hope as Beth settles into her new life while she remembers her old one ("In the battle between turkey and lasagna, turkey doesn't stand a chance"). The author handles the domestic violence theme deftly, and the ending is fearless. Begin your discussion with the final events.

Don't miss: The exchanges between Beth and the elderly Mrs. Levitt, one of her home care patients, who invariably greets her with a "Sit, Mrs. Nurse." The layer of humanity offered by Mrs. Levitt and the other Florida characters make Bobby's past and future actions all the more harrowing and humiliating to Beth/Fran.

Nonfiction alert: *A Private Matter*, Victor Rivas Rivers's memoir of growing up with a terrorizing father, portrays the horror of family violence firsthand. Though Rivers became a professional athlete and escaped, the story retains its grit. Domestic violence in the news has been the basis for many discussions and gives real-life resonance to Quindlen's themes.

Furthermore: Anna Quindlen's other novels (*One True Thing*, *Blessings*) are beloved by book clubs, and the author is also known as an inspirational author (*Being Perfect*, *A Short Guide to a Happy Life*, *How Reading Changed My Life*).

The Corrections
(2001) by Jonathan Franzen

Is this family yours? Did Chip Lambert dispatch one of his nephews to spy on you and your parents, capturing every argument, sigh and pitiless remark? The power of *The Corrections* grows each year and though we don't have the definitive answer to the oft-asked book club question—Is this a great American novel?—we will do our best with the question before us. How do parents of grown children continue to exert an influence over their lives, and how do the children best care for these parents when they grow old? Many household objects serve the theme of anomie: "It's the fate of most Ping-Pong tables in home basements eventually to serve the ends of other, more desperate games."

The Corrections is a sprawling nineteenth-century novel set in an America at the end of the twentieth century. Enid and Al Lambert raised their three children—Gary, Chip and Denise—in a polite America where Al ran the engineering department of the Midland Pacific Railroad. Metaphors abound as each Lambert child lights out for the East as fast at they can for lives of disappointment, dissipation and absurdity. Meanwhile, Enid is a woman of appearances and is worried sick over the kids and her husband, who is sinking into Parkinson's disease—or is it his attitude?—and wants everyone home for one last Christmas. A minor, often hilarious Narnia theme can be detected in this rich novel where corrections are offered as tantalizing, fleeting solutions or observations. Did you find every single reference?

Discussion questions, Picador: Good, but all over the place. There are spoilers in the middle, and each main question has too many subquestions. But they make dramatic points, and don't miss the question about the pivotal liver dinner in the Lambert family's early years.

Cocktails: Gary's Bombay Sapphire martinis, and Enid's cocktails du jour, Lingonberry Lapp Frappe, Spogg and cloudberry aquavit served aboard the Nordic Pleasureliner, the Gunnar Myrdal.

Selling *The Corrections* to the club: Oprah selected it, then ditched it after Jonathan Franzen expressed ambivalence. It became a best seller anyway. Don't be put off by talk of "hype," or "self-involvement" about the author. *The Corrections* stands alone among contemporary novels and we are lucky to have it. A selection of the Colin Firth Book Club (*O* magazine, January 2005).

■ ■ ■

The Handmaid's Tale
(1986) by Margaret Atwood

In the Republic of Gilead, formerly the United States, women are put into categories depending on their function for the state: Marthas, Aunts, Econowives, Unwoman, Wives and Handmaids. In Margaret Atwood's chilling dystopia, the tale we hear from Offred (as in "of Fred") is one of state-sponsored terror, made all the more horrific because our handmaid remembers the not-too-distant past before her world was destroyed by the true believers. Offred is serving a Commander, with the one and only goal of reproducing. And the Wives? "Wives do a lot. It helps their husbands' careers."

1984 anybody? Atwood's "republic" is one of such exacting detail, the official corruption makes utter sense. The Commanders are driven in "long murmurous cars," and Offred is offered forbidden glimpses of magazines "from the time before." Its haunting allusions to today's political and reproductive issues make *The Handmaid's Tale* a valuable go-to discussion book for every kind of club. What really happens to Offred, and what is

Atwood saying about our time? The ending is smashing and Atwood poses the most delectable discussion questions in the epilogue, an academic symposium in the way-future that considers Offred's case amid professorial asides and in-jokes.

Discussion questions, Anchor Books: The basics. Questions concern the novel's epigraphs and Atwood's use of language—from the symbolism of the characters' clothes to her storytelling style. But you really don't need them—you will be quickly on the case Atwood puts before us.

Compare and contrast: *Gilead* is the name of Marilynn Robinson's book where spirituality is a central theme and Gilead is a real town. How is Robinson's Gilead different or similar to the Republic of Gilead?

Fun Fact: *1984* and *The Handmaid's Tale* have both been made into operas.

Selling *The Handmaid's Tale* to the club: A provocative fable presented as an intellectual sci-fi thriller, it is made for discussion.

■ ■ ■

House of Sand and Fog
(1999) by Andre Dubus III

A dark thriller, a study in alienation and a cautionary tale about the American Dream, *House of Sand and Fog* is a runaway train of drama and suspense. In classic noir fashion, northern California does double duty as setting and metaphor for one contested house on Bisgrove Street, two cultures on a collision course and two characters who are the instruments of their fate. Colonel Behrani, a power in the old Iran of the shah, lives an immigrant's life as a garbage collector. His one hope is the investment he is making in the house, owned or formerly owned by Kathy Nicolo. She is an alcohol-dependent young woman just out of rehab, but always on the edge. The aptly named Sheriff Lester Burdon becomes Kathy's lover and pivotal crisis instigator.

Discussions often center on the competing first-person narratives of

Behrani and Kathy, the immediacy of their thoughts and actions and how the author creates the impenetrable atmosphere of doom based on what we know each is thinking. Clubs spend many hours on Kathy's addict personality and her battles with her inner beast. Dubus is equally good setting up the contrasting cultures, one that recalls a luxe Persian past, and the other showing two Americans on the way down, every step of the way.

Discussion questions, Vintage Books: Very good, going straight to the heart of the book's conflict. The taut narrative may cause readers to switch their sympathies several times, and many of the questions reflect this. Especially provocative is the question based on one thing Behrani tells his sons about Americans: "Remember what I've told you of so many Americans: they are not disciplined and have not the courage to take responsibility for their actions."

Selling *House of Sand and Fog* to the club: A central conflict, almost brutally simple—and Dubus is thoroughly successful in updating the classic thriller.

◼ ◼ ◻

The Moviegoer
(1961) by Walker Percy

On the brink of his thirtieth birthday, stock and bond trader Binx Bolling moves through the quiet, New Orleans suburb of Gentilly the week before Mardi Gras, one of life's exiles. Searching, seeking, questioning "not one but two American dreams" while attending movies, addressing God, and riding around in his lucky, malaise-free MG. He dates Sharon Kincaid and muses, "Towards her I keep a Gregory Peckish sort of distance." But he really loves the suicidal Kate, and perpetually ponderers this and everything else about modern life. Binx's interior monologues are wry and thought-provoking, especially as he contemplates the grip of everydayness. He is brought down to earth mercilessly by his Aunt Emily, reader of great books (she discusses Binx at her society meetings).

Winner of the National Book Award in 1962, *The Moviegoer* deserves to be rediscovered by clubs, doubly so as a tribute to New Orleans and the

Gulf Coast. It is an encapsulation of mid-twentieth-century America in which moviegoing is actually named by Binx as "certification." Interspersed with all the existentialism is the radio program *This I Believe*, which Binx listens to before bed. "The search is what anyone would undertake if he were not sunk in the everydayness of his own life," he says. Is this a novel only about searching? Does Binx find what he's looking for? What does Binx really believe?

DVD alert: In the age of Netflix, so many of the movies Binx loves are available to contemporary viewers. *Stage Coach, It Happened One Night, The Oxbow Incident, The Third Man, Red River* and *Panic in the Streets* are now enshrined as classics of the cinema. Discover for yourself why Binx was so profoundly affected by these films and the act of moviegoing. And consider this: if Ingmar Bergman had ever made a movie about New Orleans, would *The Moviegoer* be it?

Selling *The Moviegoer* to the club: Join the Krew of Comus for a profound, yet entertaining conversation about faith, observation and relationships. Although the epigraph is from Kierkegaard, don't let that scare you.

■ ■ ■

The Plot Against America
(2004) by Philip Roth

Hero aviator Charles A. Lindbergh strides into the 1940 Republican Convention in complete flying costume, takes the nomination and defeats Franklin D. Roosevelt for president. A simmering, official anti-Semitism ensues as historical and imagined-historical events are seen through the extremely precocious eyes of a young Philip Roth. Once again, he is a character and the Roth family is very much like his own Jewish, lower-middle-class, Newark, New Jersey family. But in this novel, fear and uncertainty about the future reign. Should the family move to Canada? Who is a true American?

Philip Roth's instant classic is an alternative history, a nostalgic recreation of Roth's actual family and an entirely plausible thriller. The family mingles with little people who become horrifyingly prominent while historical figures have fictional roles to play: gossip columnist Walter Winchell is the unlikely presidential candidate who challenges Lindbergh and exposes the Icelandic Understanding, the Munich-like agreement President Lindbergh signs with Hitler.

Did Roth go far enough in his alternative history, or did he fall short of the full Orwell? How many plots were there against America, and what actually happened to President Lindbergh? Why did the author drop hints about real future events such as the assassination of Robert Kennedy? Big subjects like patriotism and the political climate are sure to be on the agenda.

Sinclair Lewis alert: There is a mini-groundswell of appreciation for Sinclair Lewis, the first American to win the Nobel Prize for Literature. In the wake of *The Plot Against America*'s publication, clubs are rediscovering *It Can't Happen Here*, and then it's onto *Elmer Gantry*, *Arrowsmith*, and *Dodsworth*.

Philip Roth Founder's Day: Roth's books are joining the Melville, Longfellow, Welty and other immortals in Library of America collections. *Goodbye Columbus*, *Letting Go* and *Portnoy's Complaint* are collected in the first two published volumes—there will be eight volumes. Get a jump on the later volumes and select *The Ghost Writer*, *The Human Stain* or any of the maestro's work in a special tribute.

■ ■ ■

Revolutionary Road
(1961) by Richard Yates

Frank and April Wheeler are an attractive couple with the two young children, residing on Revolutionary Road in suburban Connecticut. Frank works in New York at Knox Business Machines, while April raises their family. Both believe they are above the squares living among them. They strive to find happiness and their true selves, but feel defeated and blame it on "the hopeless emptiness of everything in this country." To resolve all difficulties, they make plans to drop everything and move to Paris. But they are lost. " 'I'm afraid it wouldn't help, because you see I don't know who I am, either,' " April tells the lovelorn Shep Campbell after a dismal sexual encounter in the backseat of a car.

Richard Yates gives us a version of the 1950s that may surprise you: it's a period of immense social change under its placid façade. Though Revolutionary Hill Estates is not designed for tragedy, the narrative says otherwise. Yates's story is suspenseful, grimly funny, with dialogue that is at a perfect hard-boiled pitch, and those are just a few reasons why *Revolutionary Road* has a unique reputation as the favorite of many novelists. It was nominated for a National Book Award in 1961.

Revolutionary Road is also known for its shocking ending as well as its theme of American discord. It is a strange brew comprised of the aftereffects of the recently concluded world war, marital despair and the working life of 1950s America with its impossibly long, boozy lunches.

Cocktails: The three-martini ("or was it four?") lunch, and that's just a setup for the rest of the day.

Dressing thematically: Country casual or tweed jacket and washed-out khakis, the uniform that says "veteran" and "intellectual."

Selling *Revolutionary Road* to the club: Make no mistake: *Revolutionary Road* is a disturbing book, but many members relish this kind of thing. The novel provides the cathartic experience that only great literature can provide, and besides, how many uplifting novels with happy endings can you read?

■ ■ ■

The Secret History
(1992) by Donna Tartt

An elite group of classics students at Vermont's Hampden College takes its toga parties a bit too seriously, resulting in what is called "the first murder." But the real suspense in *The Secret History* comes from our participation in the discovery and investigations of the murders and our delight in following the sinister clues sprinkled along a swanky, but infinitely sinister, path.

How does each of the characters—Henry, Bunny, Camilla, Charles, Francis and our narrator, Richard—gradually come into focus? What is their respective relationship with the alarmingly charming and godlike professor, Julian, who offers the ominous toast, "Live forever"? Who is playing whom? Among Tartt's greatest creations is the doomed Bunny who alternates between amiable wannabe ("So what's the story, deerslayers?") and obnoxious, maniacal blackmailer. While *The Secret History* is a psychological thriller, it is also an unsettling depiction of class in America where characters would rather die than get a job—quite literally.

The Secret History juxtaposes the banality, hurt feelings and hangovers of college life (Hamden College is said to be a thinly veiled version of Bennington, Donna Tartt's alma mater) with the outré actions of the protagonists. And they are one depressed group of hothouse flowers. Literary allusions abound, and Tartt weaves them into the plot deftly.

Discussion questions, Vintage Books: Excellent, a parallel reading experience. Many questions helpfully reference the ancient rituals, while others ask about Bunny's behavior and how the story develops around it. One question describes the ownership of *The Secret History*'s film rights. Don't you wish all the publishers would keep us similarly informed?

Cocktails: Open bar. Six vodka tonics per person, Bloody Marys from dawn to dusk, martinis from thermos bottles, and a fifth of Famous Grouse.

■ ■ ■

White Oleander
(1999) by Janet Fitch

Fitting niftily into the great tradition of Los Angeles crime fiction, Janet Fitch combines the coming-of-age story with a classic portrait of the city of dissonance. Astrid Magnussen tells two tales: one about mothers and daughters and the other one about the foster care system that turns her high school years into a perfectly conceived trip through every circle of hell ("Stick around, muchacha," Astrid is warned). As the only child of beautiful poetess and single mother Ingrid Magnussen, Astrid is trained to love beauty. She is also taught that men are for manipulating and that mother and daughter are Vikings. When Ingrid murders a lover who scorned her and is sent to prison, Astrid is forced into survival mode.

For Ingrid is a monster who smells like violets, and you will dine on her letters and choice pieces of advice all night long. ("Never lie down for the father," Ingrid writes Astrid from prison. "I forbid it, do you understand?") Each foster care nightmare is believable even when Astrid is shot, but that's only the beginning. The large cast of secondary characters such as the evil Marvel Turlock or her luminous neighbor Olivia Johnstone, "poor Claire," street-smart Russian immigrant Rena and Ingrid's rich, feminist lawyer Susan D. Valeris contribute to the often droll reality.

Discuss how the author cleaves to her themes, creating suspense around the idea that Astrid may not get out of this alive, and how she punctuates these themes with a catalogue of seasonal blooms and deadly symbolism.

Discussion guide, Back Bay Books: The interview with Janet Fitch is excellent as she traces the origin of the book from the original conception of the Ingrid character. The discussion questions are good, especially those concerning Astrid's role as "snake in the garden" and, alternatively, as caregiver.

Dressing thematically: A white kimono and nothing else, worn Ingrid style; Jackie O sunglasses, white jeans and loafers a la Olivia; vintage Jessica McClintock or anything *Melrose Place* in honor of Rena's sarcasm.

Don't miss: The paragraph that thrusts the March sisters into Astrid's world. This is what reading is all about.

No Leader, No Problem: Customizing Discussion Questions

There is no such thing as "official" discussion questions. The publishers provide the discussion guides online or in the books themselves to help you and give you ideas, not because they decree that these are the perfect topics. Groups love to criticize them as too high school essayish, too simplistic, too intellectual—but then complain when there are no guides for nonfiction, or for just-released hardcovers. We're so demanding!

Still, the more you adapt the publishers' questions to your own club, or find other sources that work for you, the more satisfying your club. Sometimes a character in a historical plot acts in an anachronistic way, but this would not necessarily be explored in the guides. But you can and should cite examples. And if the opposite is true—the author created a historical period convincingly—give credit and explore how he or she succeeded.

And save introductions for last. They function as a wonderful overview of the book you have just read—and a smashing source of discussion ideas.

Use the discussion questions as jumping-off points, but develop your own ideas about how the discussion might go. What would you most like to explore and don't have a ready answer for? Consider these points:

- Do the questions approach the writing style, the point of view of the narrator, the way the characters grow, the language the author uses and why? If not, adapt.

- Are several discussion questions bunched together in one question? If so, break them up, simplify and choose only the ones relevant to your group.

- Are the questions getting at some of the less attractive—and hottest—elements of the book?

- Are the discussion questions dull, inscrutably worded and leading nowhere? If so, look for a helpful phrase or just move on.

- What are your own thoughts about the characters? Keep character trait lists so you can share your impressions with the group.

- If an author is writing about a historic period and tends to the anachronistic, do the questions draw attention to this narrative pitfall?

Focus on a couple of aspects of the book that are meaningful to you, and most of all, listen to your fellow members. After all, their opinions count the most.

When Pets Misbehave: The Fearful Guest

Not every club member or guest is as enamored of your snuggly mastiff as you and the rest of the club are. In many cases, too much time goes by before a host makes a decision in the pet-versus-the-fearful-guest scenario, while the rest of the club munches on carrots and bonbons.

Some guests may be completely straightforward about their dislike: "You have animals," they will sniff as they step into the house. Others, who are allergic or genuinely frightened, can't help but express this. Too often these fears are shrugged off as the guest's problem, or not a problem, and the entire club thus makes the fearful guest feel even worse—bullying by ignoring.

"Any person that has clear discomfort around a specific animal should not have to defend their personal fears or health issues," says veterinarian Dr. Merry Crimi.

THE FEARFUL GUEST CHECKLIST

- It cannot be overstated: open the issue of pets before the club begins, especially if there is a new member or a guest, or you are hosting for the first time.

- If new members or guests are expected, keep the animal crated or in another room.

- At the first expression of a guest's fear, put the pet out of the room and leave them enclosed for the rest of the club meeting. Don't let them back in for a good-bye, dessert or nightcap. The guest or member will relax only when they know their evening will not be disturbed.

- Take responsibility for the comfort of the group by being sensitive to each member's pet-related concerns.

- Do not begin animal training at the book club. Practice is fine, but the course should not start the minute the members arrive.

Touring Thematically:
Authors at the Lectern

The venue invariably drips with marble, ornate cornices, Gilded Age private libraries or soaring, dramatic space with floor-to-ceiling windows overlooking the best cityscapes. Best of all, one of your favorite authors will be speaking and you will be turning up with most of your club. Other clubs will also attend, so it's a great opportunity to see and be seen and find out what everyone else is reading.

Audrey Niffenegger appeared at the Harold Washington Library in Chicago; Marilyn Robinson, Russell Banks, Yann Martel, Jonathan Franzen, Karen Joy Fowler, Jane Hamilton and Chang-rae Lee spoke at the Folger Shakespeare Library in Washington, D.C. David McCullough lectured at the Antiquarian Society in Worcester, Massachusetts; Stewart O'Nan, Esmeralda Santiago, Colson Whitehead and Nathaniel Philbrick read at the Boston Atheneum. John Updike, Toni Morrison, T. C. Boyle and Tracy Chevalier spoke at Thurber House in Columbus, Ohio. Were you there?

Keep your eye on schedules at your local library, historical library and other institutions. These evenings can be planned in advance—a call to the institution as early as possible will give you an indication of how tickets are selling so you can make a decision about buying tickets for the group, or making an impromptu appearance at the last minute. Sometimes the speaker isn't scheduled until later anyway and impromptu often works best for those with busy schedules. Here are a few other tips:

■ Ask about discounted tickets—venues usually offer them for parties of 10 or more.

- Always check the institution's website before you go. Area restaurants are often listed, and they may have a special price for lecture attendees. At the very least, you can discuss the author's wardrobe and most inspirational part of the talk over coffee.

- Consider joining a regular book club at the library. The Boston Atheneum, for instance, hosts clubs for members on Proust, Trollope, Shakespeare, the Civil War, mysteries, poetry and the book club classic.

- Don't forget to bring questions and your camera: photos may be permitted and you will definitely want that snapshot of you, your club and Ian McEwan or Tracy Chevalier on your wall. Make extra copies for your club scrapbook and portfolio

The Indispensable
Short Story Collection

Andrea Barrett, *Ship Fever: Stories*

Ann Beattie, *Follies: New Stories, Secrets and Surprises: Short Stories*

William Boyd, *Fascination: Stories*

T. C. Boyle, *Tooth and Claw: And Other Stories, Descent of Man*

A. S. Byatt, *The Little Black Book of Stories*

Ethan Canin, *Palace Thief: Stories, Emperor of the Air: Stories, For Kings and Planets*

Truman Capote, *Complete Stories of Truman Capote*

John Cheever, *The Stories of John Cheever*

Anton Pavlovich Chekhov, *Stories* (translated by Richard Pevear and Larissa Volokhonsky)

Colette, *The Collected Stories of Colette*

Joseph Conrad, *The Secret Sharer and Other Stories*

J. California Cooper, *The Future Has a Past: Stories*

Roald Dahl, *The Best of Roald Dahl*

Anthony Doerr, *The Shell Collector: Stories*

William Faulkner, *Collected Stories of William Faulkner, Go Down, Moses and Other Stories*

F. Scott Fitzgerald, *Babylon Revisited and Other Stories, The Short Stories of F. Scott Fitzgerald: A New Collection*

Nikolai Gogol, *The Collected Tales of Nikolai Gogol* (translated by Richard Pevear and Larissa Volokhonsky)

Graham Greene, *Complete Short Stories*

Allan Gurganus, *White People*

Nathaniel Hawthorne, *Selected Short Stories, Twice Told Tales*

Ernest Hemingway, *The Complete Short Stories of Ernest Hemingway*

Zora Neale Hurston, *The Complete Stories*

Shirley Jackson, *The Lottery and Other Stories*

Henry James, *Selected Tales*

Edward P. Jones, *Lost in the City: Stories*

James Joyce, *Dubliners*

Stephen King, *Everything's Eventual: 14 Dark Tales*

Rudyard Kipling, *Collected Stories*

Jhumpa Lahiri, *Interpreter of Maladies*

Katherine Mansfield, *The Garden Party and Other Stories*

Bobbie Ann Mason, *Midnight Magic: Selected Stories of Bobbie Ann Mason*

W. Somerset Maugham, *Collected Short Stories Volume 1 and Volume 2*

James Alan McPherson, *Elbow Room: Stories*

Lorrie Moore, *Birds of America, Who Will Run the Frog Hospital?*

Alice Munro, *Runaway: Stories; Hateship, Friendship, Courtship, Loveship, Marriage; The Love of a Good Woman; Selected Stories; Lives of Girls and Women; Open Secrets; The Progress of Love; The Beggar Maid; Something I've Been Meaning to Tell You: 13 Stories*

Flannery O'Connor, *The Complete Stories*

ZZ Packer, *Drinking Coffee Elsewhere*

Edgar Allan Poe, *The Complete Tales and Poems of Edgar Allan Poe*

Katherine Anne Porter, *The Collected Stories of Katherine Anne Porter*

V. S. Pritchett, *Essential Stories*

Annie Proulx, *Close Range: Wyoming Stories*

Saki, *The Complete Saki*

J. D. Salinger, *Nine Stories*

James Salter, *Last Night, Dusk and Other Stories*

David Sedaris, *Holidays on Ice: Stories*

Isaac Bashevis Singer, *The Collected Stories of Isaac Bashevis Singer*

Ali Smith, *The Whole Story and Other Stories*

Edith Templeton, *The Darts of Cupid and Other Stories*

Janvier Tisi, *The Usurper and Other Stories*

John Updike, *The Early Stories 1953–1975*

David Foster Wallace, *Girl with Curious Hair*
Eudora Welty, *The Collected Stories of Eudora Welty*
John Edgar Wideman, *God's Gym: Stories*
Connie Willis, *Fire Watch*
P. G. Wodehouse, *Enter Jeeves: 15 Early Stories*

Peyton Place by Grace Metalious: An Appreciation

Grace Metalious's fabulously lurid mega–best seller was published in 1956, but to this day "Peyton Place" is conversational shorthand for illicit behaviors and the dark forces of gossip they unleash. The novel's reputation is based on its nonstop sordid action and pulp-fiction scandals including rape, illegal abortion, suicide, patricide, a carnival tragedy and an encyclopedia of noirish characters, New England division. *Peyton Place* has an undeniable narrative drive, and contemporary readers will not be disappointed in the novel's delicious melodrama. In fact, many of today's best-selling authors could learn a thing or two from the muscular dialogue and quick pacing. When reading and dishing *Peyton Place*, your club can go right to the original source—dressed in 1950s-era party dresses from the Thrifty Corner, of course.

Budding girl reporter for the *Peyton Place Times*, Allison MacKenzie tells us her innermost thoughts about boys, s-e-x and all the town's dirty, hidden secrets. Chief among them is the story of Selena Cross and her twin crises of how to pay for the white dress she will wear to the spring dance and how to beat her murder rap. Allison's single mom Constance MacKenzie owns the Thrifty Corner. When hunky new high school principal Tomas Makris arrives in town, the thirtyish couple soon show the teens what real heat is all about.

In a *Washington Post* essay, the writer Nora Sayre chose *Peyton Place* as a seminal book of the twentieth century. She describes its publication as a truly fascinating moment in popular fiction because women got to have fun having sex.

But the enduring legacy of *Peyton Place* maybe the way the author uses the carefully calibrated layers of gossip to convey what it's like to live in this small town. You are who you comment upon. "The difference between a closet skeleton and a scandal in a small town," writes Metalious, "is that the former is examined behind barns by small groups who converse over it in whispers, while the latter is looked upon by everyone, on the main street, and discussed in shouts from the rooftops."

Before Allison successfully escapes to New York, she has lots of time to daydream about her future. "Someday," says Allison, "I'll write a very famous book. As famous as *Anthony Adverse*, and then I'll be a celebrity." While the world has forgotten the 1930s bestseller *Anthony Adverse*, Allison MacKenzie—and Grace Metalious—really got it right about the enduring nature of gossip and the approaching avalanche of celebrity culture.

You will not be able to resist citing your favorite lines of *Peyton Place* or one of the many sensational passages. Consider the famous description of Constance MacKenzie's figure, Tom's concept of a "date," and any scene between Selena and her wicked stepfather Lucas Cross.

Discuss the themes of gossip, the genre of "1950s best seller" and how things have changed—and how they have not. Toast the whole *Peyton Place* scene with the book's ultrafamous first line: "Indian Summer is like a woman."

GRACE METALIOUS

The life of author Grace Metalious was as sad as any of her story lines in *Peyton Place*. A native of small town Gilmanton, New Hampshire, the author based much of the book on the people and events she knew all too well. Metalious could never replicate the success of *Peyton Place*, even with the 1959 sequel *Return to Peyton Place*. She wrote very little else and died in 1964 of cirrhosis. She was 39.

FOR YOUR CONSIDERATION:
CHARLIZE THERON, CLIVE OWEN AND LINDSAY LOHAN

Who doesn't enjoy arguing the finer points of an actor's emoting capabilities, especially if he or she would be just right for the characters you have just read and discussed? *Peyton Place* was a 1957 movie starring Lana Turner as Constance MacKenzie, and the *Peyton Place* television show launched the careers of young Mia Farrow and Ryan O'Neal. Many television soap operas later, it is time for a classy, yet ever-pulpy remake.

Consider cool, no-nonsense Oscar-winning Charlize Theron (*North*

Country, Monster, The Cider House Rules) as Constance MacKenzie. She will be in demand, of course, but we've read the original text! Her co-star at the Place? It could only be the feral actor Clive Owen (*Inside Man, Closer, King Arthur*), who would brings simmering looks and faux-American accent to the role of high school principal and heartthrob Tom Makris. And Lindsay Lohan needs to add a few dramatic roles to her repertoire of cool teens. Our new Allison MacKenzie would look equally convincing on a date with Rodney Harrington at Hyde's Diner or sweating out her *Peyton Place Times* deadlines on her trusty manual typewriter.

The Indispensable Platter:
Vegetables All Year Long

Crisp and varied vegetables crudite are a book club staple, especially when you are on automatic pilot. Consider going to the next level—blanching the tougher vegetables such as the asparagus stalks, green beans and broccoli. It doesn't take long, and variety is always valued. The easiest method is to steam the vegetables in a basket, placing the vegetables in a single layer in an inch or two of water. Blanching times vary from vegetable to vegetable, but it takes about three minutes for green beans and small broccoli, cauliflower and medium asparagus stalks.

And treat your club to different condiments such as new chutneys, raita or vinaigrette in small bowls. Here are a few other ideas:

- Three kinds of cherry tomatoes in rustic basket
- Zucchini squash blossoms
- Green beans, boiled red potatoes, radishes, baby carrots
- A platter or basket of celery, three colors of peppers, asparagus stalks, cauliflower, mushrooms, green beans, broccoli
- Endive, celery, cucumbers, snow peas, zucchini

The Indispensable Dip:
Nancy Roberts's
Two Cheeses Dip

SERVES 8–10

8 ounces Parmesan cheese, cut into 1-inch cubes

8 ounces Asiago cheese, cut into 1-inch cubes

1½ cups extra virgin olive oil

1 tablespoon pressed garlic

1 tablespoon cracked black pepper

2 tablespoons chopped green onion

2 tablespoons chopped fresh basil

1 teaspoon red pepper flakes

Mix all the ingredients in a food processor or blender for about 15 seconds, or until the cheese resembles small pebbles.

Refrigerate in a sealed container. You can make this well in advance and store in the refrigerator for up to 1 week.

Garnish with fresh basil and serve at room temperature with sliced baguette, pita points, crackers, and carrots, red peppers and celery. The recipe can be cut in half.

The Indispensable Dip: Tsatziki (Yogurt and Cucumber Dip)

MAKES 2 CUPS

1 large container of Total Greek yogurt (17.06 ounces)
1 medium seedless cucumber, peeled and chopped into medium-sized pieces
   and drained
3 medium garlic cloves, minced or pressed
2 tablespoons finely chopped fresh dill,
2 tablespoons extra virgin olive oil
Salt and pepper to taste
Kalamata olives to garnish

Drain the yogurt overnight—or for at least 3 hours—in a fine sieve over a bowl in the refrigerator.

In a medium bowl, mix together the drained yogurt, the cucumber pieces, minced or pressed garlic cloves, dill and olive oil. Mix thoroughly. Salt and pepper to taste and refrigerate. Garnish with Kalamata olives and serve with toasted pita wedges or vegetables.

BOWLS

For an easy way to entertain thematically, fill big or small bowls with one of these significant foods. It's easy, visual and to the point:

Apricots
Blood oranges
Cherries
Crab apples
Cranberries
Lady apples

M&Ms
Pistachio nuts
Pomegrenates
Red and black currants
Red plums
Sweet potato chips

If You Were in a 1950s Book Club

1950

The Disenchanted
    by Budd Schulberg
I, Robot by Isaac Asimov
Kon-Tiki by Thor Heyerdahl
The Roman Spring of Mrs. Stone
    by Tennessee Williams
The Third Man by Graham Greene
A Town Like Alice by Neville Shute
The Wall by John Hersey

1951

The Ballad of the Sad Café
    by Carson McCullers
The Caine Mutiny
    by Herman Wouk
The Catcher in the Rye
    by J. D. Salinger
The Daughter of Time
    by Josephine Tey
The Day of the Triffids
    by John Wyndham
The End of the Affair
    by Graham Greene
From Here to Eternity
    by James Jones
Return to Paradise
    by James A. Michener
The Sea Around Us
    by Rachel L. Carson
Siddhartha by Herman Hesse

1952

East of Eden by John Steinbeck
Giant by Edna Ferber
Invisible Man by Ralph Ellison
My Cousin Rachel
    by Daphne du Maurier
The Old Man and the Sea
    by Ernest Hemingway
The Silver Chalice
    by Thomas B. Costain
Tallulah by Tallulah Bankhead
Wise Blood by Flannery O'Connor
Witness by Whitaker Chambers

1953

The Adventures of Augie March
    by Saul Bellow
Annapurna by Maurice Herzog
Beyond This Place
    by A. J. Cronin
Collected Poems
    by Dylan Thomas
Fahrenheit 451 by Ray Bradbury
The Go-Between by L. P. Hartley
Go Tell It on the Mountain
    by James Baldwin
Nine Stories by J. D. Salinger
Sexual Behavior in the Human Female
    by Alfred C. Kinsey
A Stillness at Appomattox
    by Bruce Catton

1954

Collected Poems by Wallace Stevens
Lord of the Flies by William Golding
Love Is Eternal by Irving Stone
Lucky Jim by Kingsley Amis
Nectar in a Sieve
    by Kamala Markandaya
No Time for Sergeants by Mac Hyman
The Ponder Heart by Eudora Welty
The Searchers by Alan Le May
Shane by Jack Schaefer
Under the Net by Iris Murdoch

1955

Andersonville by MacKinlay Kantor
Auntie Mame by Patrick Dennis
Bonjour Tristess by Francoise Sagan
A Gift from the Sea
    by Anne Morrow Lindbergh
The Ginger Man
    by James Patrick Donleavy
The Lonely Passion of Judith Hearne
    by Brian Moore
The Man in the Gray Flannel Suit
    by Sloan Wilson
Marjorie Morningstar
    by Herman Wouk
The Quiet American
    by Graham Greene
Ten North Frederick by John O'Hara

1956

The Chronicles of Narnia by C. S. Lewis
The Fountain Overflows
    by Rebecca West
Giovanni's Room by James Baldwin
The Last of the Wine by Mary Renault

The Mandarins by Simone de Beauvoir
Peyton Place by Grace Metalious
The Search for Bridey Murphy
    by Morey Bernstein
The Talented Mr. Ripley
    by Patricia Highsmith

1957

The Assistant by Bernard Malamud
Atlas Shrugged by Ayn Rand
Compulsion by Meyer Levin
A Death in the Family by James Agee
From Russia With Love by Ian Fleming
Memories of a Catholic Girlhood
    by Mary McCarthy
On the Beach by Nevil Shute
On the Road by Jack Kerouac
Please Don't Eat the Daisies
    by Jean Kerr
The Scapegoat by Daphne du Maurier
The Wapshot Chronicles
    by John Cheever

1958

Aku-Aku by Thor Heyerdahl
The Best of Everything by Rona Jaffe
Breakfast at Tiffany's
    by Truman Capote
Doctor Zhivago by Boris Pasternak
Lolita by Vladimir Nabokov
The Magic Barrel by Bernard Malamud
The Once and Future King
    by T. H. White

1959

Act One by Moss Hart
Advise and Consent by Allen Drury

Exodus by Leon Uris
The Flame Trees of Thika
    by Elspeth Huxley
Goldfinger by Ian Fleming
Goodbye, Columbus by Philip Roth
Hawaii by James Michener
Henderson the Rain King
    by Saul Bellow
Invitation to a Beheading
    by Vladimir Nabokov
Lady Chatterley's Lover
    by D. H. Lawrence
The Manchurian Candidate
    by Richard Condon

Mrs. Arris Goes to Paris
    by Paul Gallico
Mrs. Bridge by Evan Connell
The Rise and Fall of the Third Reich
    by William L. Shirer
A Separate Peace
    by John Knowles
The Status Seekers
    by Vance Packard
The Tin Drum by Gunther Grass
The Ugly American
    by William J. Lederer
    and Eugene L. Burdick

LITERARY
RESPITES

*"In idle moments, when there were no pressing matters
to be dealt with, and when everybody seemed to be
sleepy from the heat, she would sit under her acacia tree."*
—The No. 1 Ladies Detective Agency

The gang's all here at Literary Respites. Old friends, neighbors, colleagues—everyone is dropping by to visit and, let's face it, complain and sometimes dodge the law. But it's mostly convivial, even when the setting is a gleaming spaceship of cheery nihilism. During cherry blossom time or deepest fall, from Alabama to Botswana to outer space, the books of Literary Respites are filled to the brim with folks settling in to talk about the day's events, large and small.

The books of Literary Respites share themes of fellowship, adventure and in many cases, goodness. A sense of place is ever present and sharing food is often a communal experience. You wish you could visit the Whistle Stop Café or drop in for a magical *atole* at Tita's ranch. A welcoming cup of bush tea, peanuts dropped in a bottle of Dr Pepper or the intergalactic gargle blaster will get you through any fraught situation.

Many of these books are the first in series, addicting as they are short. Agatha Christie is the literary idol of Literary Respites, though traditional genres are often stood on their heads. The detective story is updated, tweaked and displaced, but cozy fires are going somewhere nearby, sherry is consistently poured and tea is available iced or hot.

Lovers of book design need look no further. The books of Literary Respites have dreamy covers, illustrations, maps and inspirational design. And when we are finished admiring the intricate shells and fanciful type, we wonder when can we drop by.

The Ten Indispensable Titles

■■■

At Home in Mitford
(1994) by Jan Karon

Jan Karon's first book in her wildly popular Mitford series offers the unalloyed pleasure of the prototype. Here, we first meet Episcopal rector Father Tim who ministers to his sometimes unruly flock with gentle, self-deprecating humor, honesty and some scripture thrown in for good measure. Many problems are solved over a steaming cup of coffee at the Main Street Grill, at the rectory or via Father Tim's homemade meatloaf strategies.

Karon's theme? Mitford, North Carolina, may be a small town, but the interpersonal issues are the same everywhere—minus the author's gentle plot twists, which keep things interesting. Father Tim is challenged by his sudden role as guardian of adolescent Dooley Barlowe, the dognapping of his large pooch Barnabas, his own diabetes and the illnesses of his parishioners. He is also wryly burdened with the particulars of everyone's romances, not to mention the appearance of attractive new neighbor Cynthia Coppersmith. And Father T. has a rival: suave, cashmere-wearing Andrew Gregory. Will Father Tim take the plunge? Or will he ever really take a break and buy that small thatch cottage in Ireland?

At Home in Mitford is also a cozy mystery. It's so mild you might miss it, but charming enough to savor with a cup of Darjeeling or a nip or two of sherry. Discussions will center around how Mitford and its inhabitants are like or unlike your town (or club!). And it will be hard not to touch upon that other famous town in North Carolina—Mayberry.

Penguin Reading Group Guides: An excellent guide to the series, it includes an introduction, an interview with Jan Karon in which she discusses the writing process and her relationship with her most famous character,

Father Tim, and the idea of daily faith in everyday life. The seven discussion questions are a good place to start.

Dessert Bar: Fresh lemon pie from the Local, gingerbread, deep-dish apple pie, Winnie Ivey's doughnuts, cream horns, coconut cake, fudge pie, the famous orange marmalade cake—there are no end to the wonderful desserts served piping hot or iced cold in Mitford. For recipes see Jan Karon's *Mitford Cookbook and Kitchen Reader*.

Furthermore: Karon recently concluded the Mitford series with her last book, *Light From Heaven*.

■ ■ ■

Durable Goods
(1993) by Elizabeth Berg

Deceptively simple but filled with honesty and humor, *Durable Goods* was Elizabeth Berg's first novel. It's a tone poem about adolescence. Katie Nash is a precocious twelve-year-old growing up on an Army base in Texas. Her mother has died, her father can be violent and her older sister Diane has one foot out the door. Katie copes by keeping a poetry notebook, checking for breasts and spending time with her best friend, a wonderful character in her own right, fourteen-year-old fashion plate and know-it-all Cherylanne. Her advice? Shave your legs "before the event," take Midol, and the more makeup the better. Katie calls her Makeup Queen of the Universe.

Does any writer describe the days of late-childhood summers past better than Berg? You can hear the crickets, smell the chlorine and feel the heat. That Katie Nash is a born observer helps the reader understand her pain and her happiness, as well as her growing interest in boys. How does Berg achieve that delicate balance between the fun and yearning of adolescence and the very real pain of living with loss?

Discussion questions, Ballantine Reader's Circle: Excellent, a parallel reading experience. The questions reflect the depth of *Durable Goods* and how a coming-of-age story with a small number of characters can lead to a far-reaching discussion. Who is the novel's narrator? The novel's themes of coping with grief, the meaning of the title and the ways in which the author creates immediacy are among the topics.

Dressing thematically: Evening in Paris perfume, a Grecian ponytail hairdo, bangle bracelets and Love that Mango lipstick in honor of Cherylanne.

Entertaining thematically: Cherylanne's mom, Belle, treats the girls to whole cases of Coca-Cola, bowls of potato chips and pretzels, and California French onion dip (see "Pan-Fried Onion Dip," page 240), just like another evening at the book club.

Furthermore: *Durable Goods* is the first in the Katie Nash series, which includes *Joy School* and *True to Form*. But clubs love this prolific author and have made hits out of *Talk Before Sleep* and *Pull of the Moon*, among many others.

■ ■ ■

The Eyre Affair
(2002) by Jasper Fforde

The first in the series of Thursday Next adventures, *The Eyre Affair* is a spirited mixture of droll detective story, romance and literary time travel—into the pages of *Jane Eyre*. The novel introduces us to Special Ops literary detective par excellence Officer Next. If you are confused for a single second, not to worry. Each chapter begins with a summary, sometimes written by Millon de Floss, Thursday Next's official biographer.

In Great Britain of the 1980s, things are a bit totalitarian and the Crimean War has been ranging for well over a century. But in a neat twist, literature is the pop culture of this world. Characters escape into Wordsworth poems and manuscripts are always at risk for true crime. Changing one's name to that of a famous author is in fashion, and there are four thousand John Miltons in the London telephone directory. If Dr. Evil had majored in English Lit, he might become our villain, Acheron Hades.

When Hades kidnaps Jane Eyre from the pages of Brontë's novel, Thursday Next is on the case. Don't miss the clever tweak at the end when Mr. Rochester asserts his human rights.

Penguin Reading Group Guide: A good introduction to *The Eyre Affair* and the series that follows, there is an interview with the author, and the discussion questions are light and fun, especially those about time traveling in novels.

Furthermore: The Thursday Next series includes *Lost in a Good Book* (Thursday has to rescue the significantly named Jack Schitt from "The Raven" and then must study at the feet of Miss Havisham in *Great Expectations*); *Something Rotten* (Thursday takes Hamlet on a PR tour and then must battle the ever-encroaching Goliath Corporation); and *The Well of Lost Plots* (Thursday and pet dodo Pickwick reside in the unpublished crime novel, Caversham Heights). *Nursery Crime: The Big Over Easy* is a non–Thursday Next novel in which detectives Jack Spratt and Mary Mary are on the case of Humpy Dumpty's demise—you get the picture.

Selling *The Eyre Affair* to the club: Hop in the Prose Portal for this delicious romp. And your next selection is an easy choice: the one and only *Jane Eyre*.

■ ■ ■

Fried Green Tomatoes at the Whistle Stop Café
(1987) by Fannie Flagg

Surrender to the vanished world of the Whistle Stop Café, the spot for coffee, pie and barbecue in Depression-era Whistle Stop, Alabama. Meet owners Idgie and Ruth, their son Stump, superb master of the barbecue Smokey, the upright Sipsey, sheriff and part-time Klansman Grady Kilgore, the sexually liberated Eva Bates and the evil Frank Bennett. When you figure out what happens to him, don't tell anyone until you get to the club. Meanwhile, everyone will be kept superbly informed by Dot Weems and her deadpan but hilarious bulletins.

Fried Green Tomatoes at the Whistle Stop Café is one of those books that is much admired and copied. The action moves back and forth between the heyday of the café where no hobo is turned away and a mess of fried green tomatoes sizzle on the stove, to the "present," the 1980s. Here, Mrs. Evelyn Couch learns the true history of the place from old-timer Ninny Threadgoode, now in a nursing home. Fannie Flagg never sentimentalizes her characters, though you may shed a tear or two. The author even makes important points about race relations, aging and just what feminism was like in the 1980s through Evelyn's real significant other, Towanda the Avenger. Recipes famously included.

Discussion Guide, Ballantine Reader's Circle: Excellent. It includes an in-depth interview with Flagg in which she talks about her careers as an actor and a writer, and is followed by the discussion questions. Topics are numerous and pointed, helpful and heartfelt: nontraditional families in the novel, the characteristics of small towns and the fading of this one as the railroad closes down.

Fannie Flagg Founder's Day: Included in *Fried Green Tomatoes at the Whistle Stop Café* are Sipsey's recipes—everything from buttermilk biscuits to coconut cream pie to the iconic tomatoes. Assign each member a dish and celebrate Flagg's other works such as *Welcome to the World, Baby Girl, Standing in the Rainbow* and *Daisy Fay and the Miracle Man*. For further recipes consult Fannie Flagg's *Original Whistle Stop Café Cookbook*.

Club scrapbook: Grab onto those moonbeams and add a few articles in the style of Dot Weems to your club scrapbook. Remember, no event is too minor. A group trip to see a performance by playwright Mr. William Shakespeare, meteorites falling or a funny story about someone's other half are not to be left out.

Gift from the Sea

(1955) by Anne Morrow Lindbergh

Anne Morrow Lindbergh's tiny, inspirational book recently celebrated its fiftieth anniversary of continuous publication. That her lovely extended metaphor still speaks to us—especially women who are on the verge of seeing children leaving the Argonauta (a Nautilus shell)—is a measure of Lindbergh's achievement as a poet and diarist.

Alone at a sea cottage in Florida, the author walks the beach, collecting and discarding shells, creating stories around them ("Solitude, says the moon shell"). She is on a retreat, away from her five children and husband, and she imparts her wisdom. Keep life simple ("the art of shedding") and recognize changes in the tides. Each cycle is valid and that relationships—especially in marriage—change. "Patience, patience, patience, is what the sea teaches." Lindbergh is later joined at the cottage by her sister, and another meditation on sharing together and alone is considered.

And that is a fine place to begin the discussion: Are the cycles Lindbergh identified still valid today? Isn't time and space the ultimate luxury? She argues one has to fight for it, but is this practical? Though Lindbergh's life was unique, did she anticipate the age of Oprah where advice to women is administrated on 24/7 basis? Read your favorite portions aloud and see where *Gift from the Sea* still resonates.

Audio alert: Claudette Colbert narrates a two-disc audio of *Gift from the Sea* (Random House Audio Publishing). Her signature cultured yet vulnerable voice magnifies the elegant simplicity of Lindbergh's words. With a moving forward by the author's daughter, Reeve Lindbergh.

Cocktail: Sherry by the fire.

Furthermore: Anne Morrow Lindbergh's life is intricately described in A. Scott Berg's Pulitzer Prize–winning biography *Lindbergh*. It is an unflinching look at the life of the aviator and the author he married. Berg had full cooperation with Anne Morrow Lindbergh in his writing and research.

And for a fictional, distinctly non–Literary Respite, look at both Lindberghs, see Philip Roth's *The Plot Against America* (chapter 5).

■ ■ ■

Hens Dancing
(1999) by Raffaella Barker

As much as she tries to persuade us that she is a madly disorganized single mum with two young boys and a baby, Venetia Summers is really the opposite number. She is capable, funny and a complete knockout after a variety of beauty treatments. Her family could not be more charming, especially adorable baby named The Beauty, a living Teletubby dressed in gingham bloomers, blowing fat kisses to everyone. Venetia's party-loving mum can be called upon day or night and a wonderful assortment of friends and country characters wander in and out of *Hens Dancing*. Instead of wringing her hands over Charles, her charmless ex, Venetia turns him into an object of ridicule, along with his new wife ("the poison dwarf") and the weird pet crematorium business called Heavenly Petting.

This doesn't stop Venetia from using her dividend checks to buy up plant nurseries, seed catalogues and glamorous peonies. Raffaella Barker is a columnist for Britain's *Country Living* magazine and she uses her skills delightfully. *Hens Dancing* is divided by seasons, with tantalizing descriptions of the countryside in each of its respective glories ("Spring pours in through every window on a tide of blossom-scented air"). There is extremely mild romantic suspense with Venetia's true-love interest never in doubt. Is he too good to be true? Who cares? When a household is as warm, active and filled with children, piglets and puppies as Venetia's, anything goes.

Cocktails: Bloody Marys from little bottles hidden for the adults at the Easter Egg Hunt; extravagant, fruit-laden Pimms complete with pink paper umbrella; Americanos in smart hotels; gin and tonics all around.

Dressing thematically: If babies and toddlers are permitted visits to your club, show them off in true The Beauty style: shocking-pink tights and leopard-skin miniskirt, purple dungarees, and the cherry-red velvet coat with ermine trim and white fur hat, creating that "majestic effect."

Furthermore: One of Venetia's great escapes are the novels of Georgette Heyer (1902–1975). Heyer is currently enjoying a revival of her swash-buckling romances, which usually take place in Regency England. Begin with *Regency Buck*, *The Grand Sophy*, *Devil's Cub* or this character's name-sake book, *Venetia*.

Selling *Hens Dancing* to the club: Not the deepest book on the shelf, it will nonetheless delight a wide constituency, including lovers of animals, ba-bies, sophisticated country living, gardening and excellent book design, as well as anyone celebrating a "divorci-versary." Choose a season and gather in the bluebells, buttercups, lavender or holly.

■ ■ ■

The Hitchhiker's Guide to the Galaxy
(1979) by Douglas Adams

Grab your towel, adjust your setting to Monty Python and get your geek on for this profound and silly, deep and crazy, arch, scary and wryly funny journey through time and space in search of the Ultimate Question.

Are you thinking ultimate discussion question? Definitely! *The Hitch-hiker's Guide to the Galaxy* begins when an ordinary Earthling, Arthur Dent, lies in the mud in front of the bulldozers about to demolish his house. He need not have bothered—all of Earth is destroyed to make way for a galactic freeway. Dent hitches a ride with his pal, Ford Prefect, who is not an out-of-work actor but an intergalactic contributor to the mostly impractical reference book "The Hitchhiker's Guide to the Galaxy."

Clubs will discover why this cult favorite has made acolytes of so many. Seventies space-age obsession meets the big computer as Earthling and star-ship crew trade barbs and catapult through some of the more unfashionable backwaters of space. Like George Orwell, Adams turns the reigning bureau-crats and the supercomputer Deep Thought into recognizable types, even as they rock Arthur Dent's world. The plot is at warp speed as Arthur Dent incredulously tries to ingest the news about his favorite planet's fate and absurdist news flashes: " 'There's an infinite number of monkeys outside who want to talk to us about this script for Hamlet they've worked out.' "

Discussion Sourcing: The truth may be out there but you need to make it club-ready. Your first stop should be the BBC's website for all things Hitchhiker, including a guide, news about the show and the author, and a trivia quiz: http://www.bbc.co.uk/cult/hitchhikers/quiz/. Portions of the original radio program are now available (Audio Partners)—select your favorite track and play it at the club.

About Douglas Noel Adams: Known to his fans as DNA, the author of *The Hitchhiker's Guide* series was a script doctor for the cult TV classic *Doctor Who*. *The Hitchhiker's Guide* started out life as a radio show for the BBC in 1978, became a series of novels and then a TV series, and is now a movie. Adams died in 2001 at the age of 49, and there is an asteroid named for his protagonist, Arthurdent.

Cocktails: The Pan Galactic Gargle Blaster, nicely chilled.

Editions that make a difference: The new gift edition from Random House features a foreword by Terry Jones and appreciative essays by Terry Pratchett and Neil Gaiman.

Selling *The Hitchhiker's Guide to the Galaxy* to the club: And now for something completely different. Bring out the Poetry Appreciation chair, strap in the prisoners and discuss the Ultimate Question.

■ ■ ■

Like Water for Chocolate
(1992) by Laura Esquivel,
translated by Carol Christensen and Thomas Christensen

A superior example of the fable as novel (*Balzac and the Little Chinese Seamstress, Chocolat*), Laura Esquivel combines traditional Mexican family recipes with a mystical love story. After all, its subtitle is "A Novel in Monthly In-stallments with Recipes, Romances and Home Remedies." In early twentieth-century Mexico, the De la Garza ranch is ruled by the iron fist of Mama Elena. Her last daughter Tita is not permitted to marry because she must, by tradition, take care of her mother until her death.

Tita's true love, Pedro, marries her sister Rosaura at Mama Elena's insis-tence. He thinks this is a fine idea because he can be nearer his heart's de-sire, Tita, who is then named official ranch cook. Several magic realism events, beautiful images amid tragedy and incredible dishes made "for the gods" later, you will be treated to a few wonderful twists. This is a story told as a cookbook, with recipes that the publisher does not recommend as real recipes. But each offers the flavor of time, place and Tita's personality. Discuss how the author mixes so many elements—family drama, especially between the sisters and their mother; historical facts about the Mexican revolution; ranch culture; culinary history; the Latin American style of magic realism—into a real romance.

Entertaining thematically: It would be hard to resist preparing any one of these dishes for your club. Simplest would be watermelon, eaten during the dog days of summer, especially to cool down at night. Mama Elena, a mas-ter of destruction, recommends a sharp knife to penetrate "just the end of the green part of the rind." Never touch the heart of the melon.

DVD alert: The 1993 movie starring Lumi Cavazos as Tita is as sensual as the book. Screen for the club between tomes.

Furthermore: Esquivel's newest novel is called *Malinche*, the story of a Mex-ican woman named Malinalli who guided Cortez.

■ ■ ■

Lying Awake
(2000) by Mark Salzman

The cloistered world of a Carmelite monastery outside Los Angeles is a place of prayer, meditation and silence. Sister John of the Cross has spent her adult life here and is a model for the other sisters—the brilliance of her visions and the beauty of her spiritual writing is well known. Her books even bring in much needed funds to the order. But Sister John has increasingly experienced excruciating headaches, resulting in a diagnosis that affects the whole meaning of her life as a servant of God.

The exquisite writing, descriptions of silence and meditation, and sense of place makes *Lying Awake* a memorable read and a small but fascinating world to explore and discuss. Mark Salzman tells the story by subtly juxtaposing the religious thought behind "God's hidden garden," and the actual hermitage with its mulberry and ginko trees, thicket of bamboo, eucalyptus leaves and mockingbirds, roses and flagstones. Sister John's life before the monastery is convincingly told, and her meditations and poetry are lovely (and worthy of being read aloud). The other sisters are characters in their own right: they often show a sense of humor in the face of their chosen vocations and the silences. The author creates a contemplative yet realistic atmosphere set against Sister John's test of faith and life decision.

Discussion questions, Vintage Books: Provocative, striking at the novel's themes of faith and devotion. Questions about Sister John's relationships with the other sisters, her mother and God are explored at length. Especially interesting is the question posed in the book itself about creative work and mental imbalance exhibited in such artists as Dostoevsky and Van Gogh.

Book design that makes a difference: Simple yet meaningful black and white illustrations open each chapter of *Lying Awake*. What do they mean and what do they say about the lives of the sisters?

■ ■ ■

The No. 1 Ladies Detective Agency
(1998) by Alexander McCall Smith

Who could resist Precious Ramotswe, a full-figured, traditionally built woman who is the only lady private detective in all of Botswana. Traveling to her cases in a tiny white van, she is inspired by Agatha Christie ("Mma

Christie") and the manual "The Principles of Private Investigation." Mma Ramotswe has many friends and several suitors who recognize her great integrity, pluck and sense of humor. And though this may be considered a detective story, Alexander McCall Smith's great achievement is in this glorious character and her delightful community of associates.

We feel we have made a marvelous new friend who invites us along to her investigations. Cases of missing husbands, disobedient teenage daughters and most poignantly, a missing child who is thought to have been kidnapped for witchcraft purposes, are treated with humanity and perception by our lady detective. Clubs love to discuss how cleverly *The No. 1 Ladies Detective Agency* achieves its balance between a naïve charm and a sophisticated knowingness about human nature.

Discussion Questions, Anchor Books: Very good. Although *The No. 1 Ladies Detective Agency* is a wonderful read, clubs may be stumped when it comes to starting and sustaining a discussion. The guide takes you through Mma Ramotswe's past and her realization that she had a calling to help fellow Africans. Especially effective are the questions about Precious's father, whom she adored, and her husband, whom she most emphatically did not.

Bush tea: You can order Precious Ramotswe's favorite from the Republic of Tea (republicoftea.com). The company calls it Botswana Blossom Red Tea. Mma Makutsi, Mma Ramotswe's crackerjack assistant, served it with a tin of condensed milk she kept in her handbag.

Furthermore: This was the first book of the series starring Precious Ramotswe. Other titles include *The Kalahari Typing School for Men*, *Tears of the Giraffe* and *The Full Cupboard of Life*, which follow the adventures of Precious and the rest of the gang. Smith is an incredibly prolific author and has several series with different characters going at once. Clubs have also relished *Friends, Lovers, Chocolate: The Sunday Philosophy Club* and are especially taken with Isabel Dalhousie.

Selling *The No. 1 Ladies Detective Agency* to the club: Perfect in its way. Discuss over coffee on Zebra Drive or on the verandah of the President Hotel.

Six Questions for Alexander McCall Smith

How would you suggest book clubs approach discussing a series such as yours, and series in general?
I think that one thing that readers can get out of reading a series is a sense of the writer's development as a writer. I would encourage book clubs to consider the question of how writers "grow into" their series, and how their perspective may change as they go along.

What do you think about the idea that the Precious Ramotswe series is about goodness?
I think that the series probably is about goodness, although I did not deliberately set out to write about that subject. Mma Ramotswe's response to people is the sort of goodness that one finds in people in that part of the world.

If a book club has completed all or most of the series (or even one), how would you suggest they celebrate?
I think that on completing the series, one way in which members could celebrate would be to sit down with a cup of red bush tea.

Have you been back to Botswana recently?
I go to Botswana each year, and I was there three months ago. I am very fond of the country, and it is always a wrench when I have to leave.

Have you ever participated in a book club?
I have not been to a book club—I wish that I had time to do so!

What are your favorite classic books? Which ones influenced you most?
I very much enjoy the R. K. Narayan "Malgudi" series [*Bachelor of Arts, Swami and Friends, A Tiger for Malgudi, Malgudi Days*]. A wonderful writer.

The Best Generic Questions for Discussing Series

If you look at the first in the series as the prototype, how well does the author succeed in developing the series and the main characters?

How does the protagonist stay the same or change over the course of the series?

Are these changes for the good?

How does the author use the secondary characters? How does he use the minor characters who may or may not come back to the series?

How does each book in the series advance the theme? Why do some titles succeed and others do not?

Over the course of the series, has the author employed different literary techniques? How does the author keep the series fresh?

How is the setting a character in the series? Is the setting beset by change from one book to the next and how does this affect the characters?

How does the author create suspense over a long period of time? Do the characters grow older or stay the same age?

How is the beloved book series like a TV series? If it is a TV series or movie, what are the differences and similarities between the book and live version?

New Year's Resolutions
for Book Clubs

1. We will review our book lists from the past year and talk about what worked and what did not.

2. We will adapt our best new ideas to the upcoming year.

3. We will not heap scorn on a member for choosing a more adventurous book.

4. We will read beyond the best-seller list and the latest "it" book.

5. We will choose one forgotten classic or "surprise selection" per year.

6. We will read at least one work of classic fiction, a book in translation or a genre we have yet to read, such as science fiction or biography.

7. We will start keeping a list of club books and authors we have read that can be updated and sent around.

8. We will not just wish for better discussions, we will make it happen.

9. We will spend more time on discussion preparation—we will even take notes in the margins of our books or corner the market in stickies.

10. We will start a club scrapbook filled with members' great lines, menus, wine labels, tickets and mementos of every type.

11. We will do that extra bit of Internet or library research.

12. We will establish rules for personal charity solicitations at the club and plan for one group charity or mentoring initiative a year.

13. We will buy an annual club present—a bookstore gift certificate would be a capital idea!—for the member we just assume will come through and make our club what it is today.

14. We will resist a consensus mentality and explore minority opinions of the book.

15. We will make it a rule that if a member has picked an especially challenging book, he or she must show up to the meeting.

16. We will submit to an Extreme Book Club Makeover if membership has slipped.

17. We will communicate clearly on e-mail, giving all the facts in one place.

18. We will never forget to RSVP to any club event.

19. We will always follow through and host when we say we will host.

20. We will make time in our schedule for fellow book club members because we know that where they are going is always wonderful, interesting and too much fun.

Book Club Craft Essentials

Many clubs use the traditional scrapbook method, glueing, photo cornering and matching images with photos for a more finished look for each page. Others are adapting an easier, portfolio style. The portfolio usually has front and back sleeves for books lists and club invitations; memorabilia from holiday, anniversary or birthday parties; shopping lists; recipes; cards; and printed e-mail. Menus and photographs can be slipped in each page easily.

Have access to a variety of type fonts for invitations, take-home souvenirs, name tags and book lists. If you want to take your club crafts a step further, typeface fonts can be bought at high-end stationery stores or online from Two Peas in a Bucket. Warning: Buying special fonts—in designs of every season, whim and fancy, retro, serif and san serif—has become quite an addiction for those who can barely leave the Craftetorium.

A note about special paper stock and ribbon: When you see it, buy it, especially if it is a package for $1. When it's time for a club craft or invitation, you know just where it is.

The Essentials:
An excellent printer
A varied collection of papers
Craft scissors with fanciful borders
Hole puncher
Light card stock
A varied ribbon collection for all purposes, seasons and events
Small cellophane and paper bags

Sources:

Crane & Co. (crane.com)

Kate's Paperie (Katespaperie.com)

Michaels (Michaels.com)

Paper Source (paper-source.com)

Two Peas in a Bucket (twopeasinabucket.com)

The Tween Book Club:
A Christmas Memory
by Truman Capote

"Buddy, do you think Mrs. Roosevelt will serve our cake at dinner?"
—*A Christmas Memory*

The quintessential Christmas story beloved by clubs of every type is also quintessential Truman Capote. In *A Christmas Memory* (1956) Capote writes the most lovely, just-this-close to sentimental evocation of a Depression-era, rural Christmas you will ever hope to read. The narrator recalls his days as a seven-year-old, and his memory is of his sixtyish cousin with whom he lives in a house of other elderly relations. "We are each other's best friend. She calls me Buddy, in memory of a boy who was formerly her best friend. The other Buddy died in the 1880s, when she was still a child. She is still a child."

When it's fruitcake weather, the odd friends assemble the ingredients for Christmas fruitcake. First they collect pecans in an old baby carriage. Next they buy ingredients with the coins they saved up all year and placed in the Fruitcake Fund. Finally, they bake thirty cakes for people who have struck their fancy, including President Roosevelt, the bus driver Abner Packer and the frightening dancing-café owner Mr. Haha Jones, who surprises the cousins with his generosity.

The two odd friends exchange their usual Christmas presents—homemade kites—and there will not be one dry eye.

Capote is a recognized master of the short form, and you should discuss how he does it over fruitcake, or Buddy's favorite supper: cold biscuits, bacon and blackberry jam. Take turns reading the story aloud—it's impossible not to sound like Geraldine Page, who played the cousin in the splendid 1966 TV movie. Or plan to make a batch of collaborative fruit-cakes with as many ingredients specified by Capote as you wish (cherries, citron, ginger, Hawaiian pineapple, raisins and "oh so much flour, butter, so many eggs") for those you love or those in need.

And if you are preparing one for a Mr. Haha Jones, don't forget the extra cup of raisins.

Book Club Style:
Gift from the Sea

Anne Morrow Lindbergh found inspiration and perceived life patterns from her time at the cottage and her shell collections. Adapt some of her strategies and have an early breakfast book club at the beach, in a park or at a serene early-morning place. Think about it creatively—where would your club go early in the morning for an inspirational sunrise club, filled with images of nature?

Invitations: Use a simple typeface (Australian Sunrise, Bradley ITC, for example), add your favorite quote and choose a thematic paper. Or make your own with a rubber-stamp border of shells. Affix a tiny starfish charm, shell stickers or any other decorative detail you wish.

Show your shell collections: Your choice of shells, adding your own meaningful explanation a la Anne Morrow Lindbergh.

Compare editions: From first editions to fiftieth anniversary editions, well-worn library books to bright and shiny gift editions, hardcovers to paperbacks, compare and contrast. Photograph the varied covers and add to your club scrapbook or portfolio, along with snaps from your sunrise club.

Serve: Lindbergh prescribes simplicity. Coffee, corn muffins, biscuits—a perfect club breakfast.

Take-home gifts: Tiny bags of seashells, tied with raffia and paired with little cardboard books in which to record sunrise thoughts.

<u>Gift from the Sea</u> Sunrise Book Club

"Patience, patience, patience, is what the
sea teaches. Patience and faith."
—ANNE MORROW LINDBERGH

Time: 7 A.M.

Place: The Beach

Bring: Gift from the Sea by Anne Morrow Lindbergh, muffins, biscuits and coffee.

Show: Channelled whelk, moon shell, double-sunrise, oyster shell, argonauta or a few other shells

Holiday Celebration

At holiday times, clubs celebrate in every way. Some go wild hosting parties and catered events with DJs. Others meet for sedate lunches and gift exchanges attended by harp music at a hotel. Still others have a regular club meeting with or without gift exchanges. Here, you can discuss the year that has passed in books and the year ahead.

The simplest, most thematic way to celebrate the season is the wrapped book exchange. Choose a book from your shelf that club members may like and has not been a selection of your club. Wrap it in festive paper and bring to your December club. You may consider books you bought at the library sale, but do not go out and buy a book. This is about sharing, not buying.

Selections can be by grabbag, by numbers or by assignment. One thing is certain: when everyone reveals their book selection, it's a perfect opportunity to discuss each title and whether it should be considered for the club itself. It will definitely remind you of whole categories previously not considered.

Best in show: Wrap your book in an exciting way. You might choose literary-themed paper that you buy exclusively for this purpose. These papers can be found at local bookstores, and at library and museum gift shops. And there is no shortage of seasonal gift wrap that you could choose for maximum effect.

The differently wrapped books can be used as a centerpiece, books with the best wrapping paper are always picked first and the paper itself is a whimsical take-home memento or can be added to the club scrapbook or portfolio.

Discuss the year past and the year ahead with a special cocktail: the CranberryOlada.

CranberryOlada

SERVES 8

This drink can also be made in a nonalcoholic version by omitting the rum.

1 cup cranberry juice

1 cup pineapple juice

2 cups fresh pineapple, cut up into small chunks

1 cup cream of coconut

Juice of 4 limes

2 teaspoons grenadine syrup

1 cup light rum

½ cup dark rum

Crushed ice to taste

Dried cranberries, fresh pineapple or variations for garnish

Combine all ingredients except the rum and ice in a blender. Gradually add both rums. The mixture should be foamy. Add crushed ice. For garnish: Alternate dried cranberries and fresh pineapple on a skewer.

Travel trip: Blend all ingredients except the ice right before you go and pour into a jar with a screw-top lid. If you know the host will be busier than usual, bring crushed ice separately, as well as spoons, garnishes and anything else you will need. *Optional but worth it*: Bring festive paper cups of the season and amusing cocktail napkins. Never underestimate the power of these small statements.

Snacking at the Club: Ina Garten's Pan-Fried Onion Dip

MAKES 2 CUPS

In *Durable Goods*, Cherylanne's mom serves California French onion dip with potato chips and pretzels for a teen party, pre–spin the bottle. This recipe is a gourmet version of the classic dip.

2 large yellow onions
4 tablespoons unsalted butter
¼ cup vegetable oil
¼ teaspoon ground cayenne pepper
1 teaspoon kosher salt
½ teaspoon freshly ground black pepper
4 ounces cream cheese, room temperature
½ cup sour cream
½ cup of good mayonnaise

Cut the onions in half, and then slice them into ⅛-inch-thick half-rounds. (You will have about 3 cups of onions.)

Heat the butter and oil in a large sauté pan on medium heat. Add the onions, cayenne, salt and pepper and sauté for 10 minutes. Reduce the heat to medium-low and cook, stirring occasionally, for 20 more minutes, until the onions are browned and caramelized. Allow the onions to cool.

Place the cream cheese, sour cream and mayonnaise in the bowl of an electric mixer fitted with a paddle attachment and beat until smooth. Add the onions and mix well. Taste for seasonings.

Serve at room temperature.

By combining butter and oil, you get the best properties of each: the flavor of butter and the high smoking point of oil.

Diana Kennedy's Guacamole

MAKES ABOUT 2⅓ CUPS

In her classic cookbook, *The Essential Cuisines of Mexico*, Diana Kennedy tells us the history of the word "guacamole." It comes from the Nahuatl words that combine "avocado" (ahuacatl) and "concoction" (molli). She advises to never use a blender for its preparation and that guacamole is best eaten the moment it is prepared. **Note**: The chiles are extremely hot. Adjust to taste.

2 tablespoons finely chopped white onion
4 serrano chiles, or to taste, finely chopped
3 heaping tablespoons roughly chopped cilantro
Salt to taste
3 large avocados (about 1 pound, 6 ounces)
4 ounces tomatoes, finely chopped (about ⅔ cup)

For serving:
1 heaping tablespoon finely chopped onion
2 heaping tablespoons roughly chopped cilantro

Grind together the onion, chiles, cilantro and salt to a paste.

Cut the avocados into halves, remove the pits, and squeeze the flesh out of the shells and mash into the chile base to a textured consistency—it should not be smooth. Stir in all but 1 tablespoon of the tomatoes, adjust seasoning and top with the remaining chopped tomatoes, onion and cilantro.

Serve immediately at room temperature.

Easy Golden Margaritas

MAKES 6 DRINKS

½ cup fresh orange juice
½ cup fresh lime juice
½ cup Cointreau
1½ cups tequila
Chopped ice
Limes or orange slices for garnish

In a blender mix together the orange juice, lime juice, Cointreau and tequila for about a minute. Gradually add ice to taste and blend. Pour into margarita glasses and garnish with lime or orange slice.

Option: Have salt ready on a flat surface for pressing to the rim of the glass.

If You Were in a 1960s Book Club

1960

The Alexandria Quartet
    by Lawrence Durrell

Lady Chatterley's Lover
    by D. H. Lawrence

The Leopard
    by Giuseppe di Lampedusa

Night by Elie Wiesel

Ourselves to Know by John O'Hara

The Sot-Weed Factor by John Barth

Strangers and Brothers by C. P. Snow

To Kill a Mockingbird by Harper Lee

Two Weeks in Another Town
    by Irwin Shaw

1961

The Agony and the Ecstasy
    by Irving Stone

Black Like Me by John Howard Griffin

The Carpetbaggers by Harold Robbins

Catch-22 by Joseph Heller

Franny and Zooey by J. D. Salinger

A House for Mr. Biswas
    by V. S. Naipaul

The Making of the President, 1960
    by Theodore H. White

Mila 18 by Leon Uris

The Moviegoer by Walker Percy

The Prime of Miss Jean Brodie
    by Muriel Spark

Ring of Bright Water
    by Gavin Maxwell

The Winter of Our Discontent
    by John Steinbeck

1962

A Clockwork Orange
    by Anthony Burgess

Fail-Safe by Eugene Burdick
    and Harvey Wheeler

The Golden Notebook
    by Doris Lessing

The Guns of August
    by Barbara Tuchman

One Flew Over the Cuckoo's Nest
    by Ken Kesey

Pale Fire by Vladimir Nabokov

The Prize by Irving Wallace

The Reivers by William Faulkner

Seven Days in May
    by Fletcher Knebel
    and Charles W. Bailey II

Sex and the Single Girl
    by Helen Gurley Brown

Ship of Fools
    by Katherine Anne Porter

Travels with Charley in Search of
    America by John Steinbeck

Youngblood Hawke by Herman Wouk

1963

The American Way of Death
    by Jessica Mitford

Cat's Cradle by Kurt Vonnegut

The Centaur by John Updike

The Fire Next Time
    by James Baldwin

The Group by Mary McCarthy

On Her Majesty's Secret Service
    by Ian Fleming

Profiles in Courage: Inaugural Edition
    by John F. Kennedy

Raise High the Roof-Beam, Carpenters
    and Seymour by J. D. Salinger

The Sand Pebbles by Richard McKenna

The Shoes of the Fisherman
    by Morris L. West

V by Thomas Pynchon

1964

Call It Sleep by Henry Roth

Herzog by Saul Bellow

I Never Promised You a Rose Garden
    by Joanne Greenberg

A Moveable Feast
    by Ernest Hemingway

This Rough Magic by Mary Stewart

The Spy Who Came in From the Cold
    by John Le Carre

The Wapshot Scandal
    by John Cheever

1965

The Garden of the Finzi-Continis
    by Giorgio Bassani

The Looking Glass War
    by John Le Carre

The Making of the President, 1964
    by Theodore H. White

Manchild in the Promised Land
    by Claude Brown

The Mandelbaum Gate
    by Muriel Spark

The Painted Bird by Jerzy Kosinski

The Rector of Justin
    by Louis Auchincloss

The Source by James A. Michener

A Thousand Days
    by Arthur Schlesinger Jr.

Up the Down Staircase
    by Bel Kaufman

1966

The Crying of Lot 49
    by Thomas Pynchon

The Fixer by Bernard Malamud

Flowers for Algernon by Daniel Keyes

In Cold Bold by Truman Capote

In God We Trust, All Others Pay Cash
    by Jean Shepherd

The Jewel in the Crown by Paul Scott

The Magus by John Fowles

Rush to Judgment by Irving Greenfield

Speak Memory by Vladimir Nabokov

Tai-Pan by James Clavell

Valley of the Dolls
    by Jacqueline Susann

Wide Sargasso Sea by Jean Rhys

1967

The Arrangement by Elia Kazan

The Chosen by Chaim Potok

The Confessions of Nat Turner
    by William Styron

Death of a President
    by William Manchester

Diary of a Mad Housewife
    by Sue Kaufman

Nicholas and Alexandra
  by Robert K. Massie
North Toward Home
  by Willie Morris
Our Crowd by Stephen Birmingham
Rosemary's Baby by Ira Levin

1968

The Armies of the Night
  by Norman Mailer
The Cancer Ward
  by Aleksandr Solzhenitsyn
Couples by John Updike
The Electric Kool-Aid Acid Test
  by Tom Wolfe
A Fan's Notes by Frederick Exley
Myra Breckinridge by Gore Vidal
The Naked Ape
  by Desmond Morris
Papillon by Henri Charriere
Slouching Towards Bethlehem
  by Joan Didion
Soul on Ice by Eldridge Cleaver
Steps by Jerzy Kosinski

1969

The Andromeda Strain
  by Michael Crichton
The Apprenticeship of Duddy Kravitz
  by Mordechai Richler
The French Lieutenant's Woman
  by John Fowles
The Godfather by Mario Puzo
The House on the Strand
  by Daphne du Maurier
Miami and the Siege of Chicago
  by Norman Mailer
Mr. Bridge by Evan Connell
Mr. Sammler's Planet
  by Saul Bellow
Portnoy's Complaint
  by Philip Roth
The Selling of the President 1968
  by Joe McGinniss
Slaughterhouse Five
  by Kurt Vonnegut
Them by Joyce Carol Oates
An Unfinished Woman: A Memoir
  by Lillian Hellman

7

BLACK LIT

"Ships at a distance have every man's wish on board."
—*Their Eyes Were Watching God*

They are dreamy, timeless, contemporary, magical, funny and real. The novels of Black Lit show the dazzling talent of African American writers whose subject matter knows no bounds and who work in every literary genre. Poetic images of self-discovery from one author, sister-girl sarcasm from another, it's a different mood every month as clubs sample the new and return to favorites. Richard Wright was of his time and of ours.

In book clubs, we are always waiting for the next big thing. It doesn't always come to us on the night we summon it. So we return to the classics—contemporary and from the time when the Nobel laureate's goal was the "reclamation of racial beauty." As we all know by now, Toni Morrison succeeded wildly. Today, racial beauty can be seen in characters as diverse as the Buppie next door to the struggling teen in Harlem.

From up-to-the-minute or timeless dialogue to word portraits so vivid we visualize the characters' quilts, black doll collections and contemporary art on the walls, the authors of Black Lit always deliver. Realism, hyper-realism and fantastical myths are all part of an evening at the club. But, it's not all timeless prose about the natural world. Just ask the legions of Zane fans. Or Terry McMillan. "I also believe in creating realistic characters with realistic problems and who deal with them in a realistic manner," the author said recently. "We do everything."

These writers take on the big subjects—rascism, injustice, natural and man-made disasters—with characters of authenticity and truth. Yancey and Basil, Celie and Shug, Easy and Mouse—the ways in which they interact with each other and with us is a big reason why we gather. It's a continuing story, filled with drama. New authors wait in the wings as the immortals take center stage. One of these nights, though, the spotlight might be on an author we have yet to hear of. And that anticipation is the very best part.

The Ten Indispensable Titles

■■■

Any Way the Wind Blows
(2001) by E. Lynn Harris

Young women will come to town and try to make it against all odds. Bling will be acquired and lost. Songs about you-know-who will climb the charts. Older women will attempt to stay young while meddling, all in vain. Too many will be unlucky in love but will sigh knowingly, move on and laugh about it, planning and plotting for next time.

You will read this plot hundreds of times and the authors will all be different. But there is only one author king and you will accept no substitutes. You can argue about the best of E. Lynn Harris night and day, but many club members chose *Any Way the Wind Blows* as the height of E. Lynn mania. Picking up the story from *Not a Day Goes By*, fabulous sports executive John "Basil" Henderson is his old self, seeing men and women simultaneously, giving new meaning to the concept "on the down-low." Meanwhile, his jilted bride Yancey Braxton has a song climbing the charts. Its title? "Any Way the Wind Blows," with not so subtle lyrics about Basil and the way he "drop-kicked" her mercilessly. Add several secrets and revenge subplots (the best involves hunky, gay Bart Dunbar) to the emotional searching that Harris brings to his swinging, modern characters that sets them apart from all others and you will have the best of E. Lynn Harris's world. We just live in it.

Any Way the Wind Blows anticipates our present, blog-saturated media whirlwind, but have you discussed the second meaning of the title? It may surprise you.

Discussion questions, Anchor Books: Excellent. All of the characters, including the secondary but important Harris types such as gossip columnist

LaVonya, Wylie, Windsor, Raymond and that lost black Gabor sister, Ava, are always on call to harass, motivate and listen. How do they drive the plot?

Dressing thematically: Does anyone dress better than John Basil Henderson and Bart Dunbar, especially when their fashion concepts run to fruit and vegetable colors? White leather pants and body-hugging pumpkin-colored sweater for Bart and cashmere jacket over a sweater the color of ripened limes for Basil. Of course, Yancey is no slouch in her white, sleeveless sweater and capri pants.

Entertaining thematically: Yancey's favorite dish: deviled eggs with a touch of caviar (see page 273).

E. Lynn Harris Founder's Day: *And This Too Shall Pass, Invisible Life, Just As I Am, Abide With Me, Not a Day Goes By, A Love of My Own, If This World Were Mine*, the maestro's autobiography *What Becomes of the Brokenhearted*. While anticipating the next novel, pour yourself an apple martini (see page 275) or, if you dare, a "thug passion" made of cognac and Alize, revisit the *B.A.P. Handboook*, choose your favorite E. Lynn and start making your case.

■ ■ ■

The Bluest Eye
(1970) by Toni Morrison

It's almost unthinkable that Toni Morrison was once a first-time novelist, but every author has to start somewhere. And what a place to start! Considered one of her classic works, *The Bluest Eye* is told as a brutal fairy tale by a young narrator who sees it all. It is the fall of 1941, a year the marigolds did not grow. "We thought, at the time, that it was because Pecola was having her father's baby." Eleven-year-old Pecola Breedlove who has been increasingly ostracized by the entire community in little and big ways, fervently prays for the bluest eyes ("Prettier than Alice-and-Jerry Storybook eyes") as the answer to her humiliation and bitter family life.

Throughout the story, it is our growing sympathy with Pecola's plight that makes her tragic and heroic at the same time.

In between the unstoppable, awful magic, Morrison gives us satire in the "perfect" persona of green-eyed Maureen Peal, dressed in brown velvet coat trimmed in white rabbit fur. The beauty of the natural world set against the brutality of the man-made one is Morrison's hallmark as she poses the question (the why and how) and then proceeds to not turn away. In the majestic afterward written in 1993, Morrison meditates on the subject of race and beauty, and the times in which she began writing *The Bluest Eye*—1962. The writer's process and the autobiographical elements of the author's life growing up in Lorain, Ohio, are not only an indispensable part of the discussion for this novel, but might just be used as a template for every other book.

Discussion questions, Penguin Reading Group Guides: Excellent. The questions concern the varied styles of language from reading primer ("Here is the house. It is green and white.") to issues of social class through all the instances of rape in *The Bluest Eye*. Comparisons between the time Morrison wrote the novel and today are a must-discuss.

Selling *The Bluest Eye* to the club: Elegantly written, both the ghostly and earthbound characters have horrifying wishes—and it's short. This novel is a gold standard.

■ ■ ■

Cane River
(2001) by Lalita Tademy

Lalita Tademy offers a superbly detailed fictional history of her ancestors' lives along Louisiana's Cane River. It is a community only Louisiana could produce, comprised of French planters, free people of color called *gens de couleur* and slaves. Their interaction is the heart of the story and one of the reasons *Cane River* has been embraced by clubs for its authenticity.

The novel tells the story of four women who were born slaves and who struggle to survive before, after and during the Civil War. Written with precision, each character frankly assesses her chances, or lack thereof, slavery and its generation-spanning legacy. Both the white and black characters' thoughts and actions are often unpredictable, but the threat of violence is always present. The sense of joy and relief the author feels after telling her family's story is palpable.

The style of *Cane River* is unusual because it is called a novel, but it is still an intimate family history, filled with historic and family documents. Why did the author make this choice of narrative style? Begin your discussion here.

Discussion questions, Warner Books: Thorough. There are thirty questions, so you will have more than enough to choose from. Among the topics: the different losses suffered by each generation of women, their relationships, the promise of freedom and all the exceptions and contradictions inherent in Cane River.

Club scrapbooks: One of the most effective sections of the book was the endearing remembrances from Cousin Gurtie Fredieu. In a letter she wrote about her family's history in 1975, she evokes the vanished world with simplicity and eloquence. This scrapbook style might be adapted to your club, where each member writes a short family remembrance and accompanies it, if possible, with a photo.

The Color Purple
(1982) by Alice Walker

The most magical of stories, *The Color Purple* unfolds gradually. The fantastic twist still jolts happily, and the experience of reading, rereading and discussing Alice Walker's Pulitzer Prize–winning novel is all the more delicious. It opens with a shocking admission from a fourteen-year-old Celie in her letters to God about her threatening father: "You gonna do what your mammy wouldn't." Celie is raped by him and watches helplessly as her two children are taken away. Celie is pawned off on Mister as a combination wife, prisoner and housekeeper.

But changes are in store for our heroine when she falls in love with glamorous, sexy singer Shug Avery, the Queen Honeybee. Mister also loves her and instead of jealousy, there is compassion and humor. The entire book is told through a series of achingly honest letters a lonely Celie writes to God and then in an exchange with her beloved missing sister Nettie. The hard lives of these women in the South during the Depression is so intimate, you imagine your own family.

If you are reading *The Color Purple* with a new club, for the second time, or preparing to see the musical, concentrate on the language: How does Celie's writing style change subtly? Can you see the influence of Zora Neale Hurston on the characters' country speech? Revel in the symbolism and the superb secondary character Sofia ("White folks is a miracle of affliction"). Put on some Bessie Smith or Duke Ellington and take another walk in the fields filled with the color purple. (See "The Color Purple Flower Celebration," page 265.)

Dressing thematically: The perfect pair of pants in the style of Celie—colors of the sunset in soft, flowing fabric that catch the light.

■ ■ ■

Little Scarlet
(2004) by Walter Mosley

It's 1965 and though the Watts riots in Los Angeles are just beginning to subside, a real war has been declared. In this burnt-out landscape, a man is pulled out of his car by a mob, escapes into a building where the body of a red-haired black woman nicknamed Little Scarlet turns up. This set-up calls for a hero of middle-aged proportions: Easy Rawlins.

In one of the very best books in the series, Walter Mosley's Easy is tough, thoughtful—dare we say, romantic *and* a good dad—But he never lets up as he tracks the killer through a swirling, racially charged cityscape. The black neighborhoods are ringed with white cops who really need Easy this time and call on his special private-detective skills of "Research and Delivery" to find out the truth. ("Who knew when the Molotov cocktails would start exploding in Beverly Hills?") It turns out that the killer is some twisted wreck, but Mosley manages the feat of all great writers in making you almost care about his fate.

Fans of the series will be rewarded with a few great plot twists. And club members who enjoy contemporary history will savor a discussion about a city that exploded, and the reasons behind the explosion, explained eloquently by Easy and his friends. ("They all come from the South. They all come from racism so bad that they don't even know what it's like to walk around with your head held high.") Plus, Mouse is back! The secondary characters are always a treat, and in *Little Scarlet*, a visit from irrepressible temptress Juanda is a sight to behold. How does Mosley use a historical event to turn up the volume on favorite characters?

Discussion sourcing: *Little Scarlet* was chosen for the Los Angeles One Book, One City program. An illuminating interview with Mosley can be found at powells.com. Here, he discusses his great themes, including the Los Angeles riots and racial strife.

Audio alert: Michael Boatman is a terrific actor and narrates the audio version of *Little Scarlet* (Time Warner Audio Books). He supplies all the voices and though it's hard to pick out a favorite, Boatman's characterization of Juanda alone is worth the price of admission.

Walter Mosley Founder's Day: Everyone has a favorite Walter Mosley mystery. Choose a date, introduce to the group your favorite Easy Rawlins mystery and plan to honor *Devil in a Blue Dress*, *A Little Yellow Dog*, *Black Betty* or *Gone Fishin'*. And don't forget Socrates Fortlow, the protagonist of *Always Outnumbered, Always Outgunned*. Read passages aloud or dress thematically in your favorite Ezekiel Rawlins outfit. Sixties-era two-piece ensemble with a single-button jacket, anyone?

Entertaining thematically: Easy loves breakfasts at Nip's Coffee Shop on Olympic and the lemon-filled donuts at Trini's Creole Café at 105th and Central. Looters and cops sit at Trini's counters throughout the riots (" 'Dollar don't make itself, brother.' ") Dinner at Pepe's at the small hotel, The Oxford, features Pepe's famous "green salad of frisee lettuce, cherry tomatoes, cut green beans and a strong garlic vinaigrette."

■ ■ ■

Native Son

(1940) by Richard Wright

Written in shades of black, white and red, it's as if Richard Wright wants us to be always horrified, always engaged by this story of Bigger Thomas. A poor, uneducated black man and petty criminal in 1930s Chicago, Bigger becomes a chauffeur in the employ of a liberal, wealthy white family, the Daltons. He becomes angry and confused by the chumminess of the Dalton's daughter, Mary, and her Communist boyfriend Jan. The evening ends in the accidental death,—or was it accidental?—of Mary at Bigger's hands.

Divided into three sections, "Fear," "Flight" and "Fate," we understand exactly what the future holds for Bigger Thomas. But that does not minimize the suspense or the uncomfortable questions: Does the author want us to sympathize with Bigger, whose murder of Mary and the burning of her body is described in excruciating detail? How accidental was the murder? Do the brilliant interior monologues combined with the *Day of the Locust*-type newspaper and newsreel coverage increase our empathy with the isolated murderer?

Wright builds his scenes with precision dialogue, and his use but not overuse of symbolism and metaphor could be the entire basis of a discussion. Who is really blind?

The controversial summation at the end of the trial by the Communist lawyer, Mr. Max, continues to be a key discussion event.

Discussion questions, Harper Perennial: Very good, though you wish for more than six questions. Particularly provocative is the question about James Baldwin's essay "Everybody's Protest Novel" where he dismisses *Native Son* and its author as self-righteous and for relying on stereotypes.

Audio alert: Don't miss the Recorded Books version of *Native Son*, narrated by Peter Francis James, who voices every character. James masterfully conveys the thrilling, awful chaos swirling around Bigger as the narrative becomes a nightmare newsreel.

Selling Native Son to the club: Your last books were *The Vow* and *Confessions of a Video Vixen*—it's time for a literary classic. Your job is to pitch *Native Son* as a maximum literary thriller.

■ ■ ■

72 Hour Hold
(2005) by Bebe Moore Campbell

Keri Whitmore is facing the crises of her life when her daughter sinks deeper into bipolar disorder. Trina is eighteen years old and about to enter Brown University when her disease seizes her. In *72 Hour Hold*—the title refers to the amount of time a parent can seek help for an adult child while he or she is held in the hospital—beloved novelist Bebe Moore Campbell gives us a remarkable story of a mother and daughter, wrapped up in a thriller set in that land of the thriller, Los Angeles. "My child had been swallowed up by the Los Angeles night."

Who is in denial and when do they see the light? What would you do in these circumstances? Keri must make instant decisions that will have huge implications on her daughter. The words "spiral," "control," "stigma" and "health insurance" are touchstones in this world as Keri does everything in her power to keep Trina on track. We are inside her head as her emotional barometer rises, falls and measures everything in between. Ex-husband Clyde, boyfriend Orlando and Keri's workplace mates are characters in their own right. Campbell also looks at a contemporary phenomenon— the black conservative as radio host, Clyde's chosen profession.

A must-discuss: Keri compares living with the Trina's illness to slavery ("Now normal has been sold deep south") and the radical treatment offered by Brad and his team to the underground railroad. Harriet Tubman herself visits Keri's thoughts, along with Keri's grandmother Ma Missy. She cracks bitter jokes: "I went to bed, warning myself not to feel better. That would be like Sally Hemings sending out wedding invitations." It's an original and jarring juxtaposition of past and present events; start your discussion here.

Discussion questions, Knopf: Very good. There are fifteen questions and topics, including Keri's guilt and her mother's alcoholism. Watch out for spoilers in some of the early questions.

Dressing thematically: When juggling your exes, vintage Armani, DKNY or Dolce and Gabani from Keri's successful resale shop As Good as New. Or Keri's Saturday uniform: sweats and sneakers, no makeup.

Furthermore: Clubs have fully embraced the entire Campbell spectrum, including *Singing in the Comeback Choir, What You Owe Me* and *Your Blues Ain't Like Mine*. Discuss your favorite after yoga and tea.

Selling *72 Hour Hold* to the club: With a contemporary theme that fits beautifully into a suspenseful genre, *72 Hour Hold* will have you talking all night. It will especially resonate with parents of teenagers.

■ ■ ■

Their Eyes Were Watching God
(1937) by Zora Neale Hurston

From the famous opening sentence, you know you are being treated to a work of genius. But for all the justifiably acclaimed imagery and dialogue in *Their Eyes Were Watching God*, it is also a ripping love story. If you are reading the novel for a second time, concentrate on Zora Neale Hurston's beguiling language. If you keep a reading journal, your pen will not stop. And if you are the one who loves to read aloud, fellow members will soon be telling you to cease and desist—there are simply too many exquisite passages of self-discovery: "She had been getting ready for her great journey to the horizons in search of *people*: it was important to all the world that she should find them and they find her."

West Florida teenager Janie Mae Crawford is a dreamer in the great literary tradition of women who yearn for something better. She and her grandmother live in a plantation shack on a rural farm when Janie soon finds herself in an unhappy arranged marriage with an older man. She flees this marriage when she meets Joe Starks, an up-and-coming man who becomes mayor of the black town Eatonville and who tells her what is best for her.

After Joe's death, Janie has many suitors, but there is only one for her: the incomparable Tea Cake, a man of many talents not the least of which is his courtship style. Janie is hooked and the two move to Jacksonville and then on to the muck of the Everglades with a hard-drinking, hard-working crowd, presided over by the royal couple, Janie and Tea Cake. It's the adventure and love story of a lifetime, told in the most lyrical prose you will ever encounter.

Discussion questions, Harper Perennial: Very good. Many of questions explore the nature of relationships of men and women, the author's use of vernacular dialect and what it reveals about the characters.

About Zora Neale Hurston: Though the setting of *Their Eyes Were Watching God* was the Eatonville, Florida, of her birth, Zora Neale Hurston went to Howard University and later studied anthropology at Barnard College in New York. She was a star of the Harlem Renaissance, a folklorist and writer. But her later years were marked by poverty and anonymity. In the 1970s, Alice Walker led a smashingly successful effort to restore Hurston's grave and her all-but-forgotten reputation.

Dressing thematically: Anything and everything blue, the color Tea Cake insisted Janie wear. And when she did, town gossip had her looking like "some young girl."

Selling *Their Eyes Were Watching God* to the club: Oprah presented it, Halle Berry starred in it, now it's time to read and discuss the real thing.

■ ■ ■

Upstate

(2005) by Kalisha Buckhanon

Told entirely through letters between Harlem teenagers Antonio and Natasha, *Upstate* is at once a love story, a "making it" tale and a portrait of two talented young people in crisis. Seventeen-year-old Antonio is sent "upstate" after being convicted of killing his father, though he took a plea for involuntary manslaughter. He and Natasha swear eternal love in their letters, and we know where that might lead as Natasha takes advantage of the opportunities she is given.

Clubs will enjoy discussing the style of Kalisha Buckhanon's stunning debut novel, how she creates suspense, who are the guilty parties and just who is a better writer—Antonio or Natasha? Each is gifted as they describe their different worlds. Antonio tries to survive in his tough, lonely cell ("I'm cold. I'm so cold I can feel my bones inside of me"), and it is heartbreaking as he recalls his vanished youth of movies, friends, trips to McDonald's, cherry bombs from Mister Softee and even high school ("I kind of hoped that you might be standing there waiting for me after lunch the way you used to"). The ending is remarkable. *Upstate* is set in the 1990s, so members will naturally want to talk about their own whereabouts.

1990s download: Old school Queen Latifah and Natasha's mother's favorites, Chaka Khan, Patti Labelle and Regina Belle. Don't forget the soundtrack to *Boyz N the Hood*.

From Antonio's bookshelf: *The Catcher in the Rye* by J. D. Salinger, *The Autobiography of Malcolm X* by Malcolm X, *The Outsiders* by S. E. Hinton, *The Jungle* by Upton Sinclair and *Short Eyes* by Miguel Pinero.

Selling *Upstate* to the club: Buckhanon is a fresh and exciting new voice, and this small, fine novel is one of the best evocations of young love you will ever read.

Waiting to Exhale

(1992) by Terry McMillan

It's a towering, best-selling game changer, and when you revisit *Waiting to Exhale* you think: what makes it a modern day classic? Then you think, forget about all that, this is a great, funny book—maybe the best ever about female friendship. We care intensely what happens to these characters and the men who love them—and the men who don't. Sometimes, we even want to stop them, but who would want to? Then we would miss Robin's description of Russell ("a lying, sneaky, whorish Pisces") or Bernie's ultimate revenge fantasy come to life or Savannah's road trip recollections where she found a cheap motel for her annoying traveling companion and "politely dropped his ass off." In the end, Terry McMillan knows what's best for them.

Savannah, Bernadine, Gloria and Robin are four close professional black women in their thirties who now live in Phoenix around the time the state made headlines around the world for not passing the Dr. Martin Luther King Jr. holiday. It turns out to be an inspired choice of locations for this issue, underscoring the characters' relative isolation in a town not know for a large black population. As they look for love, struggle with job issues and get together to discuss all of the above, the women's stories often end satisfyingly, but the trip is unexpected. Can you name all the ways the characters exhale?

Drinking thematically: White zinfandel, margaritas and champagne. Just bring your toothbrush and plan to spend the night.

Casting call: The original movie (a treat for DVD night) starred Forest Whitaker, Whitney Houston, Angela Bassett and Dennis Haysbert among the stellar cast. Is it time for a remake or is it perfect the way it is? Would you like to see these actors performing the same roles at their current ages?

Old-school download: *Waiting to Exhale* is filled to the brim with songs from the 1980s, fueling one of the book's most famous scenes: the slumber party and "the list." Create your own "Exhale" download featuring Rick James, vintage Whitney Houston, Minnie Ripperton, Teddy Pendergrass, and Bobby Brown, and get in the way-back machine for Aretha, Gladys and the Temptations.

Furthermore: Everyone has a favorite McMillan—*Disappearing Acts*, *Mama*, *How Stella Got Her Groove Back*, *A Day Late and a Dollar Short*. And if imitation is the sincerest form of flattery, McMillan would be even richer. In her latest blockbuster, *The Interruption of Everything*, the heroine is forty-four-year-old Marilyn Grimes who is in the sandwich generation of looking out for her grown children and taking care of her mother and foster sister. A major plot development leaves a McMillan character facing yet another big choice.

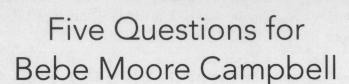

Five Questions for
Bebe Moore Campbell

72 Hour Hold *can be read as a thriller and as contemporary novel with several themes. And it can also be appreciated by any parent with a teenager. How would you suggest clubs approach your novel?*
Book clubs should approach the book with the expectation of reading a good story. The theme of mental illness from the family members' point of view will definitely resonate with some readers. The most important aspects of the book are the characters and the story. I want readers to see themselves in Keri's struggle. I want them to empathize with her. I want them to savor and appreciate the language and the metaphors I've chosen. I hope this book will be a sensory experience.

The events in this book and Keri's emotional state are so precise. Have you had personal experience in dealing with this disorder?
I have a family member who has a mental illness, so I know firsthand the experience of dealing with a loved one who is manic. In addition, I've become active in the National Alliance of the Mentally Ill (NAMI), an advocacy group for the mentally ill and their families. Some women and I have cofounded NAMI-Inglewood, a chapter in Los Angeles. My mission is to get mental illness out of the black community's closet.

Are there groups as you depicted in the novel who "kidnap" patients with parental approval?
I don't know if there are such groups. There are "boot camps" for children with problems such as Trina's, but I've never found any that were willing to kidnap adults.

Have you ever been in a book club? If so, what are your favorite books?
I've never been in a book club. Too busy writing, I guess. My favorite books: *Sula* by Toni Morrison, *The Paperboy* by Pete Dexter, *The Mambo Kings Play Songs of Love* by Oscar Hijuelos, *Sister Carrie, An American Tragedy* and *Jenny Gerhardt* by Theodore Dreiser, *Disappearing Acts* by Terry McMillan, to name a few.

Which classic books have particularly influenced you?
The works of Theodore Dreiser, Louisa May Alcott, Charles Dickens, Mark Twain, James Baldwin and Zora Hurston have been very important to my development as a writer. Those books made me fall in love with the written word.

No Leader, No Problem:
The Flip Side

What would a book be like if it was told from the point of view of another character? It would not be the book you are talking about tonight, but it would be a very interesting jumping off point for a discussion.

Consider these flip side questions and adapt your own:

- What if one or all of the male characters in *Waiting to Exhale* told his own side of the story? What would it be like and how would the issues change?

- What if *72 Hour Hold* was told in diary form by the daughter and became more like *The Bell Jar* with a teen narrator and less a mother's anxious story?

- What if Walter Mosley moved his crew to Atlanta instead of Los Angeles? How would the stories change?

- What would an E. Lynn Harris novel be like if the Mama Dearest character either narrated from her point of view or transformed into someone with more endearing qualities? How would she see the other characters?

- Can you think of an example of an author answering the previous question in a sequel or a prequel to one of his or her books?

Book Club Style: A Color Purple Flower Celebration

What kind of trees all them flowering? ast Shug. I don't know, I say.
Look like peach, plum, apple, maybe cherry.
But whatever they is, they sure pretty.
—*The Color Purple*

In tribute to divine narrator Celie, glamorous Shug Avery and Nettie, Sofia and the rest of the gang, prepare a Color Purple flower celebration. Gather spring flowers and branches and plan and assign platters. For the largest selection of flowers, the best time to have this club is spring; the best time for fruit and vegetables is summer. But substitutes can be made all year long, a concept book clubs perfected long ago.

Set out for the green market, farm stand, nursery, gourmet grocery or all-in-one supermarket together. If it is spring, you are on the lookout for Easter lilies and blossoming branches of any kind, including peach, apple, almond or dogwood. Bunches of lilies, jonquils and daffodils as well as early wildflowers were on Celie's list, so add it to yours.

If it is summer, you will search for blackberries of all types at the markets and fruit stands. Along the way, you will discover new herbs in large bouquets, poultry, and pork (goose breast, smoked duck, organic pork or wild turkey anyone?). You might even find vegetables you have never heard of to add to the fiddlehead ferns or ramps you might now always throw in your weekly shopping cart. Best of all, you are discovering the market together, so start the celebration early.

And for your salad, don't forget to check for a wide variety of lettuces, cucumbers, radishes and peas in season.

Arrange the branches and don't forget to include Celie's favorite: fortune cookies.

The Indispensable Reading List: Memoir and Nonfiction

MEMOIR

The Autobiography of Malcolm X by Malcolm X as told to Alex Haley

The Autobiography of Martin Luther King, Jr. by Martin Luther King, Jr.,
   Clayborne Carson (editor)

The Autobiography of Medgar Evers edited by Medgar Evers, edited by
   Myrlie Evers-Williams, Manning Marable

Black Boy * by Richard
   Wright

Dreams from My Father: A Story of Race and Inheritance by Barack Obama

Don't Play in the Sun * by Marita Golden

Dust Tracks on a Road by Zora Neale Hurston

Finding Fish by Antwone Fisher

The Fire Next Time by James Baldwin

Gifted Hands by Ben Carson, M.D.

I Know Why the Caged Bird Sings * by Maya Angelou

Life After Life: A Story of Rage and Redemption by Evan Hopkins

Makes Me Wanna Holler: A Young Black Man in America by Nathan
   McCall

Q: The Autobiography of Quincy Jones by Quincy Jones

Soul on Ice by Eldridge Cleaver

What Becomes of the Brokenhearted by E. Lynn Harris

*Publisher includes discussion questions.

NONFICTION

The Angry Black Women's Guide to Life by Denene Millner, Mitzi Miller, Angela Burt-Murrary

At the Hands of Persons Unknown: The Lynching of Black America ★ by Philip Dray

Before the Mayflower: A History of Black America by Lerone Bennett

Blood Done Signed My Name by Timothy B. Tyson

Bright Boulevards, Bold Dreams: The Story of Black Hollywood by Donald Bogle

Carry Me Home: Birmingham, Alabama by Diane McWhorter

Is Bill Cosby Right? by Michael Eric Dyson

Live from Death Row by Mumia Abu-Jamal, introduction by John Wideman

No Disrespect by Sister Souljah

On Her Own Ground: The Life and Times of Madam C. J. Walker ★ by A'Lelia Bundles

The Pact: Three Young Men Make a Promise and Fulfill a Dream by Samson Davis, George Jenkins, Ramek Hunt

Race Matters by Cornell West

Swerve: Reckless Observations from a Post-Modern Girl by Aisha Tyler

Unforgivable Blackness: The Rise and Fall of Jack Johnson by Geoffrey C. Ward

Wrapped in Rainbows: The Life of Zora Neale Hurston by Valerie Boyd

POETRY

Collected Poems of Langston Hughes by Langston Hughes, edited by David Roessel

The Collected Poems of Maya Angelou by Maya Angelou

Love Poems by Nikki Giovanni

The Tween Book Club:
Roll of Thunder, Hear My Cry
by Mildred D. Taylor

Smart, observant Cassie Logan is the narrator in this coming of age story set in Depression-era Mississippi. Readers have long identified with Cassie girl, who loves to hide in small places just to report to us on the action in her close-knit family and the often scary world around her. Cassie, her parents and her tight sibling unit navigate their less happy surroundings, a deeply segregated world.

Mildred D. Taylor's 1976 Newbery Medal–winner is not only a loving portrait of a family, but some of it is also based on her own family's experiences. *Roll of Thunder, Hear My Cry* is also an adventure story in the classic mold. Its action-packed conclusion gives Cassie much to think about and a lot to discuss. "And it came to me that this was one of those known and unknown things, something never spoken, not even to each other."

For every triumph, there is payment due. Everyday events like the distribution of new books have sickening undertones: the children understand that the books they are receiving are the ones deemed worn out and unacceptable by the white students at Jefferson Davis County School. And even young readers might imagine the fate of the Logans' lively friend and troublemaker T. J., who develops a fatal attraction to a pearl-handled pistol. But there was never a dreamier older brother than Stacey Logan.

Roll of Thunder brims with humor, pranks and typical pre-teen behavior—even Cassie can be mischievous. The Depression was a time when a Christmas celebration with gifts was never assured, but always appreciated. The children received books, clothes and oranges as gifts, and they were happy to get them. Life was a shared adventure for the Logan children, who were sometimes rescued by the mysterious, heroic lodger

Mr. Morrison. How could they not learn numerous life lessons? Are there parallels to these experiences today? You can reminisce about sibling adventures, Christmas's past, delicious family picnics, parents' wisdom in the face of adolescent concerns, the arrival of beloved uncles and far-flung family members and as always, trouble at the fair.

The real-life fears of losing everything is all too convincing, but the nostalgic glow is also contagious and will get you imaging a time before TV. Remember copying your name into your first books? Cassie's inscription in *The Three Musketeers* reads: "This book is the property of Miss Cassie Deborah Logan. Christmas, 1933."

Tween satellite club: Some books clubs have junior membership programs to encourage younger people to read and talk about books. Their activities include special annual clubs for adults and young people, service projects and annual parties and teas. If your club doesn't have an outreach for younger members, consider starting one — and inaugurate it at a picnic, Logan family style.

Casting Call

The Boyz N the Hood was beloved by Harlem teen Natasha in *Upstate*, and *The Godfather* is beloved by everyone. *Sparkle* was one of Yancey Braxton's favorite movies of all time. In *Any Way the Wind Blows*, she was offered the lead role in a biography of Lena Horne—shutting out Vanessa Williams, Halle Berry and Sanaa Lathan in the process. Hey, that's why they call it fiction!

Movies throw a big shadow on our favorite characters and serve a purpose for our authors: we can know more about a character by who they follow on the big screen. And casting books and remaking movies is always a big book club activity. We simply must keep up with the new stars on the rise and old stars who are given new orbits (paging Alfre Woodard).

Nick Cannon and Naomie Harris as the thwarted Antonio and Natasha in *Upstate*? Gabriel Union in a remake of *Waiting to Exhale*? Kerry Washington as Shug Avery *or* Celie in the new movie version *The Color Purple* based on the Broadway show? And who could fill Denzel Washington's shoes as Easy Rawlins? Many filmgoers thought the 1995 movie of *Devil in the Blue Dress* starring Denzel Washington, as well as actor's actor Don Cheadle as Mouse, and directed by Carl Franklin was a classic, if underrated, movie. "I don't see why Denzel can't continue," says Kamal Larsuel-Ulbricht, also known as The Diva on her definitive movie website 3blackchicks.com

Her other picks? "I would like to see Will Smith or Jamie Foxx take on *To Kill a Mockingbird*, which is a hard sell because the first version is nearly perfect," she says. Larsuel-Ulbricht would also like to see an updated version of *Wuthering Heights* and *Little Women* with Regina King, Vivica Fox and Kimberly Elise. As for the remake of *The Color Purple*, Elise is up again as Celie.

Remember *Coffy* ("You're in danger, girl"), *Black Heat* and *Foxy Brown*? Larsuel-Ulbricht would love a full slate of these blaxplotation classics remade. "I think that would be fun," she says.

Book Club Supper:
Edna Lewis and Scott Peacock's
Macaroni and Cheese

MAKES ENOUGH TO SERVE 10

1¾ cups (8 ounces) elbow macaroni

Salt

5 ounces extra sharp cheddar cheese cut into ½-inch cubes (about 1¼ cups)

2 tablespoons plus 1 teaspoon all-purpose flour

1½ teaspoons salt

1½ teaspoons dry mustard

¼ teaspoon freshly ground black pepper

⅛ teaspoon cayenne pepper

¼ teaspoon freshly grated nutmeg

⅔ cup sour cream

2 eggs, lightly beaten

⅓ cup grated onion

1½ cups half-and-half

1½ cups heavy cream

1 teaspoon Worcestershire sauce

1⅔ cups grated extra sharp cheddar cheese (6 ounces)

Cook the macaroni in a large pot of boiling salted water until just tender. Drain well and transfer to a buttered 9 × 13 × 2-inch baking dish. Mix in the cubed cheddar cheese.

Preheat the oven to 350 degrees.

Put the flour, 1½ teaspoons salt, dry mustard, black pepper, cayenne pepper and nutmeg in a large mixing bowl, and stir to blend. Add the sour cream, followed by the eggs, and stir with a wire whisk until well blended and homogenous. Whisk in the onion, half-and-half, heavy cream and Worcestershire sauce until blended. Pour this custard over the macaroni and cubed cheese, and stir to blend. Sprinkle the grated cheese evenly over the surface of the custard. Bake in the preheated oven until the custard is set around the edges of the baking dish but still a bit loose in the center, about 30 minutes.

Remove from the oven, and cool for 10 minutes to allow the custard to thicken.

Deviled Eggs Yancey Braxton

MAKES 24 HALVES

Yancey liked her deviled eggs "with a touch of caviar," but you can choose from a variety of toppings. Yancey should note, there is a wide selection of caviar, salmon roe or golden trout caviar in every price range in the supermarket or gourmet groceries.

    1 dozen large eggs, hard-boiled, and cooled
    4 tablespoons mayonnaise
    1 tablespoon Dijon mustard
    Salt and pepper to taste
    Hot sauce to taste
    Topping options: Caviar, salmon roe, golden trout caviar, sliced sweet pickle,
        fresh cracked pepper, fresh chopped chives or any other fresh herbs, or
        sweet paprika

Peel the eggs and cut them in half lengthwise. Carefully remove the yolks and place in a large bowl. Mash the egg yolks with the mayonnaise until smooth, then add the mustard and salt, pepper and hot sauce to taste.

Spoon this mixture back into the egg halves and refrigerate. When ready to serve, add the caviar Yancey-style or your own choice of toppings.

Cooking hard-boiled eggs: Everyone has a favorite cooking method for hard-boiled eggs. Edna Lewis and Scott Peacock suggest putting the eggs in a large saucepan, pouring in enough water to cover them by 2 inches. They further suggest adding a tablespoon of salt and a tablespoon of vinegar, bringing the eggs to a hard boil over high heat, and then removing from the heat immediately and covering. "Let sit covered for exactly 10 minutes. Pour off the hot water and immediately run cool tap water over the eggs to cool them and stop the cooking. Shake the pan as you do so, to crack the eggshells gently all over," according to Lewis and Peacock.

Frisee Salad with Garlic Vinaigrette in Honor of Easy Rawlins

SERVES 8

Easy Rawlins loved the green salad at The Oxford, especially the strong garlic vinaigrette component. Adjust garlic to taste.

- 4–5 whole, large cloves garlic, peeled and minced or pressed
- 4 tablespoons vinegar
- 1 teaspoon salt
- ⅔ cup extra virgin olive oil
- 2 heads frisee lettuce or a combination frisee and mixed lettuces including romaine
- 2 cups whole cherry tomatoes
- 2 cups cut green beans, fresh or frozen

In a medium bowl, mix together the garlic, vinegar and salt. Add the olive oil in a stream and blend. In a salad bowl, toss the lettuce and vegetables with the dressing. Or serve as a salad compose: a bed of lettuce on each plate, adding the vegetables and dressing, restaurant style.

Apple Martinis in Honor of E. Lynn Harris

MAKES 6 DRINKS

The apple martini became hugely popular in the 1990s and shows no signs of slowing down. Several E. Lynn Harris characters are devoted to them—and these sparkling green drinks look festive at the club.

1 cup apple schnapps
1 cup vodka
2 tablespoons Cointreau
Ice
Thinly sliced Granny Smith apple for garnish

Combine the schnapps vodka, and Cointreau in a pitcher. Transfer to cocktail shaker and shake vigorously with ice. Pour into chilled martini glass, garnish with apple slice and serve.

If You Were in a
1970s Book Club

1970

The Bluest Eye by Toni Morrison

Deliverance by James Dickey

Love Story by Erich Segal

One Hundred Years of Solitude
    by Gabriel Garcia Marquez

Rich Man, Poor Man by Irwin Shaw

The Rising Sun by John Toland

Time and Again by Jack Finney

1971

Angle of Repose by Wallace Stegner

*The Autobiography of Miss Jane
    Pittman* by Ernest J. Gaines

Being There by Jerzy Kosinski

The Bell Jar by Sylvia Plath

Bury My Heart at Wounded Knee
    by Dee Brown

The Day of the Jackal
    by Frederick Forsyth

84 Charing Cross Road
    by Helene Hanff

Eleanor and Franklin by Joseph P. Lash

The Exorcist by William P. Blatty

The Female Eunuch
    by Germaine Greer

Honor Thy Father by Gay Talese

Inside the Third Reich by Albert Speer

Rabbit Redux by John Updike

Summer of '42 by Herman Raucher

The Winds of War by Herman Wouk

1972

August 1914
    by Alexander Solzhenitsyn

The Best and the Brightest
    by David Halberstam

Captains and Kings by Taylor Caldwell

Fear and Loathing in Las Vegas
    by Hunter S. Thompson

Fire in the Lake by Frances Fitzgerald

My Name Is Asher Lev
    by Chaim Potok

The Optimist's Daughter
    by Eudora Welty

Semi-Tough by Dan Jenkins

1973

Breakfast of Champions
    by Kurt Vonnegut Jr.

Burr by Gore Vidal

*Fear and Loathing on the Campaign
    Trail* by Hunter S. Thompson

Fear of Flying by Erica Jong

Gravity's Rainbow
    by Thomas Pynchon

The Honorary Consul
    by Graham Greene

The Odessa File by Frederick Forsyth

Pentimento by Lillian Hellman

Portrait of a Marriage
    by Nigel Nicholson

Sula by Toni Morrison

1974

All the President's Men
   by Carl Bernstein
   and Bob Woodward
All Things Bright and Beautiful
   by James Herriot
Dog Soldiers by Robert Stone
The Gulag Archipelago
   by Aleksandr Solzhenitsyn
Pilgrim at Tinker Creek
   by Annie Dillard
Plain Speaking: An Oral Biography of
   Harry S. Truman by Merle Miller
The Seven Per-Cent-Solution
   by John H. Watson,
   edited by Nicholas Meyer
Something Happened
   by Joseph Heller
Tinker, Tailor, Soldier, Spy
   by John Le Carre
The War between the Tates
   by Alison Lurie
Watership Down by Richard Adams
Zen and the Art of Motorcycle
   Maintenance by Robert Pirsig

1975

Bring on the Empty Horses
   by David Niven
The Choirboys by Joseph Wambaugh
Heat and Dust
   by Ruth Prawer Jhabvala
Humboldt's Gift by Saul Bellow
JR by William Gaddis
Looking for Mister Goodbar
   by Judith Rossner
Ragtime by E. L. Doctorow

The Raj Quartet by Paul Scott
Shogun by James Clavell
Terms of Endearment
   by Larry McMurtry
Without Feathers by Woody Allen

1976

Beautiful Swimmers
   by William W. Warner
Blind Ambition: The White House
   Years by John Dean
Chilly Scenes of Winter by Ann Beattie
The Final Days
   by Bob Woodward
   and Carl Bernstein
The Great Santini by Pat Conroy
Ordinary People by Judith Guest
Passages: The Predictable Crises of
   Adult Life by Gail Sheehy
Roots by Alex Haley
Trinity by Leon Uris
Woman on the Edge of Time
   by Marge Piercy
The Woman Warrior
   by Maxine Hong Kingston

1977

All Things Wise and Wonderful
   by James Herriot
Beggarman, Thief by Irwin Shaw
Blood Tie by Mary Lee Settle
Daniel Martin by John Fowles
Falconer by John Cheever
The Grass Is Always Greener Over
   the Septic Tank
   by Erma Bombeck
Haywire by Brooke Hayward

The Honourable School Boy
by John Le Carre
The Last Cowboy by Jane Kramer
The Shining by Stephen King
Song of Solomon by Toni Morrison
Staying On by Paul Scott
The Thorn Birds
by Colleen McCullough

1978
The Beggar Maid by Alice Munro
The Book Shop
by Penelope Fitzgerald
The Cement Garden by Ian McEwan
*A Distant Mirror: The Calamitous
Fourteenth Century*
by Barbara W. Tuchman
Dress Grey by Lucian K. Truscott
Evergreen by Belva Plain
Eye of the Needle by Ken Follett
The Far Pavilions by M. M. Kaye
Going After Cacciato by Tim O'Brien
Mommie Dearest
by Christina Crawford
*My Mother/My Self: A Daughter's
Search for Identity*
by Nancy Friday
The Sea, the Sea by Iris Murdoch
The Stories of John Cheever
by John Cheever

Tales of the City
by Armistead Maupin
War and Remembrance
by Herman Wouk
The World According to Garp
by John Irving

1979
A Bend in the River by V. S. Naipul
A Dry White Season by Andre Brink
Endless Love by Scott Spencer
The Executioner's Song
by Norman Mailer
The Ghost Writer by Philip Roth
Good as Gold by Joseph Heller
The Hitchhiker's Guide to the Galaxy
by Douglas Adams
*If Life Is a Bowl of Cherries What Am I
Doing in the Pits*
by Erma Bombeck
I'm Dancing as Fast as I Can
by Barbara Gordon
Ironweed by William Kennedy
Sally Hemings
by Barbara Chase Riboud
Smiley's People by John le Carre
Sophie's Choice by William Styron
The Things They Carried
by Tim O'Brien
The White Album by Joan Didion

8

NONFICTION THAT READS LIKE FICTION

"Forgive me, Stephen,
but you give the impression that you are lying down."
—Bill Bryson to Stephen Katz, *A Walk in the Woods*

Have you ever considered how important a character the author is in a work of nonfiction? Bill Bryson and Jon Krakauer may be omnipresent in their books, but can you imagine *A Walk in the Woods* or *Into Thin Air* without them? They would become mere entries into the dullest encyclopedia instead of the crackling portrayals of geography as psychodrama.

We like our authors active—climbing, hiking, and coping or foundering in a foreign land. We like it when they expose themselves to countries and cities, civilizations and historical moments on the rise or on a sad, downward spiral so that they may bring back the real scoop. If they behave as nincompoops in our service, isn't that what they signed up to do? In order to create the atmosphere of a real tale of adventure or history come to life, our authors plunge right in. And as we read and discuss these books, we often stop to wonder: are we reading a novel?

The brand-name authors we follow up the trail and down the dusty streets, around the charming, historic squares of mystery and death and into history and back can be as beloved as fiction favorites Kingsolver, Patchett and McMillan. They render the historic periods and exotic places intimate and understandable. Are people alike everywhere? Doesn't that Chinese auntie remind you of your own and didn't we just see that Afghani uncle at our family reunion? Or do they remain fixed in the exotic and unfamiliar? This is what we are here to discuss.

Pour glasses of Great Wall wine in honor of all foreign babes, any old brewski in honor of Katz or an apple schnapps to recognize the character that is Lady Chablis and discuss how true-life people become larger than life at the hands of the authors who have been there and back.

The Ten Indispensable Titles

■■■

The Devil in the White City: Murder, Magic, and Madness at the Fair That Changed America
(2003) by Erik Larson

A gleaming man-made dreamland of a city built in two years, a serial killer on a quiet, methodical rampage and the world on the brink of the twentieth century. Erik Larson brings together these elements in the story of the 1893 Chicago World's Fair. The narrative techniques are so suspenseful, you will wonder if that Ferris wheel really did succeed.

The task that lay before Daniel Burnham and the top architects of the day was to turn a city best known for its bloody slaughter yards into an exemplar of progress. That the fair became popularly known as "the white city" is a testament to people's faith in that man-made progress. And the descriptions of how the fair was a precursor of our own consumer culture will fascinate. In the book's alternate, ghoulish history, Dr. Henry H. Holmes's chilling ingenuity in luring and destroying young women also reflected the age of science, innovation and the historical moment when huge numbers of young women were coming off the farm into cities for the first time. Holmes took advantage of this situation in ways that are shocking to this day.

Members will enjoy a wide-raging discussion about an era that was filled with optimism and electricity amid crime and poverty. Larson consistently hits the theme of how the fair presaged our own age of entertainment culture with such attractions as Buffalo Bill's Wild West show sensation and the probable influence the fair had on a young Walt Disney: his father, Elias Disney, was a carpenter and furniture maker who was one of the fair's 4,000 workers.

Discussion questions, Vintage Books: Excellent. The major subjects to explore include the late-nineteenth century concept of civic honor, the contrasts between good and evil in a unique setting, and just how Holmes got away with his crimes for so long.

Fun fact: It's the Gilded Age, so Larson includes banquet menus in their entirety. Did you know there was course for cigarettes?

■ ■ ■

Foreign Babes in Beijing:
Behind the Scenes of a New China
(2005) by Rachel DeWoskin

With rudimentary Chinese and a sharp eye for cultural disconnect, Rachel DeWoskin sets off for Beijing to work for an American public relations agency. It is 1989 and big changes are affecting China. One of them is a growing consumer culture, and the author is smack in the middle of it all—she is cast as American vixen Jiexi in a television show called "Foreign Babes in Beijing." A metaphor for the new China and a real experience, *Foreign Babes in Beijing* is DeWoskin's candid story of the expatriate life and a wild, too-funny tale of the show's production, eventually watched by about 600 million viewers. Here, she learns that the Chinese think every American is fat, overly casual in every aspect of life and most of all, over-sexed. (" 'You see what I mean?' the director of photography said to the assistant director. 'Foreign babes are tigers.' ")

Brimming with historical and literary asides and at least one ugly American, the book combines actual lines from the "Foreign Babes" script and dissections of the Chinese language filled with "density and ambiguity." We, like DeWoskin, are offered "dizzying lessons on the intersections between an antique past and a global present." DeWoskin is a charming guide and many of your preconceptions about China will be turned upside down. Begin your discussion here.

Discussion questions, W. W. Norton: Basic. Most useful are the questions about the author's role as outsider and the stereotypical thinking exhibited by both sides.

Furthermore: For a much different approach to the subject of globalization, consider *The World Is Flat* by Thomas L. Friedman. Best-selling author and *New York Times* columnist, Friedman posits that everyone is interconnected globally, rendering borders obsolete. His writing is big picture, while DeWoskin's is at street level. Compare and contrast.

Selling *Foreign Babes in Beijing* to the club: A contemporary story, you could not ask for a more personable portrait of a country on the move. It's also a hilarious look at first job foibles, and certainly the wellspring of many "first job" discussions.

■ ■ ■

In Cold Blood
(1965) by Truman Capote

Considered Truman Capote's crowning and final achievement, *In Cold Blood* places the reader unequivocally in Holcomb, Kansas, in 1959. There, four members of the Clutter family are murdered and the killers have left few clues. Capote famously interweaves the story of the often-frustrating murder investigation with the still-shocking, sympathetic portraits of the killers, Richard Hickock and Perry Smith. "Dick and Perry" are alternately specimens, perpetrators and protagonists, but their execution provides Capote what he needed the most—an ending. *In Cold Blood* is currently enjoying the ultimate resurgence in clubs, spurred on by the uncanny portrayal of Truman Capote by Philip Seymour Hoffman in an Oscar-winning performance.

The author's unmatched skill in rendering real-life people such as Nancy Clutter, the killers and FBI agent Alvin Dewey as characters is child's play compared to his literary pyrotechnics. The language and structure of *In Cold Blood* may be the biggest character of them all. Begin your discussion here: What is in Capote's bag of literary magic tricks that makes *In Cold Blood* a page-turner decades after we know what happened? How does he present the thoughts of the killers, especially Hickock, enabling us to really see the crime? What is real and what does the novelist imagine?

Choose a passage about the wind-bent wheat on the plains of western Kansas and start your investigation.

Audio alert: Scott Brick narrates the exemplary audio version of *In Cold Blood* (Random House Audio Publishing).

DVD alert: *Capote* is a mandatory viewing experience when discussing *In Cold Blood*. Best of all, Catherine Keener costars as Capote's witty sidekick and conscience, Harper Lee.

■ ■ ■

Into Thin Air:
A Personal Account of the Mount Everest Disaster
(1997) by Jon Krakauer

What is the nature of truth in telling a story that results in several deaths? How is blame apportioned? Could a tragedy be avoided and is that even a fair question? Jon Krakauer is on assignment for *Outside* magazine in 1996 to cover a big-ticket expedition to Mount Everest for which each climber has paid up to $65,000 "to be taken safely up Everest." There, he witnesses a natural and human disaster resulting in the deaths of four teammates and several other experienced climbers in a murderous, rogue storm.

One of *Into Thin Air*'s ponderables is the role of Krakauer as a climbing participant, a historian and guide to the history of climbing Everest and, ultimately, as a character in the drama and eyewitness to the impending disaster. Though there have been modern advancements in climbing since the days of Sir Edmund Hillary, who successfully ascended in 1953 to world acclaim, Everest is a beautiful, forbidding landscape of unpredictability and death. Present at Everest during this period were several groups of international climbers and a group of wealthy amateur climbers who are often painted as villains for their indulgences. The most famous of all is "millionaire socialite-cum-climber" Sandy Pittman, who you will talk about all night long. Does it help that Krakauer compares her obliviousness to Jane Austen's Emma?

Foolish mortals versus nature, the role of the Sherpas in the business of climbing Everest, Sandy Pittman versus nature, Krakauer as journalist and moralist—the discussion topics are precise and wide reaching at the same time. He is frustrated and outraged over the decisions made and agonizes often. *Into Thin Air* is a morality tale packed into an adventure story where the heroes are obsessed with the dead.

Furthermore: Jon Krakauer has become a brand-name author of utopian ideas that go awry. Clubs know they are in for a cage match in discussing *Under the Banner of Heaven: A Story of Violent Faith* and *Into the Wild*, true tales told by a master.

■ ■ ■

Midnight in the Garden of Good and Evil
(1994) by John Berendt

New York editor and journalist John Berendt goes native in Savannah, Georgia, and returns with a terrific blend of travel writing at its best, true crime, and memorable, eccentric characters that you will miss and wonder: where are they now? *Midnight in the Garden of Good and Evil* is a story about a town as far away from Mitford as you can possibly get, but the inhabitants are just as engaging. The rogues gallery includes vivacious drag queen Lady Chablis, the matrons of the Married Woman's Card Club and antiques dealer Jim Williams, accused of shooting a small-time hustler, Danny Hansford, and put on trial many times. Williams seems to be channeling Oscar Wilde while at home in his mansion, Mercer House, thus becoming the source of drama, wit and outrage in a book where the spirit of songwriter Johnny Mercer is just one of the many ghosts.

Berendt skillfully informs on matters of race, class, history and even voodoo in a town of semitropical otherness evocatively portrayed here. When discussing *Midnight in the Garden of Good and Evil*, think of other books where the location is the major character and the cover is as important to the story as any of the words.

Discussion questions, Vintage Books: Very good—a useful and clever stroll through the characters' foibles and their importance to the story. The heart of the matter is Jim Williams, and there are several questions about him, the Nazi-flag episode, his character and the role of his homosexuality in a town preoccupied with class.

Cocktails: In Savannah, the locals' first question is always, "What would you like to drink?" Here, the answer is champagne cocktails, martinis delivered in wicker baskets, pitchers of Manhattans, sherry and tea punch, and an apple schnapps for Lady Chablis.

Furthermore: *The City of Falling Angels*, Berendt's latest book, takes us to Venice where we meet the usual cast of eccentric characters in another city where restoration is a serious matter.

Selling *Midnight in the Garden of Good and Evil* to the club: Though it's a nonfiction classic, you will often mistake it for a novel.

■ ■ ■

Parallel Lives: Five Victorian Marriages
(1983) by Phyllis Rose

If the tabloids dispatched their paparazzi to the Reform Club, this is what the crew would turn over to its gleeful editors: unconsummated marriages, cohabitation, joint delusion, secret journals, Thackeray doing the electric slide at a Christmas party arranged by Charles Dickens. *Parallel Lives* is an unfettered series of literary marital portraits, all meticulously presented by Phyllis Rose, a noted scholar of the Victorian era.

It is quite a litany of dysfunctional unions including that of John Ruskin and Effie Gray (unconsummated), Charles Dickens and Catherine Hogarth (they had ten children together before the internationally famous author judged her unworthy and cast her aside), John Stuart Mill and Harriet Taylor (platonic), Thomas Carlyle and Jane Welsh (Jane was reduced to unappreciated drone) and George Eliot and George Henry Lewes (the happiest couple, they never married, preferring to live in sin).

The title itself may begin the discussion. What is the author telling us about these marriages and the times? Is the concept of "parallel" and non-intersecting relationships strictly a Victorian one or is it also a contemporary concept? Clubs will also want to discuss the era's ideas about chastity, courtship and marriage, and especially the role of women viewed legally as the husband's property. How strange and unhappy these couples appear to us, and though the growing reform movement resulted in the Marriage Reform Act, divorce was rare until after World War I. Have a ripping discussion of these exceptional people in exceptional times.

Your favorite villain: One fiery discussion may involve who comes off the worst in *Parallel Lives*. There are many villains from which to choose (John Stuart Mill, anyone?), but most have the most famous author in their crosshair: Charles Dickens. The beloved Father Christmas becomes cruel and unfeeling in the Scrooge or Uriah Heep mode.

Selling *Parallel Lives* to the club: So many of our subjects—love, marriage, relationships, power, authority—are encapsulated here, you will be thoroughly engrossed.

■■■

The Planets
(2005) by Dava Sobel

Book clubs' favorite science writer, Dava Sobel (*Longitude, Galileo's Daughter*) returns with *The Planets*, a dreamy meditation on the solar system. It is an unexpected treat, even for the nonscientifically inclined. Using a combination of techniques from memoir to imagined history (a letter from Caroline Herschel to American astronomer Maria Mitchell, two female pioneers in the field), Sobel makes us care about each and every orb in the sky. Her planetary character studies are filled with mystery and drama. Don't miss the Venus chapter ("Beauty") where all of the poets including William Blake, Tennyson, Wordsworth and Frost are called forth to comment on her. Virgin or vamp? Begin your discussion here.

The "limitless strangeness of the planets constrasted sharply with their small census" is one way to describe each planet's mysterious appeal to the young Dava—and to the poets and ancient masters. Sobel often poses discussion questions in the form of musings: "Is it an accident that the Solar System's sole inhabited planet possesses the only satellite precisely sized to create the spectacle of a total solar eclipse? Or is this startling manifestation of the Sun's hidden splendor part of a divine design?" Choose your favorite planet and its most alluring poem and defend it as you would a character in a novel.

Poor Pluto! Discussion sourcing: Discoveries of new planets and discussions of demoting Pluto from the "cultural" solar system we know so well is big news. To the accompaniment of "The Planets, Suite for Orchestra" by Gustav Holst ("Music of the Spheres" is one of the chapters), discuss recent articles ("You Call That a Planet?" by Megan O'Connor, for example, appeared as an Explainer column on slate.com, August 2, 2005) and create your own solar system. Consider calling in an expert—scientist, librarian, theologian or poet—to help you discuss the state of the galaxy and beyond.

Selling *The Planets* to the club: Sobel's tone poem will appeal to all club members who love astronomy *and* astrology, colors, etymology and poetry.

■ ■ ■

The Professor and the Madman:
A Tale of Murder, Insanity,
and the Making of the Oxford English Dictionary
(1998) by Simon Winchester

Gather round the Scriptorium and consider the tale of Dr. W. C. Minor, a former U.S. Army surgeon who may or may not have been driven around the bend by the Battle of the Wilderness when he had to brand deserting Irish soldiers during the Civil War. Moving to London, he commits a random murder and is sent to what was then an enlightened insane asylum, Broadmoor. During his long imprisonment, he submitted over 400,000 definitions to the Oxford English Dictionary and began a long, poignant friendship with Professor James Murray, the brilliant editor of the dictionary.

Master storyteller Simon Winchester describes several shocking crimes and one even more shocking instance of self-mutilation amid a portrait of an era of premodern medicine. For those of us who love words, *The Professor and the Madman* cleverly combines palpable history, the personal story of these two men and a short history of the dictionary. Did you know that our word "serendipity" came from Serendib, the name Arab sea traders gave to Sri Lanka, further enhanced by a fanciful story by Horace Walpole? For a book about a dictionary begun in 1857 and not completed until 1927, *The Professor and the Madman* is suspenseful and sometimes astonishing. Dictionary definitions of key words ("murder," "polymath," "philology," "lunatic," "bedlam") lead each chapter, and fans of book design will enjoy the Victorian type illustrations.

Discussion questions, Harper Perennial: Basic, the many short questions will get you started. The question about the mutilation is handled with sensitivity and gives nothing away. Much of the discussion will center around our shifting sympathies with the sad, mad doctor.

Futhermore: Winchester is a master of popular history and he is prolific. *Krakatoa: The Day the World Expoded: August 27, 1883* tells the story of the volcanic island's violent eruption followed by a tsunami that killed 40,000 people. In *A Crack at the Edge of the World: America and the Great California Earthquake of 1906*, he creates suspense though we know the story so well.

■ ■ ■

Seabiscuit: An American Legend
(2001) by Laura Hillenbrand

An exuberant, suspenseful depiction of the 1930s horse-racing culture that produced national idol Seabiscuit has made Laura Hillenbrand's book a beloved nonfiction must-read. She treats the major figures as characters, especially Charles Howard, Seabiscuit's owner and California rancher who was General Motors' largest distributors of cars and is a character in his own right. Seabiscuit's trainer Tom Smith, the original horse whisperer, who the Indians nicknamed "Lone Plainsman," and Red Pollard, a poor, accident-prone jockey who understood and rode the Biscuit in some of his greatest races, round out the cast.

It is a western story and the ironies are not lost on the author. "Throughout the West, frontier regions that had long revolved around the horse were now dotted with sleek, modern Howard dealerships." But it was the intersection of racing, radio, the frenzied media and the industry of escapism that grew out of the Depression that created the legend of Seabiscuit. When we first meet him, he is a laconic underdog who takes nothing seriously. The horse is shipped all over the Northeast and shows little potential. But then Smith sees a glimmer, and it is his training, and Seabiscuit's charming personality and winning ways that makes *Seabiscuit* a real story. As Pollard says of Seabiscuit, "So long as you treat him like a gentleman, he'll run his heart out for you." How Hillenbrand made an old Movietone newsreel such a beguiling story should be first on your discussion agenda.

Discussion guide, Ballantine Reader's Circle: Very good. A conversation with Hillenbrand depicts her own story as she is battling the debilitating chronic fatigue syndrome. There are ten discussion questions revolving around the main "characters," the popularity of Seabiscuit, the jockeys' extreme methods for making weight and the other thoroughbreds on the scene.

Cocktails: Champagne from gigantic golden loving cups at the Turf Club Ball or scotch at The Derby.

Photos that make a difference: Period photos lead each chapter of *Seabiscuit* and each is worthy of a place in your discussion. How do they contribute to your appreciation of the story and the times?

■ ■ ■

A Walk in the Woods: Rediscovering America on the Appalachian Trail
(1998) by Bill Bryson

In the great literary tradition of author as patsy, Bill Bryson sets off to hike the Appalachian Trail accompanied by yet another literary tradition, the fleshy sidekick. Stephen Katz is slothful, funny, vengeful and glorious, and just one of the reasons *A Walk in the Woods* has endeared itself to book clubs. Interspersed with the travails of hiking the trial in early spring, when the weather is more Arctic than Georgian, Bryson offers fascinating facts about the AT, its flora and fauna, its topography and what is becoming an ecological minefield growing up alongside the trails.

Clubs love to discuss Bryson's discourses on the sum of all fears a hiker can experience, including, but not limited to, bears (black and grizzly), murders, hypothermia and out-of-shape, middle-aged bodies unused to vigorous hiking, especially on a diet of noodles and Little Debbies.

We are lucky to be along for the walk. As Bryson and Katz trudge along the trail Bryson describes on the first page as "meandering in a dangerously beguiling fashion," the duo become fitter and stronger even as they take days off from the trail in small towns to eat pie, drink beer and in the case of Katz, meet Beulah ("Oh, she's a big woman") in a laundromat. He then must run for his life from her husband. Club members will not be able to contain themselves in retelling their own hiking stories and narrow escapes to compete with Bryson's. It will be a tough competition.

The correct way to serve Little Debbies: Room temperature.

Audio alert: Rob McQuay is the voice of Bryson in an audio version of *A Walk in the Woods* (Books on Tape). He is supremely droll in both roles as the author and Katz himself, with just the right touch of exasperation and hope.

Furthermore: Bryson's work is a can't-miss selection, and clubs are reading *A Short History of Nearly Everything*, *In a Sunburned Country* and *I'm a Stranger Here Myself: Notes on Returning to America After Twenty Years Away* while awaiting his next opus.

Selling *A Walk in the Woods* to the club: Fellow members will thank you with tears in their eyes for selecting it.

No Leader, No Problem: Meeting Style

Book club life is just like high school where everyone is competing for the highest possible club attendance. A few simple rules:

- Make sure you have enough of everything. You don't want to see your friends fighting over that last cracker.
- Serve the simplest food on large white oval platters.
- Make just one dish, but use only the freshest ingredients.
- Invest in a serving tray—nothing says hospitality better than twelve glasses arranged on a tray, presented to the club.
- Be on the lookout all year long for little book-related presents for your club.
- Choose the perfect paper napkins.
- Show and use your collections no matter how modest (books from the library sale) or grand (your prized porcelain teacups).
- You may not have the Duchess of Richmond's porcelain, but take charge of organizing a trip to see it at the local museum.
- Never let the summer go by without meeting outdoors.
- Keep your books, pens, pads and related papers in a beautiful woven basket, right by your chair.
- Send everyone home with a small bouquet, a book or an idea.

The Indispensable Reading List: Biographies

A Beautiful Mind: The Life of Mathematical Genius and Nobel Laureate John Nash by Sylvia Nasar

Alexander Hamilton by Ron Chernow

Desert Queen: The Extraordinary Life of Gertrude Bell★ by Janet Wallach

Founding Brothers: The Revolutionary Generation★ by Joseph J. Ellis

Galileo's Daughter★ by Dava Sobel

Isak Dinesen: The Life of a Storyteller by Judith Thurman

John Adams by David McCullough

Kate Remembered by A. Scott Berg

Lindbergh by A. Scott Berg

Mornings on Horseback: The Story of an Extraordinary Family, a Vanished Way of Life and the Unique Child who Became Theodore Roosevelt by David McCullough

Nightingales: The Extraordinary Upbringing and Curious Life of Miss Florence Nightingale★ by Gillian Gill

The Rise of Theodore Roosevelt by Edmund Morris

Saint-Exupery by Stacy Schiff

Savage Beauty: The Life of Edna St. Vincent Millay by Nancy Milford

Secrets of the Flesh: A Life of Colette★ by Judith Thurman

Theodore Roosevelt by Edmund Morris

Truman by David McCullough

Vera (Mrs. Vladimir Nabokov)★ by Stacy Schiff

Will in the World: How Shakespeare Became Shakespeare by Stephen Greenblatt

★Publisher's discussion questions available.

Savannah Style

Lucille Wright was Jim Williams' caterer and her menu for the first Christmas party (we're not exactly sure what was served at the second, "gentleman-only" party)—cheese straws, marinated shrimp, roast hams, turkey and oysters, tomato finger sandwiches—were a fixture of the Savannah party scene.

In *Midnight in the Garden of Good and Evil*, men owned their own white tie and tails and took their parties very seriously, engraved invitations and all.

Spin a few Johnny Mercer ballads, arrange the white dogwood blossoms, fresh palmetto fronds, cedar boughs and magnolia leaves, take out your silver goblets and Queen Alexandra's silverware and get ready to party—just don't ring the doorbell.

A Savannah-style menu:

- Tomato finger sandwiches
- Sherry and tea punch
- Cheese straws in tall container (small vase, glass or pitcher) lined with linen napkin.

Serve all on a silver tray, with linen napkin.

The Indispensable Reading List:
The Arcane Thriller

The Club Dumas ★
  by Arturo Perez-Reverte
The Coffee Trader★ by David Liss
A Conspiracy of Paper★
  by David Liss
The Dante Club★ by Matthew Pearl
The Da Vinci Code★ by Dan Brown
A Death in Vienna by Daniel Silva
The Egyptologist★ by Arthur Phillips
The Eyre Affair★ by Jasper Fforde
The Flanders Panel
  by Arturo Perez-Reverte
Foucault's Pendulum
  by Umberto Eco
The Geographer's Library
  by Jon Fasman

The Historian★
  by Elizabeth Kostova
Lempriere's Dictionary
  by Lawrence Norfolk
My Name is Red by Orhan Pamuk
The Name of the Rose
  by Umberto Eco
Possession★ by A. S. Byatt
The Rule of Four★
  by Ian Caldwell
  and Dustin Thomason
Shadow of the Wind★
  by Carlos Ruiz Zafon
A Spectacle of Corruption★
  by David Liss
The World to Come by Dara Horn

★*Publisher includes discussion questions.*

A Restaurant Meeting

You would gladly meet the gang at the Three Jolly Bargemen, the Blue Boar, or Pip's club, Finches of the Grove. You would take a taxi to The Saloon on Broadway or B. Smith's in New York's theater district if you were beckoned by E. Lynn Harris. Or you might gather at P. J. Clark's if you were summoning the spirit of *Breakfast at Tiffany's* or at the Berghoff in Chicago for a more grounded moment in *The Time Traveler's Wife*. You could take the prose portal for the restaurants of the imagination: crab cakes at Rick Rack's Café in *Ladder of Years* or chicken biryani at the Wayside Inn in *A Fine Balance*. You could time travel to Rectors at Clark and Monroe, Sherry's or Delmonicos in New York or a teahouse in the Gion district, Geisha style.

If you live in a big city, your club can often pinpoint the same restaurant the characters inhabited, or a reasonable facsimile. If you don't, you can get close by choosing the cuisine and even the right kind of atmosphere. But some clubs meet in restaurants all the time, finding one at the midway point, especially when they live far away from each other. Or they celebrate birthdays and club anniversaries. Others think of a restaurant meeting as a treat for holiday time or as a reward for the completion and discussion of a particularly large or challenging book.

Whether you go all the time or rarely, here's how to plan:

- Make a reservation on the early side, before the dinner rush for maximum face time with the waiters and minimum interruptions by everyone else.

- If it's a relatively expensive restaurant, consider a lunch or early dinner if the restaurant can give you special prices.

- Confirm your reservation the day before or the morning of the club with the exact number in attendance. Your consideration will be much appreciated.

- Book a table in the back or in the section of the restaurant where the club's raucous laughter and never-ending banter will least offend other diners.

- Or if you want to be seen, demonstrate the book club spirit in the way-front.

- Consider going to the same restaurant on a regular or semiregular basis so the staff can get to know your preferences. It will become a club within a club.

- Ask the restaurant if they have a prix fixe menu—or can develop one just for your club—that includes appetizers, main course and desserts. Planning in advance will get you over the time-wasting ordering part, and facilitate the discussion.

- Consider a field trip to another city for a specific cuisine mentioned in your favorite book.

- Save all menus and restaurant memorabilia for your club scrapbook or portfolio. In a few years when you look back on your cocktail-napkin notes, you will howl with laughter and recognition.

CLUB COCKTAIL

You mean your club doesn't have one? If you go to your favorite restaurant, they might be able to develop one for you—and you can take the recipe back to your club to make as many times as you wish. You might even be able to work with the bar staff on the literary cocktail of the evening.

Best Generic Discussion Questions for Nonfiction

Using fiction discussion techniques, discuss the protagonist as a character. Who were his or her antagonists? How does he or she overcome obstacles and achieve goals? How does he or she respond to unpredictable events and change?

What narrative techniques did the author use to create the scene, add suspense and tell the story? How well did the author succeed as this?

Did the author succeed in creating a dramatic arc?

Discuss the secondary characters. Did the author develop them? What was their role in the central drama?

What were your original thoughts about the events portrayed? How did they change after reading this book?

How was the factual material presented?

What was the protagonist's legacy?

If the book is historical, what comparisons can you draw to today's world?

Who would you cast for the movie or miniseries?

Supper at the Club:
Anytime Pasta Salad

SERVES 8

½ cup fresh lemon juice

¾ cup extra virgin olive oil

½ teaspoon red pepper flakes

One 1-pound box fussili, rotelle or other small pasta, cooked al dente

1 pound large shrimp

3 tablespoons chopped fresh dill

1 teaspoon chopped fresh tarragon

1 10-ounce package frozen peas, organic if possible, cooked

Shaved Parmesan cheese to taste

Salt and pepper to taste

Optional ingredients to include or substitute:

Roasted Cherry Tomatoes (see recipe chapter 4)

Steamed broccoli

Fresh herbs such as rosemary or thyme

Red, yellow and orange peppers, diced raw or roasted

Fresh peas

Asparagus cut on the diagonal

Plum tomatoes diced and seeded

Grilled eggplant

In a large bowl, mix together lemon juice, olive oil and pepper flakes. Add the pasta, shrimp, herbs and peas (and/or any of the substitutes). Garnish with shaved Parmesan, salt and pepper to taste.

Travel tip: This is a perfect last-minute dish to bring to the club, depending on what you have on hand. Mix all ingredients, leaving out the shrimp and peas until ready to serve.

Mixed Greens with Blackberry Vinaigrette

SERVES 8

2 cups fresh blackberries or frozen blackberries, drained

¼ cup apple cider vinegar

2 tablespoons honey

1 cup extra virgin olive oil

Salt, pepper and fresh herbs to taste

Assorted baby greens including mesclun, Bibb lettuce or curly endive, rinsed
   well and dried

1½ cups walnuts, toasted

Small package (about 6 ounces) goat cheese, sliced or crumbled

Blend 1 cup of the blackberries in a blender until smooth. Add the apple cider vinegar and honey and blend. Blend in the oil in a thin stream.

Strain the mixture into a medium bowl adding salt, pepper and fresh herbs to taste, and refrigerate.

When ready to serve, toss the vinaigrette with the greens. Add toasted walnuts and goat cheese. Garnish with remaining fresh blackberries.

Ina Garten's
Chocolate Chunk Cookies

MAKES 36–40 COOKIES

These cookies are so good. They're crisp on the outside and creamy on the inside, and the chocolate chunks make them just so gooey. Be sure to use chocolate chunks because chocolate chips don't have enough chocolate flavor. It's important to underbake the cookies to get the right texture.

—Ina Garten

½ pound unsalted butter at room temperature

1 cup light brown sugar, packed

½ cup granulated sugar

2 teaspoons pure vanilla extract

2 extra-large eggs at room temperature

2 cups all-purpose flour

1 teaspoon baking soda

1 teaspoon kosher salt

1½ cups chopped walnuts

1¼ pounds semisweet chocolate chunks

Preheat the oven to 350 degrees.

Cream the butter and two sugars until light and fluffy in the bowl of an electric mixer fitted with the paddle attachment. Add the vanilla, then the eggs, one at a time, and mix well. Sift together the flour, baking soda, and salt and add to the butter with the mixer on low speed, mixing only until combined. Fold in the walnuts and chocolate chunks.

Drop the dough on a baking sheet lined with parchment paper, using a 1¾-inch–diameter ice cream scoop or a rounded tablespoon. Dampen your hands and flatten the dough slightly. Bake for exactly 15 minutes (the cookies will seem underdone). Remove from the oven and let cool slightly on the pan, then transfer to a wire rack to cool completely.

Nestlé makes chocolate chunks that are perfect for this recipe.

If You Were in a 1980s Book Club

1980

The Clan of the Cave Bear by Jean Auel
A Confederacy of Dunces
    by John Kennedy Toole
Cosmos by Carl Sagan
Loon Lake by E. L. Doctorow
The Lords of Discipline by Pat Conroy
Midnight's Children by Salman Rushdie
The Third Wave by Alvin Toffler
Thy Neighbor's Wife by Gay Talese
The Women of Brewster Place
    by Gloria Naylor

1981

The Chaneysville Incident
    by David Bradley
The Glitter Dome
    by Joseph Wambaugh
Gorky Park by Martin Cruz Smith
The Hotel New Hampshire
    by John Irving
Housekeeping by Marilynne Robinson
An Indecent Obsession
    by Colleen McCullough
*Mrs. Harris: The Death of the Scarsdale
    Diet Doctor* by Diana Trilling
Noble House by James Clavell
Rabbit Is Rich by John Updike
The Soul of the New Machine
    by Tracy Kidder
The White Hotel by D. M. Thomas

1982

The Color Purple by Alice Walker
Dinner at the Homesick Restaurant
    by Anne Tyler

The Fate of the Earth
    by Jonathan Schell
Growing Up by Russell Baker
Is There No Place on Earth for Me?
    by Susan Sheehan
Master of the Game
    by Sidney Sheldon
The Mists of Avalon
    by Marion Zimmer Bradley
The Mosquito Coast by Paul Theroux
Sassafras, Cypress and Indigo
    by Ntozake Shange

1983

At the Bottom of the River
    by Jamaica Kincaid
Blue Highways: A Journey into America
    by William Least Heat Moon
Fatal Vision by Joe McGinnis
A Gathering of Old Men
    by Ernest J. Gaines
The Little Drummer Girl
    by John Le Carre
*Motherhood: The Second Oldest
    Profession* by Erma Bombeck
The Name of the Rose
    by Umberto Eco
Out on a Limb by Shirley MacLaine

1984

". . . And Ladies of the Club"
    by Helen Hooven Santmyer
Empire of the Sun by J. G. Ballard
Flaubert's Parrot by Julian Barnes
*The Good War: An Oral History of
    World War Two* by Studs Terkel

Hotel du Lac by Anita Brookner
Love Medicine by Louise Erdrich
Small World by David Lodge
Stones for Ibarra by Harriet Doerr
The Unbearable Lightness of Being
    by Milan Kundera
Wired: The Short Life and Fast Times
    of John Belushi
    by Bob Woodward

1985
The Accidental Tourist by Anne Tyler
The Beans of Egypt, Maine
    by Carolyn Chute
The Bone People by Keri Hulme
The Cider House Rules by John Irving
Continental Drift by Russell Banks
Dancing in the Light
    by Shirley MacLaine
The Handmaid's Tale
    by Margaret Atwood
House by Tracy Kidder
The House of Spirits by Isabel Allende
Lake Wobegon Days
    by Garrison Keillor
Lonesome Dove by Larry McMurtry
White Noise by Don DeLillo

1986
Fatherhood by Bill Cosby
It by Stephen King
Perfume by Patrick Suskind
The Prince of Tides by Pat Conroy
The Sportswriter by Richard Ford

1987
Beloved by Toni Morrison
The Bonfire of the Vanities
    by Tom Wolfe
The Child in Time by Ian McEwan
The Closing of the American Mind
    by Allan Bloom

Crossing to Safety
    by Wallace Stegner
Ellen Foster by Kaye Gibbons
Fried Green Tomatoes at the Whistle
    Stop Café by Fannie Flagg
Moon Tiger by Penelope Lively
Presumed Innocent by Scott Turow
That Night by Alice McDermott

1988
The Bean Trees by Barbara Kingsolver
Breathing Lessons by Anne Tyler
A Brief History of Time
    by Stephen Hawking
Cat's Eye by Margaret Atwood
Coming of Age in the Milky Way
    by Timothy Ferris
Fair and Tender Ladies by Lee Smith
From Beirut to Jerusalem
    by Thomas Friedman
Love in the Time of Cholera
    by Gabriel Garcia Marquez
Oscar and Lucinda by Peter Carey
Paris Trout by Pete Dexter
The Queen of the Damned
    by Anne Rice
World's End by T. C. Boyle

1989
Affliction by Russell Banks
Billy Bathgate by E. L. Doctorow
Geek Love by Katherine Dunn
The Joy Luck Club by Amy Tan
The Mambo Kings Play Songs of Love
    by Oscar Hijuelos
A Prayer for Owen Meany
    by John Irving
The Remains of the Day
    by Kazuo Ishiguro
The Temple of My Familiar
    by Alice Walker
This Boy's Life by Tobias Wolff

9

THE MEMOIR

"Happy birthday. Buy some diaphanous coed a malted.
You don't mind if I say 'diaphanous,' do you?"
—Uncle Charlie, *The Tender Bar*

Everyone has a personal history. But it really comes down to this: the writers who mine the best fossils from his or her personal history will be the ones who are read and discussed. Professor Stephen King tells us this and more in his own superlative excavation, *On Writing: A Memoir of the Craft*.

These memoirists create intimacy in a story that sweeps across history or one that describes pain and love, loss and faith, and the precise color of God. Many of these authors grew up poor with the major exception of Katharine Graham. But her domineering mother and husband combined with the glittery milieu of the nation's capital made her unconfident. And that became her mining expedition.

These are tales of survival, and as we all know by now Mrs. Graham not only survived, she thrived. Almost all of our writers share a common theme: books have often saved their lives. The students in Tehran and China during their countries' cultural revolutions, a boy growing up in Maine or Manhasset or Washington—all turned to classic tales and minute biographies. Jay Gatsby is the fallen hero of the memoirist. His life—and that of his creator—was the ultimate cautionary tale.

Their mothers, fathers, uncles, siblings, friends and teachers speak to us still. What had been lost has been rediscovered and presented anew. All describe a time and place like no other, and the trip to Limerick, British East Africa, the Pacific Northwest at the end of the Eisenhower administration or the bar down the street is a trip that is ordinary and profound.

Press your khakis and prepare to take a trip with the best tour guides around.

The Ten Indispensable Titles

■ ■ ■

Angela's Ashes
(1996) by Frank McCourt

Dipping into the powerful, lyrical language of Frank McCourt's classic memoir, you will find that the immediacy of the time and place he invokes will always stay with you. From the opening page, in which the author expresses regret that his desperately poor parents left New York during the Depression to move back to an even more desperate Limerick, the McCourt family faces one tragedy after another. The deaths of baby sister Margaret, the twins Oliver and Eugene and the surviving siblings' near starvation are just part of the litany of grief. The family begs for food and fights rats and disease next to the Shannon, the river that kills.

Most poignant of all is the portrait of McCourt's parents: the long-suffering Angela of the title and the charming, drunken Malachy who asks his sons to die for Ireland and can't help but drink his wages even during World War II when everyone was working. Though the story is unbelievably sad, McCourt's great triumph is the humor and honesty reflected in the unflinching and funny writing ("Above all—we were wet"). You may sigh, but you never look away. Instead, you are delighted to have met the family.

Discussion questions, Scribner: Very good. Why, indeed, does this memoir stand out among so many others? Other topics include the originality of McCourt's style, the way in which the Catholic Church informed the lives of the McCourt family, the Irish songs and of course McCourt's father, about whom you will not stop talking about.

Furthermore: To extend the theme of New York immigrant life, revisit the beloved *A Tree Grows in Brooklyn*. Betty Smith's 1943 novel of plucky, smart Francie Nolan and her coming-of-age-story set the standard for realism that combines humor and great sadness. Francies father could be kin to Malachy McCourt and he might also break your heart.

Fun fact: *'Tis: A Memoir*, McCourt's 1999 sequel to *Angela's Ashes*, was a selection of the Carmella Soprano book club.

Selling *Angela's Ashes* to the club: Your club started meeting after *Angela's Ashes* became a huge best seller and after it won a Pulitzer Prize—do not delay selecting this book.

▪ ▪ ▪

The Color of Water: A Black Man's Tribute to His White Mother
(1996) by James McBride

Forget for a moment all of the tributes, accolades and anointments as *the* book of the One Town, One Read movement. Think of *The Color of Water* as the heartfelt, incredible life story of Ruth McBride Jordan and her children. "Mommy" was Ruth Shilsky, the daughter of a rabbi growing up in a deeply unhappy Orthodox Jewish home in Virginia. Ruth escapes to New York, falls in love with the remarkable Andrew McBride, a black man, eventually raising twelve children. All of them went to college and as McBride proudly states, many went on to graduate school.

Ruth was the family's commander in chief, a terrible church singer and an indomitable force always insisting on the best from each of her children. McBride portrays her as a strange and powerful figure, transformed by the love of her husbands and of Christianity. Gradually, we learn Ruth's American story told in her own words: "Love didn't come natural to me until I became a Christian." It is her explanation for the color of God's spirit that becomes the title. " 'It doesn't have a color,' she said. 'God is the color of water. Water doesn't have a color.' "

But for McBride, growing up the child of a white mother who described herself as "light-skinned" was not easy—or explicable—and that is the power of this story. He relates that he was embarrassed by this eccentric who never told her children the truth about her past. He was angry at the world. McBride describes his eventual turnaround movingly. Don't miss the loving portrayal of Andrew McBride's life, made all the more poignant by his death months before the author was born.

Penguin Reading Group Guide: Good. The questions cover all the basics including the siblings' different reactions to the civil rights era and especially the life and contradictions of Ruth.

For further discussion: In many memoirs, the author recalls the time in his or her life when they were struggling, living in tiny dwellings, perhaps newly married. James McBride's mother was no different and remembered a one-room kitchenette in New York City, home to two adults and four children, as the happiest of her life. What does this say about the nature of memory and what does it communicate about an author?

■ ■ ■

On Writing: A Memoir of the Craft
(2000) by Stephen King

Attention, club. Professor Stephen King, prolific and beloved novelist and sometimes journalist, is here to teach us a thing or two about writing. Short sentences can be perfect. Vocabulary goes on the top shelf of your toolbox. Toss out what is not working ("Murder your darlings"). The adverb is not your friend. King invokes this bit of advice darkly, but *On Writing* will be remembered as one of his friendliest books.

It begins as a traditional memoir of a boy who was raised by a single mother and who fell in love with writing at an early age. His first best seller, sold to classmates, was a retelling of *The Pit and the Pendulum*. King's battles with alcohol, the support of his wife, Tabitha, and the awful accident that could have killed him in 1999 are also included. But the source of *On Writing*'s profound reputation is the course King offers on his craft: how to begin writing (close the door), how much to write (every single day), what to write (doesn't matter as long as it's the truth). He'll also tell you when it's time to open the door to test your material on Ideal Reader.

Best of all, King insists that to be a writer, you have write a lot and read a lot. No problem!

King demystifies the writing experience in his own style that is by turns practical, subversive and often profane. His influences vary wildly from *The Elements of Style* by William Strunk Jr. and E. B. White to the taut dialogue of his pal, Elmore Leonard. And throughout there are love letters to his favorite subject. "Books," King writes, "are a uniquely portable magic." King concludes with a wonderfully idiosyncratic book list.

Discussion questions, Pocket Books: Excellent. The questions will work if you are in a book club or a writing group. King's themes of reading extensively, excavating a good story from the ground up "like fossils in the ground," and debunking myths about writing at a fantasy desk will engender a unique and exuberant discussion. "Life isn't a support-system for art. It's the other way around."

Selling *On Writing* to the club: This is the book everyone is reading—and marking up feverishly.

■ ■ ■

Out of Africa
(1937) by Isak Dinesen

Writing under the pen name Isak Dinesen, Baroness Karen Blixen wrote about her experiences as a coffee plantation owner in British East Africa from 1914 to 1931. Readers love her account of colonial life where our baroness bags a few lions before breakfast and nurses the Africans who consider her a healer. Her place becomes a colonial frat house where many bwanas stay when back from safari, leaving their books and gramophone records. Most notable among her lodgers is big-game hunter Denys Finch-Hatton, memorably played by Robert Redford in the 1985 movie opposite Meryl Streep as Dinesen.

Life on the farm is filled with travails but also stunning beauty, and you will love discussing the simple elegance of Dinesen's philosophy. The author was particularly apt at capturing each character's voice. After the

Prince of Wales pays a visit, her beloved cook Kamante asks: "Did the son of the Sultan like the sauce of the pig? Did he eat it all?" Throughout the book, Dinesen crafts her own African folktales of day-to-day, and often hand-to-mouth, existence.

Don't miss the antics of adorable antelope Lulu, as small as a cat, and the splendid descriptions of this deep and mysterious land of "mighty, weightless, ever-changing clouds towering up and sailing on," grass, hill and endless stars. Clubs love to discuss the baroness's flying adventures with Finch-Hatton. She equates these flights with freedom, romance, beauty and eventually death. Dinesen even poses her own discussion question: "We came to discuss the question of whether, if we were offered a pair of real wings, which could never be laid off, we would accept or decline the offer."

Cocktails: At 11 A.M. in the forest. Champagne served in Danish stemware.

Dressing thematically: Vintage Ralph Lauren safari wear or the latest in game-reserve attire.

■ ■ ■

Personal History
(1997) by Katharine Graham

Has anyone had a more dramatic arc to her life? From the cover, a movie-star-type mother of the old Hollywood system looks out sternly, pearls at the throat. But inside, the Pulitzer Prize–winning memoir by *Washington Post* owner Katharine Graham tells a story of struggle rooted in the her insecurities and the times in which she lived.

Personal History, published just four years before Graham died in 2001, has been embraced by book clubs since it came out. Members have relished the family's story and her quick marriage to the brilliant, charming but increasingly mentally ill Philip Graham. The great events of the twentieth century mingle with family friends as the author gives us Washington's real inside story. The Pentagon Papers and Watergate era, when Graham did so much to hold her company together in the face of mounting Nixon administration hardball, are especially worthy of discussion.

Clubs also relish the details of Graham's many worlds. She describes how business really gets done in Washington, upper-class life and the famous Black and White Ball Truman Capote staged in her "honor" at the Plaza Hotel. Graham relishes descriptions of the intricate workings of a great newspaper in what can often be a small town. Her confessional tone that often moves from bafflement to total mastery of any situation, from decorating a house to running a big company endears Mrs. Graham to many different types of book clubs and never falls off club reading lists.

Discussion questions, Vintage Books: Excellent. Especially good are the questions about her marriage and how a wife was treated in the halls of power before the civil rights and women's movements. Indeed, if Philip Graham had not committed suicide would Katharine Graham have become Katharine Graham?

Furthermore: For a look at Washington during and after the Watergate era, consider revisiting *All the President's Men* by Bob Woodward and Carl Bernstein and *Heartburn* by Nora Ephron.

■ ■ ■

Reading Lolita in Tehran: A Memoir in Books
(2003) by Azar Nafisi

Although Professor Azar Nafisi's university classes and private book group took place in an atmosphere of Islamic revolution and morality squads, you will immediately recognize the group: the student who loved Mr. Darcy to the exclusion of any real man, the know-it-alls and the teacher's pets who bring bunches of flowers to teacher. You will also recognize the shared intimacy that these discussion groups engendered, made all the more necessary by the world crashing down around them.

For Nafisi's themes are how books can save lives and how the great authors—Vladimir Nabokov, Jane Austen, Henry James, F. Scott Fitzgerald—can give readers the gift of empathy. Nafisi teaches her students to empathize even with Humbert Humbert. Fiction becomes "a magic eye" during the arbitrariness and uncertainty of the totalitarian regime. The students compared their predicament to that of the orphaned Lolita's, another teenage prisoner. "Like my students, Lolita's past comes to her not so much as a loss but as a lack, and like my students, she becomes a figment in someone else's dream."

Nafisi also makes an excellent case for the heroines of nineteenth-century literature as true revolutionaries, while the dialogue in Austen is "democratic." Metaphors abound. One of Nafisi's most apt is the blind censor whose decisions are designed to enforce the Islamic fundamentalists' tyrannical goals. Nafisi mentions so many books in this memoir, your club will have a syllabus for years to come.

Don't miss: The trial of *The Great Gatsby* with Professor Nafisi for the defense, and the Jane Austen Society dance where the girls performed an homage to the great Austen signature scene, the ball. One of Prof. Nafisi's students, Sanaz, demonstrates the dance, Persian-style.

Discussion questions, Random House: Excellent, a parallel reading experience. The questions connect the dots between the books discussed and how they affect Nafisi's students living in an increasingly hostile regime.

Audio Alert: South African actor and playwright Lisette Lecat narrates *Reading Lolita in Tehran* (Recorded Books), and she makes you feel as if you are in the classroom with the one of the world's greatest teachers.

■ ■ ■

The Tender Bar: A Memoir
(2005) by J. R. Moehringer

So James Joyce, Tom Seaver, Nick Carraway and Cliff Claven walk into a bar. Tonight's topics? Philosophy of women, the Mets, Rilke, Batman villains, *The Ginger Man*, *The Quiet Man*, Lincoln, *Macbeth* and the mysteries of the solar system told in bar cherries and olives. It's just one of the great nights at Publicans, magically captured in J. R. Moehringer's coming-of-age memoir. And it's lucky for us that the author took so many notes on cocktail napkins about a bar in Manhasset that was a home to so many, but most notably J. R. himself. East Egg was modeled on Manhasset and the author imagines himself walking "across Fitzgerald's abandoned stage," in one of the many apt references to *The Great Gatsby*.

A fatherless boy, J. R. and his mother live in his grandfather's falling-down house with way too many family members. Moehringer effectively makes the case that the funny, sympathetic, profane philosopher kings of the bar raised him in the manly arts. Chief among the mentors is his Uncle Charlie, a bartender at Publicans and a serious drinker and gambler. He is also a very special and profane wordsmith: cops are gendarmes, "False" is his usual comeback to questions from the Kid and thirsty customers were told to wait in so many words while he recites "To His Coy Mistress" or belted out his favorite of favorites, Anthony Newley's "What Kind of Fool Am I?"

Clubs will delight in recounting the great lines and the classic Pip-like trajectory of J. R. You will most surely debate Bill and Bud's warning about disillusionment, the role that books play in J. R.'s life, the ending of *The Tender Bar* and the true tale of the Kid. The quote in the Prologue is from Dylan Thomas's *Under Milk Wood*. Explain.

Discussion questions, Hyperion: Short and numerous. The best questions are about the men, their sports obsessions and how good they were as role models. The question about the epilogue is very good.

Cocktails: Uncle Charlie may call you a Sea Breeze Betty or a Dewars-and-Soda Dave, but all will be forgiven if you spin Sinatra, classic Doo Wop or Newley. You may start by building the following Pelican favorites: pink squirrels, the Manhasset ("a Manhattan, with more alcohol"), Bloody Marys, gin martinis (see recipe, pages 328) and pitchers of martinis, sidecars, Old-Fashioneds, gin and tonic, scotch and soda, vodka with a cranberry splash, a batch of silk panties, screwdrivers and rusty nails. Salud!

Selling *The Tender Bar* to the club: Head to the nearest Publicans and start trading all the great lines.

■ ■ ■

This Boy's Life: A Memoir
(1989) by Tobias Wolff

Before *The Tender Bar*, there was the supreme example of the form, *This Boy's Life*. Tobias Wolff's memoir of growing up in the 1950s, convertible Thunderbirds and Corvettes included, is alternately sad, entertaining, touching and timeless; it is filled with lively scenes, flawless punchlines and lessons learned.

Toby, who has renamed himself "Jack," moves with his mother to rural Washington state in an attempt to start a new life after his family splits up. They want to change their luck. Jack, endearingly honest and vulnerable as he describes himself, becomes a successful Boy Scout and a minor juvenile delinquent in the true 1950s sense of the word. He steals from local stores, drinks, hangs out with the guys going nowhere and eventually forges his transcript to prep school ("I owned some pencils myself") in an effort to get away from his stepfather, Dwight.

A walking rap sheet of human pettiness, Dwight is a household terrorist who works Jack to the bone on jobs that end badly or in great absurdity. Jack is belittled and bullied by a man who always blames the gun on his poor marksmanship. It is this relationship that burns the brightest and is the source of much exploration of this wonderful book.

DVD alert: Here is the rare case of a superb memoir that is so well served by its film adaptation that the book and the movie live on vibrantly in both forms. Can anyone forget Robert De Niro as Dwight, Leonardo DiCaprio as Jack and Ellen Barkin as his mother? The rest of the cast of this 1993 movie includes Chris Cooper, Kathy Kinney and even Tobey Maguire. After you read *This Boy's Life*, treat your club to DVD night and discuss how a movie can defeat a book's reputation or make it soar.

Selling *This Boy's Life* to the club: A favorite book of many readers and writers, it is profound and intensely funny.

Truth and Beauty: A Friendship
(2004) by Ann Patchett

When Lucy Grealy was in the hospital suffering from a life-long malady, she would call her best friend Ann Patchett. Ann would fly up from Nashville, get the complete attention of all the doctors and nurses, and buy Tupperware for Lucy's Brooklyn apartment. *Truth and Beauty* is a memoir of this friendship between the author (*Bel Canto, The Magician's Assistant*) and the writer Lucy Grealy (*Autobiography of a Face*), for whom Patchett did all of this and more. "I decided then that my love for Lucy would have to manifest in deeds," writes Patchett.

Here, Lucy and Ann become characters, with Ann as the steady worker ant and Lucy as the flamboyant, demanding diva searching for love and suffering the effects of childhood cancer. The chemotherapy and radiation treatments left her with only part of her jaw. Years of reconstructive surgeries provide the arc of this book, and test this incredible friendship.

These respective roles are torn from the pages of fiction, and lucky for us, the story is told by a true master. Though the ending is tragic, *Truth and Beauty* is filled with the fun and intimacy of deep friendship and ongoing angst. (" 'I don't have a boyfriend,' Lucy relates. 'Nobody loves me.' ")

This memoir might also be considered an inspirational work as it describes the pain of both women who are having a harder and harder time coming to terms with Lucy's health issues and her self-destructive behavior. *Truth and Beauty* also amounts to a literary memoir, giving us just enough backstory to Patchett's life as a writer to illuminate her books.

Don't miss: The amusing sequence when George Stephanopoulos answers Lucy's personal ad in the *New York Review of Books* in which she describes herself as "fetching."

Discussion questions, Perennial: There are only four questions, but you hardly need them. You will be off on your commentary about this friendship, your own friendships, *Bel Canto* revisited, Lucy's charismatic and needy personality, her intellect and exquisite letters pitted against Ann's own life, and her increasingly difficult position.

Dedications that make a difference: "LUCINDA MARGARET GREALY, June 3, 1963–December 18, 2002, Pettest of my pets." This one reads like an intimate poem, others are poignantly straightforward such as the second part of the dedication in *The Kite Runner* (". . . and to the children of Afghanistan"). Can you think of other dedications that make a difference?

Selling *Truth and Beauty* to the club: It has all of our major themes: friendship, love and literature. The memoir also illuminates the relationships we have with people after they have passed, and the medical story will fascinate.

■ ■ ■

Wild Swans: Three Daughters of China
(1991) by Jung Chang

Jung Chang's story is an epic of three generations of women, the wild swans of the title, who are at the epicenter of enormous, often tragic, changes. The saga begins when Chang's grandmother is sold to a warlord as a concubine (yes, there is a description of her bound feet). She and her daughter, Jung Chang's mother, Bao Qin, endure a terrifying Japanese occupation, civil war and eventually the Communist victory. Bao Qin becomes an activist student who falls in love with a Communist Party official. Together they implement Mao's revolution, until they, too, are caught in the crosshairs of the Cultural Revolution.

Like a novelist, the author uses drama, foreshadowing and symbolism to create suspense. How does Chang balance sweeping narrative with personal observations? Does *Wild Swans* succeed as a memoir, as an historical account or both? How does she incorporate the party's teachings ("snakes in their old haunts"—bring your favorite party sayings to the club) with her increasingly scornful observations of the famine and chaos produced by Chairman Mao's policies? The author's descriptions of her parents' plight is just one of the many disturbing events portrayed in *Wild Swans*. This is a world in which "putting family first" is a serious crime and where Chairman Mao is to be worshipped like a god.

Reading aloud: Even in the depths of the Cultural Revolution's deprivations, Chang describes the marvels of breathtaking mountains and the flowering peach trees. While a concubine, her grandmother tends hibiscus, roses of Sharon and dwarf trees in her "gilded cage." When she and her family move to their official residence, the gardens are filled with "oleanders, magnolias, camellias, roses, hibiscus and a pair of rare Chinese aspens." Choose your favorite description of the natural world and read aloud.

Selling *Wild Swans* to the club: A perennial favorite of clubs, the memoir is impossible to put down, and its history lessons are terrifying and personal.

Five Questions for Ann Patchett

Bel Canto *and* **Truth and Beauty** *are beloved by book clubs. If you could suggest one theme that clubs could focus on in each book, what would that be? Might there be a common theme?*
I think there are common themes in both *Bel Canto* and *Truth and Beauty*, though I'd never thought about it before. First, there's the theme of the redeeming power of art. In *Bel Canto*, Roxane's singing unites the terrorists and the hostages and helps them find their common humanity and decency. The people who can't hear her sing are the ones that wind up perpetrating the violence. I think the same can be said in *Truth and Beauty*. Both Lucy and I saw art as something that could save us from being boring and invisible. Art made our life worth living. It gave us something to strive for. Another theme the books share is that of unconditional love. The people in both books, both the fictional ones and the real ones, make a decision to stick by one another no matter what, to love unconditionally.

What is your relationship with Lucy now that you have finished the book? Do your thoughts about her change often?
When I wrote *Truth and Beauty* I did it in part because I wanted to paint a portrait of Lucy that I could remember her by. Memory is so unreliable, and death softens our view over time. By writing *Truth and Beauty* so soon after she died, I could get everything down on paper as fast as was possible. I feel very close to Lucy now, as I did when she was alive. I think about her all the time, but every now and then something will happen that throws off the balance of my memory. Say for example a friend of hers will tell me a story about Lucy that I didn't know, and all of a sudden my love for her and my loss of her feels very immediate and my neatly

ordered memories just fall apart. Then I'm just a wreck who wants my friend back.

I want to urge people to read *Autobiography of a Face* by Lucy Grealy with *Truth and Beauty*. I think they are best read and discussed as a pair.

You talked about Lucy wanting to have the life of a fictional character, especially one in F. Scott Fitzgerald's novels. Have you noticed how many times per day there are references to classic authors and especially **The Great Gatsby** *in newspapers, on the radio and online? What do you think it means?*
Funny you should ask that. I just reread *The Great Gatsby* for the first time in years, and I was completely bowled over by what a perfect novel it is. I don't think there are a lot of literary touchstones left. We don't all read *Moby Dick* anymore. Still, most people who make it through high school read that book, and when you reference it, chances are you'll be understood. There's also something so deeply American about Gatsby. He remakes himself and yet he doesn't get it exactly right. He's still on the wrong side of the bay. I think most of us can identify with that to some extent.

What are your most beloved classic novels?
Gatsby and *Moby Dick* by Herman Melville are high up on the list. I love Charles Dickens and Jane Austen. I'm a great fan of the Russians, especially Chekhov and Tolstoy. I love *Brideshead Revisited* by Evelyn Waugh, *Portrait of a Lady* by Henry James, *So Long, See You Tomorrow* by William F. Maxwell, *The Magic Mountain* by Thomas Mann, *One Hundred Years of Solitude* by Gabriel Marquez Garcia, *Lolita* by Vladimir Nabokov, *Miss Lonelyhearts* by Nathanael West. I could go on and on.

Have you ever been in a book club? The host of one club made a daffodil cake from **The Joy of Cooking** *when the group discussed* **The Magician's Assistant**. *Any favorite recipes to share?*
I never have been a member of a book club. That is due in large part to how many book clubs I've attended since *Patron Saint of Liars* came out— I've been to an insane number of book clubs. For me to join one would be something of a busman's holiday. Once, a book club I spoke at invited me to pick their next book. I chose Scott Spencer's *Endless Love*, which is a

brilliant novel. I went back the next month to join in the discussion and people HATED it. They were so scandalized by the sex and only wanted to talk about how the parents made all the wrong decisions for their daughter. No one was pleased, including me. As for recipes, my hands down favorite cookbook is Mark Bittman's *How to Cook Everything*. I'm very devoted to his recipes.

The Cultural Revolution,
Before and After

FICTION

Balzac and the Little Chinese Seamstress★ by Dai Sijie

Becoming Madame Mao by Anchee Min

Bridegroom: Stories★ by Ha Jin

The Distant Land of My Father★ by Bo Caldwell

Dream of the Walled City by Lisa Huang Fleischman

Empress Orchid by Anchee Min

The Girl Who Played Go by Shan Sa

Raise the Red Lantern: Three Novellas★ by Su Tong

To Live by Yu Hua

Waiting★ by Ha Jin

Wild Ginger by Anchee Min

Women of the Silk★ by Gail Tsukiyama

MEMOIR

The Concubine's Children: The Story of a Chinese Family Living on Two Sides of the Globe by Denise Chong

Falling Leaves: The Memoir of an Unwanted Chinese Daughter★ by Adeline Yen Mah

Good Women of China★ by Xinran

Life and Death in Shanghai by Nien Cheng

Red Azalea by Anchee Min

Sky Burial★ by Xinran

★*Publisher's discussion questions available.*

NONFICTION

Mao: The Unknown Story by Jung Chang and Jon Holliday
*The Rape of Nanking: The Forgotten Holocaust of World War II**
  by Iris Chang

MYSTERY

Death of a Red Heroine: An Inspector Chen Investigation by Xiaolong Qui
Dragon Bones by Lisa See

Enchanted Summer Book Club

When everyone else has left for vacations and family reunions, those of us who are left should not suspend club meetings. Instead, take advantage of the season and meet outdoors as much as possible—in the backyard or garden, on the patio or front porch, at the park or beach.

A MEETING CHECKLIST

You won't think you need any of these things until you get there. It's a book club not a picnic, right? Wrong! The person who is packing will be the hero. Don't forget:

- Utensils
- Plates
- Napkins
- Cups
- Baskets large enough for plastic serving dish
- Tablecloth: Be creative, but bring a cloth of material that will withstand any gusts or sprinkles. Avoid the lighter plastic and paper varieties.

Best practice: Place your plastic serving dish directly into a large, flat woven basket or shallow crate large enough to hold it. It will be the focal point of the table. Save wooden berry baskets for utensils, salt and pepper, and bring them all together, lined with a napkin.

Best in show: It's an old trick, but it's summertime and everyone will love it. Hollow out a cantaloupe or watermelon and carve from rudimentary points to more advanced arabesques, swirls and summer scenes. Replace with original fruit, blackberries and blueberries and even kiwis, and use as a centerpiece for your Enchanted Summer Book Club table.

FLOWERS

You may be surrounded by sea or lawn, but flowers at your summer club make it real. Look for these in the backyard or green market:

- Stargazer lilies
- Daisies of all sizes and shapes
- Black-eyed Susans
- Hydrangea—rose, blue and white
- Cosmos
- Roses
- Yellow sunflowers and black sunflowers, tall or in bowls
- Sweet William
- Gerbera daisies

Best in show: Lemon-yellow and velvety, deep magenta snap dragons; small sunflowers; and zinnias in tight bouquets on the picnic table; or wild flowers, daisies and lavender in pitchers or small glass jars.

Seasonal Fruit Platters

Strawberries and blueberries. Watermelon and plums sliced wafer think. Raspberries and blackberries. In the summer we aim for splendid color. In the winter, more strawberries, grapes and pineapple. Each fruit has to last several hours, so strawberries are the go-to book club fruit.

If you are hosting, summer or winter, think about just one platter. It could hold everything: two cheeses, fruit (grapes, cherries, book club fruit strawberries) and at least one unexpected fruit such as figs or a sprig of herb or nuts. Consider putting cookies, brownies or little loaves of nut bread on one side. Variety is key and the unexpected introduces a special entertaining element without much effort.

Winter: Pineapple, sliced paper thin; figs that are cut and whole; grapes in every shade and variety.

Spring: The real strawberries. Invest in a berry dish or small basket and place the wild strawberries, strawberry blossoms, leaves and stems at the top or at the sides so they hang down in tendrils.

Summer: Blackberries and raspberries in a favorite basket, leaves and stems intact. Bowls of blueberries, sliced watermelon, and cherries of every color and variety, and a clear pitcher of cherry juice and glasses, right in the middle of the table.

Autumn: Large, low baskets of heirloom apples of every type and color; seedless grapes.

Supper at the Club: Joan Davis's Classic Pesto with Pasta

SERVES 6

This summer dish is easy to make and easy to transport. Serve as an appetizer or main course with salad.

3 cups loosely packed basil leaves
½ cup pine nuts
½ cup grated Parmesan cheese
⅓ cup of Romano cheese
3 whole garlic cloves, pressed
⅔ cup extra virgin olive oil
Salt and pepper to taste
1-pound box penne or other ridged pasta, cooked slighty more than al dente

In a blender or food processor, puree the basil leaves, pine nuts, cheeses and garlic while slowly adding the olive oil. Blend until all ingredients form a chunky paste.

Salt and pepper to taste and toss with pasta.

Dry Gin Martini in Honor of Uncle Charlie

SERVES 1

This drink is best made one at time, Uncle Charlie Publican style, using his secret recipe. Multiply by the number of people you anticipate will be drinking.

Ice cubes
1 heaping teaspoon dry vermouth
3 ounces premium English gin
A few drops of Scotch
Lemon or olive for garnish

Fill the shaker with ice and add the vermouth and the gin. Shake and strain into a chilled martini glass. Add a few drops of scotch to the chilled drink and be sure not to overpower the original martini. Garnish with lemon twist or olive.

Debbie Finan's Candied Pecan and Romaine Salad

SERVES 8

Trader Joe's has candied pecans in 5-ounce packages.

½ cup extra virgin olive oil

⅓ cup apple cider vinegar

2 tablespoons maple syrup

2 heads Romaine lettuce

1 5-ounce package candied pecans

8 ounces crumbled blue cheese

2 pears, peeled, cored and sliced thin

In a medium bowl, whisk together the olive oil, vinegar and maple syrup.

In a large salad bowl, place the lettuce and pecans. When ready to serve, mix salad with dressing, adding the blue cheese and pears. Toss and serve.

Travel tip: Salad dressing and blue cheese should be placed in separate containers. It's best to cut the pears at the club, but if you are running short on time and don't mind a little discoloration and runniness, slice at home and add a splash of lemon juice. Place the pears in an airtight container.

Bitsy Farnsworth's
Mystery Mocha Cake

SERVES 8

A powerful chocolate–coffee combination, this cake would be favored by Professor Nafisi. It is a kind of a molten chocolate cake (thus the mystery). It's very rich and small portions go a long way.

¾ cups white sugar

1 cup sifted flour

2 teaspoons baking powder

⅛ teaspoon salt

1 4-ounce bar bittersweet chocolate

2 tablespoons butter

½ cup whole milk

1 teaspoon vanilla

¼ cup brown sugar

¼ cup white sugar

3 tablespoons cocoa

1 cup cold strong coffee

Preheat oven to 350 degrees.

In a large bowl, sift together first 4 ingredients and set aside. In a heavy saucepan, melt chocolate and butter over medium heat. Cool mixture slightly and add to the sifted ingredients, blending well.

In a separate bowl, combine milk and vanilla. Pour slowly into batter and mix well.

Pour batter into greased 8 × 8-inch pan. Combine sugars and cocoa and sprinkle over the top of the batter. Using a large spoon, pour coffee over the top of the batter evenly.

Bake 40 minutes until the top is slightly crisp.

Serve with vanilla ice cream.

If You Were in a 1990s Book Club

1990

The Burden of Proof by Scott Turow

Darkness Visible by William Styron

Devil in the Blue Dress
by Walter Mosley

Jurassic Park by Michael Crichton

The Man Who Mistook His Wife for a Hat and Other Clinical Tales by Oliver Sachs

Possession by A. S. Byatt

September by Rosamunde Pilcher

The Stand by Stephen King

The Things They Carried
by Tim O'Brien

1991

The Firm by John Grisham

The House on Mango Street
by Sandra Cisneros

The Kitchen God's Wife by Amy Tan

Me: Stories of My Life
by Katharine Hepburn

Outer Banks by Anne Rivers Siddons

Saint Maybe by Anne Tyler

Scarlett: The Sequel to Margaret Mitchell's Gone with the Wind
by Alexandra Ripley

A Soldier in the Great War
by Mark Helprin

The Sweet Hereafter
by Russell Banks

A Thousand Acres by Jane Smiley

Women of the Silk by Gail Tsukiyama

1992

All the Pretty Horses
by Cormac McCarthy

Bailey's Café by Gloria Naylor

Bastard out of Carolina
by Dorothy Allison

The Brothers K
by James David Duncan

The English Patient
by Michael Ondaatje

Like Water for Chocolate
by Laura Esquivel

Little Altars Everywhere
by Rebecca Wells

The Patron Saint of Liars
by Ann Patchett

The Secret History by Donna Tartt

A Stained White Radiance
by James Lee Burke

Truman by David McCullough

Waiting to Exhale by Terry McMillan

1993

The Bridges of Madison County
by Robert James Waller

Durable Goods by Elizabeth Berg

The Giver by Lois Lowry

Having Our Say
by Sarah Louise Delany
and A. Elizabeth Delany

Nobody's Fool by Richard Russo

Operation Shylock by Philip Roth

The Shipping News by E. Annie Proulx

The Stone Diaries by Carol Shields
A Suitable Boy by Vikram Seth
Wouldn't Take Nothing for My Journey Now by Maya Angelou

1994
Breath, Eyes, Memory
    by Edwidge Danticat
Corelli's Mandolin
    by Louis de Bernieres
The Flanders Panel
    by Arturo Perez-Reverte
The Ice Storm by Rick Moody
In the Lake of the Woods
    by Tim O'Brien
In the Time of the Butterflies
    by Julia Alvarez
Midnight in the Garden of Good and Evil by John Berendt
No Ordinary Time
    by Doris Kearns Goodwin
Schindler's List by Thomas Keneally
The Shell Seekers
    by Rosamund Pilcher
Talk Before Sleep by Elizabeth Berg
Vinegar Hill by A. Manette Ansay
The Wind-Up Bird Chronicle
    by Haruki Murakami

1995
Beach Music by Pat Conroy
Blindness by Jose Saramago
A Civil Action by Jonathan Harr
The Ghost Road by Pat Barker
The Horse Whisperer
    by Nicholas Evans
The Hundred Secret Senses
    by Amy Tan
Independence Day by Richard Ford

Ladder of Years by Anne Tyler
The Liars' Club by Mary Carr
Native Speaker by Chang-Rae Lee
Range of Motion by Elizabeth Berg
The Samurai's Garden
    by Gail Tsukiyama
Snow Falling on Cedars
    by David Guterson
The Tortilla Curtain by T. C. Boyle

1996
Alias Grace by Margaret Atwood
Angela's Ashes by Frank McCourt
Bridget Jones's Diary
    by Helen Fielding
The Color of Water
    by James McBride
The Deep End of the Ocean
    by Jacquelyn Mitchard
Divine Secrets of the Ya-Ya Sisterhood
    by Rebecca Wells
The Emigrants by W. G. Sebold
How Stella Got Her Groove Back
    by Terry McMillan
Into the Forest by Jean Hegland
Pope Joan by Donna Woolfolk Cross
Primary Colors by Anonymous
The Rapture of Canaan
    by Sheri Reynolds
She's Come Undone by Wally Lamb
Under the Tuscan Sun
    by Frances Mayes

1997
All Over but the Shoutin'
    by Rick Bragg
American Pastoral by Philip Roth
Charming Billy by Alice McDermott
Cold Mountain by Charles Frazier

The God of Small Things
  by Arundhati Roy
Harry Potter and the Sorcerer's Stone
  by J. K. Rowling
Into Thin Air by Jon Krakauer
Larry's Party by Carol Shields
Le Divorce by Diane Johnson
A Lesson Before Dying
  by Ernest J. Gaines
Memoirs of a Geisha by Arthur Golden
Midwives by Chris Bohjalian
The Perfect Storm
  by Sebastian Junger
Personal History by Katharine Graham
The Reader by Bernhard Schlink
The Red Tent by Anita Diamant
*The Spirit Catches You and You Fall
  Down* by Anne Fadiman
Stones from the River by Ursula Hegi
The Weight of Water by Anita Shreve
*What Looks Like Crazy on an Ordinary
  Day* by Pearl Cleage

1998
Amy and Isabelle by Elizabeth Stroud
A Beautiful Mind by Sylvia Nasar
Black and Blue by Anna Quindlen
Chocolat by Joanne Harris
Cloudsplitter by Russell Banks
Enduring Love by Ian McEwan
The Greatest Generation
  by Tom Brokaw
The Hours by Michael Cunningham
I Know This Much Is True
  by Wally Lamb
An Instance of the Fingerpost
  by Iain Pears
Kaaterskill Falls by Allegra Goodman
A Man in Full by Tom Wolfe

One Thousand White Women
  by Jim Fergus
The Pact by Jodi Picoult
Paradise by Toni Morrison
A Patchword Planet by Anne Tyler
The Pilot's Wife by Anita Shreve
The Poisonwood Bible
  by Barbara Kingsolver
Tuesdays with Morrie by Mitch Albom
A Widow for One Year by John Irving

1999
Ahab's Wife by Sena Jeter Naslund
A Map of the World by Jane Hamilton
Amsterdam by Ian McEwan
Back Roads by Tawni O'Dell
Daughter of Fortune by Isabel Allende
Fortune's Rock by Anita Shreve
Galileo's Daughter by Dava Sobel
Gap Creek by Robert Morgan
A Gesture Life by Chang-rae Lee
Girl in Hyacinth Blue
  by Susan Vreeland
*The Girls' Guide to Hunting and
  Fishing* by Melissa Banks
Guns, Germs and Steel
  by Jared Diamond
Interpreter of Maladies
  by Jhumpa Lahiri
The Ladies Auxiliary by Tova Mirvis
The Lexus and the Olive Tree
  by Thomas Friedman
Plainsong by Kent Haruf
River Cross My Heart by Breena Clarke
Slaves in the Family by Edward Ball
Tara Road by Maeve Binchy
'Tis by Frank McCourt
Waiting by Ha Jin
White Oleander by Janet Fitch

BIBLIOGRAPHY

Benet, William Rose. *The Reader's Encyclopedia, Second Edition*. New York: Thomas Y. Crowell Company, 1965.

Bradbury, Malcolm, general editor. *The Atlas of Literature*. London: Greenwich Editions, 2001.

Burgess, Anthony. *Ernest Hemingway and His World*. New York: Charles Scribner's Sons, 1978.

Gajdusek, Robert E. *Hemingway's Paris*. New York: Charles Scribner's Sons, 1978.

Halperin, John. *The Life of Jane Austen*. Baltimore: The John Hopkins University Press, 1996.

Hemingway, Ernest. *A Moveable Feast*. New York: Charles Scribner's Sons, 1964.

Korda, Michael. *Making the List: A Cultural History of the American Bestseller 1900–1999*. New York: Barnes & Noble Books, 2001.

Lawson, Jane. *Shaken: 250 Classic Cocktails with a Twist*. San Diego: Laurel Glen, 2004.

Long, Robert Emmet. *Henry James: The Early Novels*. Boston: Twayne Publishers, 1983.

Nabokov, Vladimir. *Lectures on Literature*. Edited by Fredson Bowers. Introduction by John Updike. New York and London: Harcourt Brace Jovanovich, 1980.

Nabokov, Vladimir. *Lectures on Russian Literature*. Edited by Fredson Bowers. New York and London: Harcourt Brace Jovanovich, 1981.

Parker, Peter, editor. *A Reader's Guide to the Twentieth Century Novel*. Frank Kermode, consultant editor. New York: Oxford University Press, 1995.

ACKNOWLEDGMENTS

This book would not be possible without the inspiration of the gracious, creative and unflappable book club hosts I have been lucky enough to know. Your generosity was unqualified, your instructions (and injunctions!) precise and I will always bow to your superior knowledge. I am also proud to know all of your pets, with a special hug to Zappa and in memory of Dudley. I am indebted to Wendy Baskin, Alex Baudouin, Laura Becker, Mary Ann Bogner, Ellen Bregman, Gerry Bush-Jeffray, Melinda Caldwell, Barbara Currie, Liz Doughty, Bitsy Farnsworth, Valerie Foote, Leslie Geller, Susan Hessney, Darryl Manning, Chris Penberthy, Jan Reenders, Nina Restieri, Nancy Roberts, Mary Sarin and Hoskins Smith. In memory of Joan Carter, an early reader of this book and a woman of dazzling intelligence, warmth and personal style.

My abundant thanks to Ginjer Buchanan and the staff of Berkley Books. I could not ask for a more experienced or patient editor—your enthusiasm and support for this project was evident from start to finish. Profound thanks to my agent John Silbersack, who shaped this book masterfully and championed its cause.

Most special thanks to authors Isabel Allende, Bebe Moore Campbell, Ann Patchett and Alexander McCall Smith for their thoughtful and fascinating answers to my questions.

For their professional advice and always witty insights, special thanks to Beth Goehring of the Literary Guild and Carol Mackey of Black Expressions. I think about your criteria for book selection every day. For their wise counsel, I would like to thank Paul Elie, Sandy Graciano, David Hirshey, Anne Kreamer, Kamal Larsuel-Ulbricht, and Spenser Lee.

This book would not exist without public librarians at their posts, in the stacks, online—and sometimes in emergency telephone sessions. I would particularly like to thank Randolph Blakemen, Karen Traynor, Molly Williams; Joan Hume, Marta Campbell and the staff of the Westport Public Library; and Mary Rindfleisch and the staff of the Ridgefield Public Library. The staff of Fiction L, the librarians' list, has been an invaluable resource for me and for everyone who loves books and libraries.

And to the girl from the fiction department of the Seattle Public Library, Jennifer Baker, my heartfelt gratitude.

For their prompt, expansive and knowledgeable responses to my pet questions, I would like to thank Dr. Merry Crimi, American Animal Hospital Association past president and owner of the Gladstone Veterinary Clinic in Portland, Oregon; William Berloni, coauthor of *Doga Yoga For Dogs* (Chronicle Books) and president of William Berloni Theatrical Animals; Debbie Tracy of the American Animal Hospital Association; Lisa Peterson, of the American Kennel Club; Lisa Radosta of the American Veterinary Society of Animal Behavior; and Nancy Peterson, Issues Specialist for The Humane Society of the United States.

For their professional assistance, thanks to Julie McCaffrey of the Chicago Botanic Gardens; Holly Shrewsbury of the Denver Botanic Gardens; Garland Scott of the Folger Shakespeare Library and to the staff of the Brooklyn Botanic Gardens.

Special thanks to Joan Davis, Debbie Finan, Cecily Gans and Charlaine Fontelieu for the use of their recipes; Beth Lipson for your suggestions (and the loans from your amazing library) and Sarah Johnson for your friendship and always wonderful advice.

To my mother and father, for your inspiration and encouragement, and for introducing me to my very first books. Finally, to Philip and Nicholas for your unwavering support (with special thanks for the superior tech support) and your astounding good humor, with much love.

RECIPE CREDITS